creative
rhythmic
movement
For Children of Elementary School Age

Shirley J. Winters

formerly of the University of Southern California

creative
rhythmic
movement

FOR CHILDREN OF ELEMENTARY SCHOOL AGE

WM. C. BROWN COMPANY PUBLISHERS
DUBUQUE, IOWA

Photographs

Location: The University of Southern California, Los Angeles, California
Photographer: John Simpson

Location: West Davis Elementary School, Davis, California
Photographer: Jeffrey Childress

Location: Young Women's Christian Association, Sacramento, California
Photographer: A.J. Hance and W.D. Winters

PHYSICAL EDUCATION

Consulting Editor
*Aileene Lockhart
Texas Woman's University*

HEALTH

Consulting Editor
*Robert Kaplan
The Ohio State University*

PARKS AND RECREATION

Consulting Editor
*David Gray
California State University, Long Beach*

**to my husband
and children**

who have constantly urged
and inspired me to go on learning.

contents

preface

This book is intended to encourage those who are involved with teaching, directing, or assisting children of the elementary school age, to try creative rhythmic movement as a means of initiating and developing self-awareness, self-esteem, and self-direction in these children.

The concepts and methods are so described—in ample detail—as to be readily available for use. Each idea is presented in a way that focuses attention on the child and how he will grow physically, mentally, emotionally, and socially through an awareness of the concepts associated with creative rhythmic movement. It is this logical, relevant kind of approach that makes the teaching of creative rhythmic movement an important and essential subject for consideration in the elementary school, and in all situations involving the psychological and behavioral development of the child.

The classroom teacher, the physical educator, the science teacher, the reading specialist, the drama, art, music, and dance teacher, and the child psychologist may all find in this book information applicable to helping children grow and learn about themselves and others. The teacher of children with physical disabilities or mental retardation may also find some of the material well suited to their needs. Despite the fact that few specific references to such material appear in the text, it is adaptable, having been used successfully with mentally retarded children.

The classroom teacher may draw many ideas from the lesson plans and various parts of the book which relate to subject matter presented in the classroom. The classroom teacher may find the ideas on space especially relevant to the study of geography; the study of rhythm especially helpful to children studying mathematics and reading; the synthesization of ideas and the development of patterns and forms useful in the development of creative writing. Of special interest to all teachers of children are the subsections of chapter three, dealing with problem-solving and other teaching methods.

The interrelationship between the concepts of creative rhythmic movement and sports is especially intense, and is stressed throughout the book, sparked by the idea that creative rhythmic movement should be more universally used as a preparatory or remedial activity for boys and girls interested in sports. Therefore, the physical educator and coach may find here many useful ideas for the development of body, rhythmic, and spatial awareness as well as motor development for children. A program of creative rhythmic movement in the elementary school de-emphasizes the need for equipment or manipulative objects, and stresses the development of the child through nongoal oriented movement. A program such as this for the physical development of children is extremely economical, and therefore highly appropriate for presentation to school administrators as an addition to the curriculum.

The creative arts teacher may discover here numerous suggestions pertinent to the teaching of dance, drama, painting, music, and the plastic arts. These suggestions emerge from sections in the book dealing with imagination, expression and communication, the creative process, music, rhythm, creative stories, vocalization of words, and the stimulation of the senses.

The science teacher may find the sections on movement education, motor learning and body awareness most applicable; while for the reading specialist references to spatial awareness, involving the patterns of movement, directionality, and tracking ability may be of great importance.

Though the book is principally directed to the teacher of elementary, school age children, there are many useful ideas for evoking a creative rhythmic movement response in the preschool child.

Since the focus of the book is mainly on children and how they develop, the child psychologist and therapist can draw many ideas for their work with children from the sections on nonverbal expression and communication, sensory perception, spatial and body awareness, and imagination.

Finally, it is the author's expectation that this book will be a useful tool for the training of those young adults in colleges and universities who will become teachers of rhythmics, physical education, dance, creative rhythmic movement, eurythmics, music, creative drama, and writing in the elementary school.

All teaching methods and movement ideas presented on the following pages have been used with hundreds of children in the dance studios at the University of Southern California, and the Sacramento Y.W.C.A., as well as in two Los Angeles and Davis elementary schools.

Acknowledgments

I wish to thank the following:

Dr. Aileene Lockhart, former Chairman of the Department of Physical Education for Women, University of Southern California, now Dean of the College of Health, Physical Education and Recreation at Texas Woman's University, for giving me the encouragement and opportunity to express my convictions concerning the value of creative rhythmic movement to the development of the child; Dr. Lois Ellfeldt, Professor of Dance, University of Southern California, for "taking me in" and giving me space at the university so that I could have the freedom to practice, develop my theories, and teach children and university students as well; and

Margaret H'Doubler, Professor Emeritus and former chairman of the Dance Department at the University of Wisconsin, Madison, who gave me my first insight into movement education, and under whose guidance my teachings developed and matured to the point at which I felt compelled to write this book.

one

Creative Rhythmic Movement

What is *creative rhythmic movement?* It is creative, it is rhythmic, and it is movement, just as the name implies. It is creative in that it calls forth new and original movement, shapes and designs—spatially and rhythmically—simply by the movement of one's body within and throughout space. The body has many mobile parts, a number of which, being highly flexible, move in several different ways, and since the space one moves in and throughout is vast, the designs produced by bodily movements are myriad in number. Add to this the infinite number of rhythmic combinations which may accrue as the result of moving slowly, quickly, jerkily, smoothly, or in a relaxed manner, and you can understand why creative rhythmic movement can be regarded as a most exciting and creative activity.

If creative rhythmic movement is so exciting, why don't more people try it? Our society has been warned of the physical and psychological disadvantages of becoming a sedentary, spectator people, but we have done very little to alter the situation. Are people reluctant to try rhythmic movement, or movement of any kind?

1

During the past fifteen or twenty years, the United States, as well as many other parts of the world, has witnessed a great surge of freedom of expression through the medium of creative rhythmic movement. Young adults have been, and presently are, creating new shapes and designs in space to the insistent and prominent rhythmic patterns of Rock and Country Music. Through these rhythmic movements, they have discovered a great release of physical and emotional tension and the excitement and self-satisfaction of creating new and original movement forms spatially as well as rhythmically. For youth it is a satisfying method of expression and communication. Rock and Roll dancing, especially in its formative stage, is Creative Rhythmic Movement.* But, it is of great importance to be aware that in Rock and Roll dancing, the music is the dominating force, while the movement remains secondary. The movement expresses the feeling of, and takes the form of, the music. In actuality, Rock and Roll music produces Rock and Roll movements.

However, in creative rhythmic movement, the process is reversed; the movement dominates. The emphasis is on the self, on the feelings and ideas expressed by the self through movement, done creatively and rhythmically. The forms taken by the movements are original designs in space created by the mover. If you can imagine the self-satisfaction derived from exploring, discovering, and executing one's movements, expressing one's feelings and ideas, then you can also imagine how these movements are enhanced by the accompaniment of music, words, or a rhythmic pattern created solely to intensify this expression. It is truly the height of freedom of expression and is within the reach of anyone who has a body of mobile parts and a brain to instigate and direct an awareness of these movements. It is movement for exercise, expression, communication, self-awareness, and self-esteem. And most of all, it is movement for fun! Creative rhythmic movement could be the answer to the pleas of psychologists, psychiatrists, and educators who urge that more self-satisfying movement activities be presented in the elementary school, movements which are not oriented toward a goal or executed to accomplish a task. However, the emphasis could be upon movements which stimulate thought and promote an awareness that can be synchronized with other activities in school.

How can this come about? There are by no means enough dance specialists to go around. Who, then, can present activities in creative

---

* NOTE: The descriptive phrase *Creative Rhythmic Movement* is, of necessity, used repeatedly throughout this volume. In the interest of smoothest reading, the abbreviation CRM appears where considered expedient.

rhythmic movement, and how? Is creative rhythmic movement dance? Does one have to know a great deal about dance or movement to teach creative rhythmic movement, and if so, how much? Before answering these questions, let us see what is entailed in the learning and teaching processes of CRM.

Since exploring and discovering one's own movements is the basic activity used to effect an awareness of the concepts of creative rhythmic movement, we should first examine how one explores and discovers self-movement. Are there any special rules involved? And, if so, what knowledge must one have in order to begin? Self-movement is discovered and explored simply by moving one's body within and throughout space. There are no rules involved. There are no right or wrong ways to move. If, through executing a movement, the person derives a sense of satisfaction, or a feeling of well-being, then, the movement is right for that person. If the movement expresses that person's feelings or ideas in a way that is satisfying to him, then the movement is right for him. Since we all have a body of movable parts, which occupies space and moves within or throughout it, no special knowledge about CRM is really required.

Presenting a program in creative rhythmic movement can be as simple as having the teacher offer the time, opportunity, and space to allow her students to express themselves through the medium of rhythmic movement. However, such a program can be a much more challenging and enriching experience for the teacher and children if approached through the solving of movement problems related to the concepts of creativity, rhythm, and movement. The process of solving these problems can initiate and nurture an awareness in each child, providing him with a greater understanding of himself and others.

Some movement problems the teacher might present are as follows: How high can you skip? What can you do to make your body go higher? Where are your elbows—your head—your knees? Can you feel where your knees are without looking at them, or moving them? Touch your shoulders. How many ways can you move your shoulders? Can you see your arms moving in the space surrounding you? Can you see John running through the space in this room? Other rhythmic problems might be so stated as: How fast can you run? How slow can you walk? How many hops does it take for you to go from here to there? How many beats does it take for you to go from here to there? Where is the first beat? Where is the last? Where in your movement do you make the greatest effort?

Typical creative problems might be stated as follows: Can you discover a movement which you like so much you want to repeat it

Can you express your feelings and ideas through
Creative Rhythmic Movement?

often? Will this movement lead you to the discovery of another movement? Can you remember the first movement as it leads you on to the
next? What kind of pattern have you discovered? Has your movement
created a pattern in space? Have you worked out a pattern on the
floor? How did you feel when you moved this particular way? *Show me
your feelings in movement.*

Can a classroom teacher, in addition to her other responsibilities,
find time to offer her students opportunities in CRM? If so, what
knowledge will assist her in presenting such a program? Moreover,
what concepts will children become aware of as they explore and
discover movement? Children will become aware of: *the anatomical
structure of their own body and how it moves; the physical laws which
act upon and govern movement; rhythm with its time and force components; and space, with its vastness, its limitations, and its psychological
factors.* Children will also become more *aware of their emotional
selves,* and the *expressive and communicative powers of creative rhythmic movement.*

To know all of the above is really *a study of being aware of one's
self in his immediate environment*—how one acts and interacts with
his environment, *not verbally, but through bodily movement.* To learn
all this through creative rhythmic movement makes this subject a
very attractive one (and an economical one) for the school curriculum.

two

Content and Criteria for the Teaching of Creative Rhythmic Movement

This chapter presents the content and criteria concerned with movement, rhythm, and creativity in concise form—readily available for clarifying the meaning of terms as used in this book. The teacher may also find this chapter a valuable source of information from which to draw when composing movement problems for the children to solve. The information is basic for initiating an awareness of the concepts of creative rhythmic movement; it is, however, the means by which this awareness is effected that will influence the development of the child physically, mentally, emotionally, and socially. Therefore, the material is presented as a fount of understanding from which the teacher and child may draw for their movement explorations, discoveries, and creativities. The study of CRM is a process through which the children should go in order to discover themselves as they solve movement problems. It is an exciting and never-ending process full of surprises, clarifications, and relevances. Acquiring this information as factual material, without focusing on the child and all that encompasses him as a person in society, is to completely misconstrue the ideals and philosophy of movement education for children as set forth in the following pages.

This chapter is divided into three main parts, the first of which deals with *bodily movement,* as an educative process, and in relation to its force and space factors. The second part details everything an elementary school teacher needs to know about *rhythm* in order to teach creative rhythmic movement. Included are suggestions for music and other accompaniment desirable for the teaching process. However, little or no reference is made to musical terms; though a knowledge of music may be helpful for teaching CRM, it is not essential. The third part emphasizes *the creative process* and its relation to the building of movement patterns and composition, and a comparison of dance, sports, and creative rhythmic movement. In this part, expression and communication through CRM are also considered.

BODILY MOVEMENT

A *bodily movement* is a stirring or shifting of the body mass or part of the body mass. In general it may refer to movement of the whole body or to a particular part of it. In this book, a bodily movement refers to the movement of more than one part of the body and usually involves the whole body. Movement of specific bodily parts are referred to by name: movements of the feet, movements of the head, movements of the shoulders, and so forth.

Doing any of the following will result in general bodily movement: Move your body in as many ways as you can imagine. Move your body from here to there. Move your body as low to the floor as it will go. Stretch your body as tall as you can.

Here are examples that will result in specific bodily movements: Move your head in as many ways as possible. How many ways can you move your fingers? Flex your legs at the knee joint. Flex your arms at the elbow joint. Hop!

Movement is the medium by which one may express feelings and ideas in CRM. The human body, when moving and at rest, is subject to the same laws of movement that govern all bodies and objects. Movement occupies space, takes time to perform, and emits a certain amount of force. Since there are no exact, established ways to move one's body in creative rhythmic movement, one builds a vocabulary or repertoire of movement for himself, depending on his own particular body structure as well as on his knowledge of how the body exists and moves through space, in time, and with force.

The body and its movable parts is the instrument of expression in CRM. There are three structural considerations in bodily movement:

—Range of joint action.
—Degree of muscle tension.
—Relationship of bodily parts.

Moreover, five basic laws of physics are involved in bodily movement:

—Movement takes place within and throughout space.
—Movement takes time.
—Movement requires force, or energy.
—Movement is an outward expression of one's inner self.
—The body, as a mass existing in this universe, is subject to those physical forces which affect all other masses.

Body movement, or movements of body parts, may be changed by altering space, time, force, and emotional factors. That is, one may change the character and/or quality of a movement by changing any of the following: its range of joint action, acceleration, rhythm, moment of execution, balance, direction, focus; the action of other bodily parts; the intent, or the idea or feeling behind it. By altering the movement a great deal of creativity can result.

The material that follows is intended to give the teacher an idea of what a particular movement looks like when executed in its most usual form. The teacher may then use this information for purposes of identification, comparison, evaluation, remedial work, and as a "takeoff" point for the presentation of movement problems.

LOCOMOTION AND NONLOCOMOTION

Bodily movement can be divided into two main groups: locomotion, and nonlocomotion. These two groups may in turn be divided into locomotion of the feet and locomotion of the body mass; and nonlocomotion of the feet and nonlocomotion of the body mass.

1. *Locomotion:* If the movement of the body results in transferring the total body mass from one locale to another, the movement is a locomotor movement. Locomotor movements occur on a horizontal plane and form a design on the floor called a floor pattern. One may locomote via movements of the feet or of the total body mass.

   Locomotor movements by way of the feet are made by using the elementary forms of locomotion, or combinations of them. The elementary forms of locomotion have specific names and exact methods for execution. They are: the walk, run, hop, jump, leap, and ball-heeling. Their most common and frequent combinations lead to the execution of the gallop, slide, or skip. These are covered in detail further on, where we describe movements of the feet. See below.

Locomotor movements by way of the motion of the total body mass are any and all movements which propel the body horizontally through space by transferring the weight from one bodily area to another, by means other than the feet. These movements are also basic, elementary, and have specific names. They are the: roll, crawl, walking on all fours, walking on the hands or forearms, squirm, wiggle, or slide. These bodily locomotor movements are detailed later on, where we describe movement of the bodily mass. See page 25.

2. *Nonlocomotion:* Nonlocomotor bodily movement is that movement of the feet or the mass of the body which does not transfer the body through space horizontally from one locale to another.

Nonlocomotor movements by means of the feet are made by using one or more elementary forms of nonlocomotion. These have specific names and methods of execution which are described under movements of the feet. They are the: ball, brush, heel, kick, scuff, slap, stamp, tap, toe, and twist or pivot rub. Nonlocomotor and locomotor movements of the feet, often combined, provide interesting movements.

Nonlocomotor movements by means of motion of the body mass or parts thereof are any and all movements, other than by the feet, which do not propel the body horizontally through space by transferring the weight from one body area to another. These body movements shape the surrounding near space. They include: flexion, extension, abduction, adduction, circumduction, rotation; also, the twist, swing, sway, rock, shake, push, pull, vibration, strike, dodge, sit, lift, suspension, and fall.

Locomotor Movements of the Feet. Six basic locomotor forms— the walk, run, hop, jump, leap, and ball-heel—provide the most natural and spontaneous means of *transporting the body mass by one or two feet* from one locale to another. These movements, often referred to as elementary forms of locomotion (of the feet), have one thing in common; all are executed naturally to beats of even duration.

Locomotor movements of one or both feet are specifically concerned with: (1) Weight transference—how and when accomplished;

(2) Foot relationship, spatially, at the moment of weight transfer; (3) Rhythm and force characteristics.

THE WALK—a locomotor movement in which there is a transference of weight from one foot to the other in smooth, somewhat swingy, even rhythm. As the weight is transferred, continual contact with the floor is maintained by one or both feet. One walk is often called a step.

Walking!

Starting Position
- Stand with body erect but without excess tension. The toes are pointed forward.
- Arms hang near the sides, relaxed.
- Shoulders are level, the head is high, and the chin is level.
- Focus eyes straight ahead.

Action
- Shift the weight to one foot and lean slightly forward.
- Swing the opposite leg forward freely from the hip and knee, raising the foot slightly off the floor.
- Place the heel on the floor.
- Push from the rear foot and transfer the weight from that back foot to the forward heel, to the ball, and finally to the entire forward foot.
- Continue this action of transferring the weight from one foot to the other by constantly placing the center of gravity over and ahead of the advancing foot. (When focusing attention on this action of the walk, one can identify a series of small falls and recoveries.)
- The arms swing in opposition to the movements of the legs.

Space Pattern
- Direction—forward.
- Level—standing, or high level.
- Size of step—varies with each individual.

Rhythm
- Tempo—moderate. The tempo most commonly identified with the average walk is that of a march, and its rhythm is frequently vocalized by repeating the words left-right-left-right, loudly and forcefully.
- Each walk (one step) takes one even beat. One may begin to count a series of continuing walking beats when the heel touches the floor. This represents the first beat.

Force
- The amount of muscle force used to perform a walk is moderate. The muscle force changes with the intent, tempo, or grade and texture of the surface.
- Other factors contribute to the quality of the walk; but in general, it is smooth, even, and has a swing.

THE RUN—a locomotor movement whereby the weight is quickly transferred from one foot to the other causing momentary loss of contact with the floor.

Starting Position
- Stand with one foot a small step forward, knees slightly bent, weight on both feet, and toes forward.
- Lean body slightly forward.
- Bend arms slightly at the elbows.
- Focus eyes straight ahead.

Running!

Action

- Shift weight to the forward foot.
- Push off with the ball, then toes of the rear foot, and at the same time, lean further forward, keeping the rear leg straight until recovering for the next step.
- Swing the rear leg forward, landing on the toes (momentarily only), ball, and heel.
- It is usually beneficial to take two or three short steps before continuing with the long, even strides.
- Swing bent arms freely in opposition to the leg movements.

Space Pattern

- Direction—forward and upward.
- Level—standing, or high level to highest level.

- Size of step—varies with the intent; however, it is generally larger than for a walk.

Rhythm
- Tempo—faster than a natural walk.
- Each run constitutes one even beat. Begin to count a continuing series of running beats as you land on the ball of one foot.

Force
- The amount of muscle force used to do a run is moderate to great. It changes however, with the intent, tempo, or grade and texture of the surface.
- Various other factors also determine the quality of the run, but it is generally smooth, even, and slightly buoyant and resilient.

THE LEAP—a locomotor movement in which there is a transference of weight from one foot to the other, with a sustained loss of contact with the floor as the body is carried a higher and greater distance than during the run.

Starting Position
- Stand with one foot positioned slightly in front of the other. Place the weight on the rear foot.
- When executing a leap to gain distance, lean forward before moving; to gain height, stand erect.
- Hang arms close to your sides, relaxed.
- Focus eyes straight ahead.

Action
- Bend the weight-bearing leg.
- Push off with the weight-bearing leg and extend the forward leg. The greater the bend and push off by the rear leg, the higher and larger the leap.
- Swing arms forward and back until they are extended in opposition to the leg movements. You should not swing the arms higher than shoulder level, and the shoulders should not be elevated during the movement.
- Land on the forward foot, first the toes, then the ball, and finally the heel.
- Bend the forward leg to absorb the shock and prepare for the next leap. It is a combination pushing and reaching action by the legs.
- Leaps are often combined with one or several runs in order to gain greatest height and/or distance. The easiest combination of runs and leaps is one or three runs, plus a leap. The result is a leap, which is always executed on the same leg. If it is desirable for the leap to occur on alternate legs, use two or four runs, plus one leap.
- Leaps are often taught so that they start off with a run, and the size of successive runs gradually increases.

Space Pattern
- Direction—forward with height and/or distance.
- Level—standing, or high to highest.
- Size of step—varies with intent. Usually larger than for a run.

Leaping!

Rhythm

- Tempo—moderate, about the same as for a walk.
- Each leap takes one even beat. The execution of a continuing series of leaps begins as the rear foot pushes off the floor. By the time the word *leap* can be verbalized, the leap should reach its greatest elevation. The first leap is counted when the ball of the foot touches the floor.

Force

- The amount of energy used to perform a leap is considerably more than that required for any of the other forms of foot locomotion. But it is easier to make several continuous leaps than it is to make one, since the force of momentum tends to act as a propellant for the movement that follows.
- Balancing the body when it is at its maximum elevation is of prime importance for the execution of a leap. The shoulders should not be elevated in an effort to gain height, but should remain in a low, steady position and serve to counterbalance the action of the leg and arm muscles at work.
- The quality of the movement depends on whether the leaps are executed to gain height or distance. A leap made for height is buoyant, and appears effortless. A leap executed for distance is more percussive and vigorous.

THE JUMP—a locomotor movement which transfers the body weight by a springing action from one or both feet into the space above the floor, to a landing on both feet. A jump is made to gain height and/or distance.

Starting Position

- Stand on one or both feet with the weight of the body distributed evenly over the base of support.
- Keep the body erect, shoulders level, and head high.
- Focus eyes straight ahead.

Action

- Bend both knees and bring the arms down and back.
- Swinging the arms forward, push off from one or both feet, and spring into the surrounding space with the toes leaving the floor last.
- Land on the balls of both feet; then lower the weight onto the soles and heels.
- Bend the knees to cushion the shock of landing.
- If jumping to attain the highest level possible, the arms should swing forward and continue upward until they are fully extended in the space above the head. Bend the knees when landing.
- The jump is often preceded by several runs in order to gain the speed and force needed to travel farther. This jump is usually accomplished by transferring the weight from one foot to two feet.
- The swing of the arms and the tucked position of the knees help to gain height and/or distance.

Space Pattern

- Direction—upward and forward.
- Level—high to highest.
- The size of the jump varies with the intent.

Rhythm

- Tempo—moderate.
- Each jump takes one even beat. Begin to count the first of a

Jumping!

continuous series of jumps when both feet land; however, the signal
to jump begins at the instant of departure.

Force

- The amount of energy used to make a jump is considerable.
- The movement quality of a jump is strong, resilient, and exhilarating.

THE HOP—a locomotor movement in which there is a spring, or
push, off the ground from one foot and a return to the ground on
the same foot. A hop is done to gain height or distance.

Hopping!

Starting Position

- Stand erect with the weight of the body centered over one foot.
- Raise the other foot to the rear, with the knee and ankle flexed. The raised foot should make no contact with the floor.
- Keep shoulders level, head high, and toes forward.
- Focus eyes straight ahead.

Action

- Bend the knee of the supporting foot.
- Push from the floor, and extend the supporting leg, springing up off the floor.
- Land on the same foot, touching the toe first, then the ball, and the heel last. Land with a bent knee.
- Continue this hopping action on the same foot. When a change of feet is desired, leap onto the other foot and continue hopping.

Space Pattern

- Direction is upward.
- Level—high to highest.
- Size of hop varies with the intent. The hop for distance uses more space.

Rhythm

- Tempo—moderate to moderately fast.
- Each hop takes one even beat. Begin to count the first of a continuous series of hops as one foot lands; however, the command to hop begins at the instant of departure.

Force

- The amount of energy utilized to execute a hop depends on the height or distance one wants to gain. The weight should be held high in the torso, and the landing should be sequentially placed from toe, to ball, to heel.
- The quality of a hop is generally light, buoyant, resilient, and staccato, although a hop for distance is heavier.

BALL-HEEL—a smooth locomotor movement which proceeds sideways and transfers the weight from the ball of one foot to the heel of the same foot, or from the balls of both feet to the heels of both feet. The side of the body leads and twists in opposition to the action of the feet. It has not been considered a basic locomotor form in the past; however, many children above the age of five do it spontaneously. Ball-heel, as a locomotor form, develops easily from "the twist," a social dance form which was prevalent throughout the sixties. This may be the explanation for its popularity among children at the present time.

Starting Position

- Stand on one or both feet, with the weight of the body mass evenly distributed over the base of support. Point toes forward.

- Bend arms slightly at the elbows.
- Focus eyes straight ahead.
- If executing the ball-heel on one foot, bend the other knee, and let the other foot hang behind, or alongside, and off the floor.

Action

(The following directions are for both feet. The same action applies if executed on one foot.)

- Bend the knees slightly and press both heels down into the floor. (The movement may also begin with the balls of the feet.)
- At the same time, lift the balls of the feet.
- Pivot slightly on the heels, so the toes of both feet are pointed diagonally toward the direction of locomotion. The movement should proceed with the side of the body leading.
- Press down into the floor with the balls of the feet, and lift the heels.
- Pivot on the balls of the feet so the movement will proceed in that same direction.
- The movement locomotes by the alternate relocation of the weight of the feet from the balls to the heels or vice versa. The shoulders move in the direction opposite from that of the toes, giving a twisting motion to the torso.

Space Pattern

- Direction is on a high horizontal plane.
- The body moves in a sideward direction, the side leading.

Rhythm

- Tempo—moderate to fast.
- Each ball-heel takes two even beats: one for the ball, and one for the heel.
- Begin to count the first ball-heel in a continuous series of ball-heels directly following the pivot, while the balls or heels of both feet are touching the floor.

Force

- The amount of energy used to do a ball-heel is moderate to slight.
- The movement quality of a ball-heel is smooth, with a twisting movement from the torso. The twisting motion very often makes the body look as if it is rocking.

     Combinations: Frequently the foregoing elementary forms of locomotion are combined, leading to the formation of three well known step patterns, which are easily and commonly executed by children: the gallop, slide, and skip. All three have the same uneven rhythmic pattern which can be verbalized as follows: long, short, long, short, . . .

THE GALLOP—a locomotor movement which combines a walk and a leap, in an uneven rhythm, with the walking foot always in the lead.

Starting Position
- Stand erect with one foot a large step in front of the other.
- Direct the toes forward, and center the weight over both feet.
- Raise bent arms slightly away from the body.
- Focus eyes straight ahead.

Action
- Place weight on the leading foot. This is the walk, or step.
- Bring the trailing foot up to meet the leading foot by leaping. Remember to not proceed further than the lead foot.
- Continue the walk, leap pattern of the gallop.

Space Pattern
- Direction is forward and upward.
- Level is high.
- Size of gallop varies with intent. The walking foot always leads, while the leaping foot comes up alongside of it.

Rhythm
- Tempo—moderate.
- Beat intervals are uneven. Begin to count the first beat of a continuous series of gallops as the lead foot touches the floor on the walk forward.
- The gallop is best performed to music in 6/8 measure. The rhythmic pattern is as follows:

	>			>		
	walk	leap		walk	leap	
6						
	1	2	3	4	5	6

- The rhythm is often described as a rocking rhythm. It suggests the gallop of a horse.

Force
- The amount of energy used to do a gallop is moderate.
- The quality of a gallop depends on the degree of joint action used. If executed with a great deal of leg joint action, the quality is lumbering and heavy gaited. If accomplished with little leg joint action, the movement quality is smoother, with a slight rock.

SLIDE (OF THE FEET)—a locomotor form which may be any one of the following:

- A smooth step-together movement composed of two walks executed sideways with a small amount of elevation at the moment of weight transference. This movement is sometimes called a glide.
- A combination of a walk and a leap, in an uneven rhythm similar to the gallop, but done sideways.
- A locomotor movement which advances the body from one locale to

Sliding!

another by slipping on a smooth surface. This slide, often preceded by several runs—is also referred to as a slippery slide.

Starting Position

- Stand on both feet, weight evenly distributed.
- Keep the body erect, shoulders level, and head high.
- Focus eyes straight ahead or sideways, in the direction of the slide.

Action and Rhythm

- Slide no. 1: Walk to the side, with the side of the body leading. Bring the other foot up to the lead foot in the form of a step, but do not pass the lead foot.

4	open	close	open	close	←── Position of feet.
	walk	walk	walk	walk	←── The side leads.
	1	2	3	4	
	1	2	3	4	

- Slide no. 2: Same as the gallop, only sideways. There is usually less flexion in the knees than with the gallop.

6	open walk	close leap	open walk	close leap
1	②	3	4	⑤	6
1	2	3	4	5	6

- Slide no. 3: Take several running steps. During the last running step, push off from the ball of the foot and step lightly onto the advancing foot. Keep the weight held very high in the torso so that the advancing foot is permitted to progress by slipping and sliding on the floor. After the slide has begun, the other foot may also rest lightly on the floor for balance and slip along with the advancing foot.

SKIP—a locomotor movement which combines a walk and a hop on the same foot in an uneven rhythm. The movement continues on alternating feet.

Starting Position
- Keep body erect, with weight evenly distributed on both feet. Direct toes forward.
- Keep shoulders level with head held high.
- Hang arms near the sides, relaxed.
- Focus eyes straight ahead.

Action
- Walk forward on one foot and then hop on it, landing on the ball of the foot.
- Simultaneously, bend the other knee and bring it forward.
- Repeat the step-hop with alternate feet.
- Swing the arms freely in opposition to the leg movement. Do not raise the arms higher than shoulder level. Do not raise the shoulders in an effort to go higher.

Space Pattern
- Direction is upward and forward.
- Level—high to highest.
- Size of skip depends on height or distance attained.

Rhythm
- Tempo—moderate to fast.
- Rhythmic pattern is uneven.

Skipping!

6	walk	hop	walk	hop

1	②	3	4	⑤	6
1	2	3	4	5	6

A strong accent on the walk provides the take-off for the hop. Begin to count the first beat of a continuous series of skips as the foot touches the floor on the walk.

Force

- The amount of energy required to skip varies with the height or distance attained, and the tempo.
- Great height may be gained when doing the skip by driving the walking foot into the floor harder, flexing more at the knee and ankle joint, and extending the push-off leg to its fullest. The arm swing also helps to gain height.

Locomotor Movements of the Body Mass

ROLL—a locomotor bodily movement which transports the body on a horizontal plane in the lowest level by progressively rotating the bodily weight from one area of the body to another sequentially.

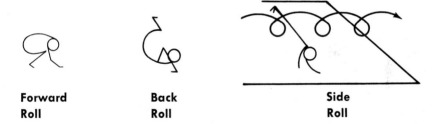

Forward Roll   **Back Roll**   **Side Roll**

CRAWL—a locomotor bodily movement which transports the body on a horizontal plane at the middle level by laterally or bilaterally transferring the body weight progressively from one knee to the opposite lateral hand (i.e., left knee to right hand, or to the right knee and the left hand), or alternately from both knees to both hands.

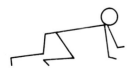

WALKING ON ALL FOURS—applies the same weight transference as for the crawl but involves the use of the hands and the feet.

WALKING ON THE HANDS OR FOREARMS—locomotor bodily movements which transport the body on a horizontal plane either at the low, middle, or high level. The transference of weight is from one arm to the other, while the rest of the body is either dragged along behind or balanced above.

SQUIRM OR WIGGLE—a locomotor bodily movement which transports the body on a horizontal plane at the lowest level by means of a series of wiggly movements which are executed by alternately unweighting a lateral side of the body (by flexing at the hip joint of that same side), and then weighting and extending the same side. The elbows are moved in opposition so as to help the forward locomotion.

SLIDE (BODY)—a locomotor bodily movement which transports the body on a horizontal plane at the lowest or middle level by means of a slipping action of the whole or parts of the body other than the feet, against a smooth surface. An example of this kind of slide is seen when a baseball player slides into a base. The body slide should not be confused with the foot slide which is an elementary form of locomotion executed by the feet.

Elementary Forms of Nonlocomotion: Movements by Means of the Feet. The nonlocomotor movements using the feet are the most basic and natural methods by which *a foot or two feet can move but not transport* the body mass. These nonlocomotor forms often combine with locomotor forms to create interesting step patterns. Nonlocomotor forms become locomotor forms by combining them with a locomotor form, or by simply transferring one's weight onto the performing foot.

BALL—executed by decisively touching the floor with the ball of one foot while supporting the weight with the other foot.

BRUSH—performed by alternately sweeping the floor with the ball of the foot, first in one direction and then in another.

HEEL—executed by dorsi-flexing at the ankle joint and touching the heel to the floor.

KICK—executed by extending the full leg in any direction in the surrounding space while the weight is supported by the other foot. Various degrees of ankle and knee joint flexion and extension are involved.

SCUFF—performed by decisively brushing the floor with the bottom and the heel of the foot in a forward direction.

SLAP—accomplished by brushing the floor with the ball of the foot in a forward direction. When executing one slap, the movement continues by touching the bottom of the same foot. In a series of slaps which locomote, the weight remains on the balls of the feet and the weight is transferred from the ball of one foot to the ball of the other. However, the ankle is very relaxed and there is a great deal of ankle joint action.

STAMP—executed by decisively and audibly striking the floor with the flat, or bottom, of the foot.

TAP—done by decisively and audibly striking the floor with the ball of the foot.

TOE AND POINT—both performed by extending the toes of one foot and either touching them to the floor or to the surrounding space.

TWIST OR PIVOT RUB—accomplished by centering the weight over one foot, pressing the ball of the other foot into the floor, and moving this foot by alternately directing the toes toward and away from the center line of the body. Movement of several other parts of the body follows sequentially in a twisting action. They involve the leg of the moving foot, the hips, and the lower torso. The arms are slightly flexed and also move across the front of the body, alternately from side to side, in opposition to the movement of the foot.

Foot Movement Combinations to Form Step Patterns. Movements of the feet may be combined to form a step pattern. Examples of the several ways this can be done follow. There are, in addition, innumerable combinations, and children should be encouraged to discover their own patterns.

Examples of locomotor plus locomotor:
Three walks and one hop

	walk	walk	walk	hop
4	1	2	3	4
	1	2	3	4

Six runs and one jump

	r r	r r	r r	jump	
4	1 +	2 +	3 +	4	r = run
	1	2	3	4	

Four hops and two jumps

	hop	hop	hop	hop	jump		jump	
4	1	2	3	4	1	②	3	④
	1	2	3	4	1	2	3	4

Four skips and four jumps

ski p	ski p	ski p	ski p	j	j		jump
4 1+ah	2+ah	3+ah	4+ah	1	2	3	④
1	2	3	4	1	2	3	4

Examples of locomotor plus nonlocomotor (When illustrating non-locomotor foot movements, it is best to indicate which foot does what. This will help to indicate where the weight changes are.)

One walk and one kick (repeated)

	walk	kick	walk	kick
2	1	2	1	2
	Right	Left	Left	Right

One walk plus one stamp plus one kick

	walk	stamp	kick	walk	stamp	kick
3	Right	L	L	Left	R	R

Four taps, four stamps, four brushes, four runs and one jump

	tap	t	t	t
4	Right	R	R	R

	stamp	st.	st.	st.
	R	R	R	R

	brush	b	b	b	r	r	r	r	jump
4	Right	R	R	R	R	L	R	L	Together

Examples of nonlocomotor plus nonlocomotor:
One ball and one heel (repeated)

	ball	**heel**		**ball**	**heel**	
2	R	R		R	R	

One heel and one toe (repeated)

	heel	**toe**		**heel**	**toe**	
2	R	R		R	R	

One brush and one stamp: one brush and one toe

	brush	**stamp**		**brush**	**toe**	
2	R	R		R	R	

Remember, there is no weight change when executing a nonlocomotory foot movement.

Popular Step Combinations. Certain step patterns have become so popular that each one of them can be identified by its name. These step patterns are used extensively in social, folk, and square dance. Their basic patterns and variations are also used in creative dance and in many sports activities. Children enjoy discovering them for themselves and varying them in many different ways.

THE SCHOTTISCHE—A combination of three runs and a hop usually done in a forward direction. The hop is done on the foot which makes the third run. When the step pattern is repeated, it begins with the alternate foot.

Rhythm
The schottische is performed to an even rhythmic pattern, as follows:

	∧ run	r	∧ r	hop
4	1	2	3	4
	1	2	3	4

Suggested Teaching Procedure:

If the children have been previously introduced to the elementary forms of locomotion of the feet, and have practiced them and explored their variations, they should be able to do the schottische just by having the teacher say: "Let's do three runs and a hop!" Have the children do any or all of these:

- listen to the drum beating measures containing four beats with a strong accent on the first beat, and a secondary accent on the third.
- clap on the major accent along with the drum.
- clap on the first three beats, accenting the first, and making no audible sound on the fourth beat.
- clap the first three beats and say "hop" on the fourth beat. Repeat often.
- say "run, run, run, hop," while teacher plays the drum or piano.
- say "run, run, run, hop," while the teacher performs the action.
- stand erect and do the schottische step pattern in place.
- locomote by doing the schottische.

Variations:

- Try moving backward and sideways somewhere within the step pattern. The change of direction will motivate the child to cross his feet in front of or behind one another, or try a step together spatial pattern of the feet in a sideward direction.
- Try doing the schottische with a partner, experimenting with different bodily facing relationships, one to another.
- Try having the schottische done by lrager groups, experimenting with varying spatial relationships among the group members.
- Do two schottische steps and add another short rhythmic pattern which can be moved to creatively. This rhythmic pattern may encourage another step pattern, or a bodily movement pattern. Return again to the two schottische step patterns. Alternate two schottische step patterns and two other rhythmic patterns.
- Because the schottische has an even, simple, and decisive rhythmic pattern, one can readily accompany it on percussion or musical instruments.

THE POLKA—A combination of slide, walk, and hop; or a combination of slide and skip. The polka begins in one of two ways: either on the hop, or on the slide.

Rhythm

The polka is danced to an uneven rhythmic pattern, as follows:

Doing the polka!

Polka no. one:

	slide	skip
	walk l	walk h
2		
	hop	

Polka no. two:

	slide	skip
	walk l	walk h
2		

l = leap
h = hop

Suggested Teaching Procedure:

Listen to the drum beating the rhythmic pattern of a slide, and clap to it.

Method no. 1.

1. Slide around the room, facing the center of it.
2. At any point during the execution of the slide, but without stopping the movement, turn to face the outside of the room (or the outside of the circle). Now, at any point during the slide and without stopping the movement, turn to face the inside of the circle again. Do this several times until changing one's facing during the execution of a slide is done with ease. Proceed to no. 3 of the progression that follows.

Method no. 2.

(The following should be done with the entire body facing the long wall. It is an excellent exercise in body facings, and also points out the sideward direction of the slide.)

1. Face one of the long walls of the room. Slide sideways to the right, to the end of the room.
2. Slide sideways to the left to the end of the room.

Progression of method one or method two. Continue either method one or method two as follows:

3. Slide eight times either facing the center of the circle (method one) or facing one long wall (method two). Now slide eight times either facing the perimeter of the circle or sliding toward the opposite wall. Accent the first step after the change. Let the children discover for themselves that they change direction on the hop. Discuss and practice it.
4. Repeat the preceding with four slides—then two. The children will now be doing the polka. The teacher may want to help the children in their execution of the polka by saying: "slide-and-change," and/or "slide-and-step-hop."

   Variations
   - The polka may be done from side to side in the same location; or it may progress through space forward, or by a series of turns. It may also be done alternately forward and backward.
   - Face to face and back to back polka: This polka is danced with a partner; the two start by facing each other, and holding both hands. They then drop hands closest to the direction in which they

wish to proceed. They do their first polka sideways, but facing each
other. They then swing the arms which are joined and firmly
extended, past the front of their bodies and point the joined hands in
the direction in which they are progressing. This action of the
extended arms swings their bodies around so that they are facing
back-to-back. They now do their second polka facing back-to-
back. On the hop or change, they swing their arms, which
are still firmly extended, across their backs to their original starting
position. The arm-swing rotates them around again to their original
face-to-face position, where they do their third polka. The movement
locomotes them always in the same direction. However, their body
positions change from face-to-face to back-to-back. Stiff arms help to
rotate the bodies easily. The hand hold is never broken. The teacher
vocalizes to the rhythmic and movement pattern by saying the
following: "face-to-face" and "back-to-back."

- Try doing the polka with a partner, experimenting with different
  body facings.
- Try doing the polka in large groups, experimenting with different
  spatial relationships to each other.
- Do two or four polka step patterns and add two or four other step or
  bodily movement patterns to the same rhythmic pattern.

THE WALTZ—A combination of three walks. The third walk is
executed by bringing the foot up alongside the second walking
foot and changing the weight next to it. During the course of
doing the three walks, the feet relate to each other spatially as
follows: open, open, close. While there are many variations of the
waltz, three of the most common are defined here. The suggested
teaching procedure which follows does not adhere to any of the
waltzes defined. Rather, the suggested teaching procedure permits the child to become thoroughly acquainted with moving
to three-quarter time—waltz time—by developing three walks
and a turn, and encourages the free-and-easy swaying feeling
one gets from moving to waltz time. From here, the child may
easily proceed to any of the many waltz variations.

WALTZ BALANCE—a combination of three walks. The first walk
is long and directed forward or backward. The second and third
walks occur in place, and are merely a shift in weight from the
ball of one foot to the ball of the other. The weight is lifted high
on the ball of the foot toward the end of the first step, and the
second and third step are taken in this high erect position.

WALTZ RUN OR THREE-QUARTER RUN—a combination of three runs
done to a rather fast three beat rhythmic pattern. The first run

The waltz run!

is accented more than the other two runs. This is done by leaning to the side on the first run and slightly flexing the knee on the same side. The second and third run are taken in progressively more elevated positions. The fact that the accent of the three-quarter run occurs first on one foot and then on the other gives the waltz run its characteristic swaying quality.

Suggested Teaching Procedure:

The children should be permitted to experience the three-beat rhythmic pattern often, and should have ample opportunity to explore moving to it. They should:

1. listen to the drum beating the three-beat rhythmic pattern and clap hard on the first beat only.
2. listen to the drum beating the four-beat rhythmic pattern and clap hard on the first beat, at the same time loudly saying "one."
3. clap hard on the first beat and softly on the second and third.
4. say "one" loudly and "two" and "three" softly, while clapping hard, soft, soft. (Method One: Do not proceed until all of the above has been practiced so often that the children strongly feel the three-beat rhythmic pattern.)
5. while sitting, sway to each side alternately on the count of one, then stand and do the same.
6. move one part of the body on the count of one in any direction. Or,
7. move another part of the body on the count of one in any direction. Or,
8. turn and face in another direction on the count of one.
9. walk three steps forward, and after the third step has been taken, make a quick turn and take another three steps in the opposite direction, then make a quick turn again and repeat.
10. be given ample opportunity to experiment with the turn. Let the children discover the turn that will get them going in the opposite direction the quickest. A description of this turn is as follows: After executing three walks forward, the feet are positioned one forward and one behind, with the weight on the forward foot. The pivot is on the forward foot so that the toes of both feet are now directed in the opposite direction. However, the back foot does not change its relative position or its spatial relationship to the forward foot. After the pivot, the back foot becomes the lead foot which will take the first walk on the count of one.
11. continue to do three walks forward and turn. The turn is on the count of "and," which occurs after the third walk and before the first walk.

walk	w	w	t	w	w	w	t	
3 Right	Left	R	R	L	R	L	L	t=turn
1	2	3		1	2	3		

The movement pattern does not locomote the body forward, but alternates it from side to side. This is because the forward direction constantly alternates. One may locomote forward by moving in a zigzag direction.

12. be encouraged to point, by extending the arm and hand, in the direction that the first step will be taken. Repeat often.
13. be encouraged to lean in the direction toward which they are extending their arm.

The child should now be moving easily to a three-beat rhythmic pattern. This should be repeated often, so that the three-beat rhythmic pattern is thoroughly enjoyed and felt by everyone. After this, the teacher may introduce other foot spatial relationships in the three-beat rhythm, being very careful not to progress too rapidly lest the children lose the special feeling of moving to waltz time.

Nonlocomotor Bodily Movements. The following movements, can be easily experienced and identified by children in the elementary school.

Flexion (commonly referred to as bending) is a nonlocomotor movement which occurs when two segments of the body approach one another, thereby decreasing the angle between them.

Extension (commonly referred to as a stretch) is a nonlocomotor movement which occurs when two segments of the body move away from each other, thereby increasing the angle between them. A stretch goes beyond the act of extension by bringing the muscles, tendons and joints of the extended segments into further use, thereby causing hyperextension of these segments.

Abduction is a nonlocomotor movement in the frontal plane which occurs when a bodily segment moves away from the midline of the body.

Adduction is the reverse of abduction.

Circumduction is a nonlocomotor movement of a bodily segment which describes a cone, with the apex at the joint and the base at the distal end of the segment.

Rotation is a nonlocomotor movement whereby a body segment turns on its own axis. When the head gestures "no," it is rotating. When the

Extend your arm in the direction you're going!

head moves in a complete circle, by reaching the chin toward the chest, the ear toward the shoulder, the back of the head toward the back, the other ear toward the other shoulder and the chin toward the chest again; the result is called circumduction.

Pronation is inward, or toward the midline, rotation.

Suppination is outward, or away from the midline, rotation.

Twist is a nonlocomotor rotating movement which combines the actions of inversion or pronation in one bodily part and suppination or eversion in an adjoining part at the same time. The shoulders may also be *elevated* or *depressed.*

The following additional movements are possible in the joints; they also have characteristic actions which are due to inward (muscular) or outward (universal) forces that depict their movement quality and give them their name.

Swing is a nonlocomotor movement which is pendular in action, and can be done by the body mass or various parts thereof. The swing creates an arc-like space pattern around a stationary center as it moves into an extension, a suspension, and a giving-in to gravity, or fall. This fall creates enough momentum to initiate another extension on the opposite side of the arc. In order to prevent a swing from dying out, a certain amount of muscular force must be applied on the upswing. This will help to keep the dimensions of the arc on each side similar. If one increases the amount of muscular power to more than is needed to maintain the arc-like space pattern, the swing will swell up and over into a full circle. The following parts of the body swing easily: arms from the shoulders; legs from the hips; the torso from the hips; and the head from the neck.

Sway is a nonlocomotor movement which is usually performed by the body mass oscillating smoothly from side to side about a fixed axis. It is a lean from side to side. In a standing position, the feet usually remain motionless as the weight is transferred from one foot to the other. The axis lies on an imaginary point halfway between the two feet.

Rock—A nonlocomotor movement similar in action to a sway, except, the body movement is from front to back instead of from side to side; a stronger tension is maintained, giving it a distinct quality.

Shake—A nonlocomotor movement of one or more bodily parts which result in short, quick, jiggling repetitive movements which are self-imposed or externally imposed. A shaking movement is slower and more defined than a vibratory movement.

Push—A nonlocomotor movement which results in a shoving action of one or more bodily parts against a real or imagined resistance, causing an extension of those parts away from the body mass. A push becomes a locomotor movement when the impetus is stronger than its resistance and the body falls outside of its base of support. The body is then forced to make one or more compensatory foot movements in order to prevent falling.

Pull—A nonlocomotor movement which results in a drawing-in action of one or more bodily parts against a real or imagined resistance, and causing a flexion of those parts toward the body mass.

Vibration—A vibration is a nonlocomotor movement which has a cause-and-effect action initiated by a strong impetus, either self-imposed or externally imposed; it results in short, quick, tremble-like movements which subside as time passes.

Strike—A nonlocomotor movement of one or both arms in any direction for the purpose of hitting a real or imagined object. The arms are usually strongly flexed to initiate a strike. They then extend, explosively, with force and speed. The movement has no follow through, and is abruptly terminated upon completion.

Dodge—A nonlocomotor or a locomotor movement which enables the body to evade rapidly. When the movement is nonlocomotor it is often called a duck.

Sequential Movement—This movement starts in one part of the body and progressively travels in succession to each adjoining part.

The following nonlocomotor bodily movements apply particularly to those movements occurring in the vertical space, surrounding the body. The positions in vertical space are called levels and are described in this chapter under *space.*

Sit—A nonlocomotor movement which transfers the body from any level to the one in which the weight is supported on the buttocks or the thighs.

Lift—A nonlocomotor movement used for transporting a real or an imagined object from one level to another in space. When one lifts his own body, he transports it from one level in space to a higher level; this is often referred to as a rise.

Suspension—A nonlocomotor movement which causes the body to assume a position in space outside the body's base of support, and thus defies the pull of gravity for a brief moment.

Fall—A nonlocomotor movement which transfers the body mass from a higher level to a lower level in space by permitting the body mass to "give in" to the force of gravity.

Combination of Foot and Body Movements. By combining foot and body movements, children will discover new and fascinating movement and space patterns to stimulate their curiosity intellectually and creatively. Because the body is equipped with so many movable parts, each part capable of being moved in several ways, the chances for any two or more combinations being alike is almost impossible. Herein lies the creativity, excitement, and thrill of discovering, bringing about, or instigating a new movement. Such a movement may not be new to the world, but it is new to the child. It is his discovery, an extension of his physical, mental, emotional, and social self, and is, therefore, self-rewarding. Combinations of foot and body movements may be done simultaneously or alternately. Some examples follow; and these are just a few of the many possibilities which exist.

Simultaneously:
Jumping, and simultaneously extending and flexing the arms alternately.

	extend	flex	extend	flex	← bodily movement pattern
4	1	2	3	4	
	jump	i	i	i	← step pattern
	1	2	3	4	

Hopping and simultaneously twisting the body alternately from side to side.

	twist R	twist L	T-R	T-L	← bodily movement pattern
4	hop	h	h	h	← step pattern
	1	2	3	4	
	1	2	3	4	

Running forward. Pulling the arms toward the body mass, while running backward.

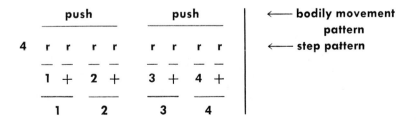

	push				push				← bodily movement pattern
4	r	r	r	r	r	r	r	r	← step pattern
	1	+	2	+	3	+	4	+	
	1		2		3		4		

Walking and shaking the whole body twice with each walking step.

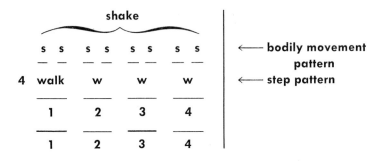

Walking while swinging the arms and head once per walking step.

Alternately:
Run, stop, extend the whole body.

Run, stop, extend, flex, extend the whole body.

	r r	r r	r r	stop		extend		flex	
4									
	1	2	3	4		1	2	3	4

	e x t e n d			
	1	2	3	4

Crawl to eight counts and roll to eight counts.

	crawl	c	c	c	c	c	c	c
8								
	1	2	3	4	5	6	7	8

			r o l l				
	1	2	3	4	5	6	7	8

Heel-toe two times and slide four times.

	heel	toe	h	t	slide	s	s	s
4								
	1	2	3	4	1	2	3	4

Run, stop, three pushes with the elbows.

	r r		r r		r r		stop	
4	1 +		2 +		3 +		4	
	1		2		3		4	

	push		p	p		
	1	2	3	4	
	1	2	3	4	

Simultaneous and alternating movement patterns: As the child becomes acquainted with the many movement possibilities of the body, he will constantly seek more intricate movement and space patterns. Two examples follow from the many existing possibilities:

Run and at the same time fully extend the body. Suspend, fall.

Run, stop, shake, and extend the whole body at the same time, shake and flex the whole body at the same time.

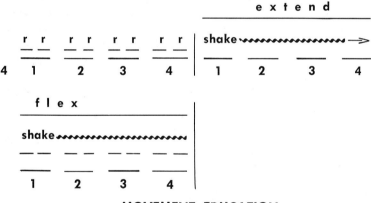

MOVEMENT EDUCATION

Movement education, as related to creative rhythmic movement, may be considered as having two main aspects. One aspect considers the *motor behavior* of the child: his performance, his skill, his fitness, and his educability. (Creative rhythmic movement is primarily concerned with observing the child's potential for engaging in efficient movement through the *greater awareness of his basic motor learning concepts,* which are mainly concerned with the cause and effect forces which act upon each child internally and externally.) The second aspect focuses upon the *maturation process of the child,* and how he develops a greater awareness of himself physically, mentally, emotionally, and socially by means of the explorations and discoveries he makes through bodily movement relative to motor learning concepts.

Both aspects are important and interrelated since they both help to prepare the child meet the problems of society by developing a thorough understanding of himself, in a very basic and observable way.

Movement Behavior, the observable movement of the body, excludes the occurrence of inner bodily changes. It is movement which has been caused by external physical forces. This observable movement, however, is a manifestation of muscle contraction acting within a system of levers and pulleys formed by the bones, tendons, and ligaments. Movement behavior is the core of CRM education in the kindergarten, second, or third grades. But as the child matures, he will be increasingly able to develop his *motor skill.* Through perceptual motor skill he will be able to recognize the more subtle cause and effect relationships of movements, especially those dealing with feelings and emotions.

Whenever movement of the body or its parts occurs, there is an observable change of position. The body may change its position by moving from one place to another, or the parts of the body may change their positions with respect to one another, producing a postural change of the entire body. In addition, these changes may take place on a moving or a stationary base of support. (Refer to bodily movement—locomotion and nonlocomotion, pp. 9–30.)

A study of motion involves consideration of three factors and their relationship to one another:

Force—the amount and method of energy release, the point of application, and the factors of resistance.
Space—the range, direction, and distance of movement.
Time—the duration, speed, and force of movement.

Once the inherent combination possibilities of these factors are grasped, there will be no limit to the patterns and forms of movement that the teacher and student may construct. Add to these factors the personality of the child and the feelings and emotions involved through the expression and communication of movement, and the possibilities for movement behavior are further expanded.

Force

The forces causing human motion may be either internal or external in origin. As related to CRM, force is mostly concerned with the mechanics of neuromuscular tension and the effect of the physical forces of the universe on the human body during rest or in movement.

It is, however, also concerned with feelings and emotions, and their power to motivate muscle activity.

Children become acquainted with these forces through movement. The teacher encourages children to test themselves against real or imagined resistances. By allowing their center of gravity to fall outside their base of support; by movng faster; or to go from slow to fast, and see how this affects their movement. The children are also encouraged to move extensively, slightly, diagonally, or smoothly, to see what happens to their movement and to their ideas and feelings about their movement.

An awareness of the ideas concerned with force as related to creative rhythmic movement is very important to the child for the following reasons:

- It increases his kinesthetic awareness.
- He becomes more *satisfied* with his movement because he understands its mechanics.
- He uses his increased perception of movement to increase his *ability to express* his ideas and feelings in movement.
- He has a greater *sense of appreciation* for the movement of others.
- He is more able to *remedy difficulties* associated with tension, relaxation, and movement of his own body.
- He is more able to increase his ability to move his body in *relation to other stationary and moving objects.*
- He will enhance his ability to *manipulate objects.*
- He will increase his movement technique and further his ability to *create.*
- He will *reduce tension* and *fatigue,* and move more efficiently.
- He will increase his ability to coordinate the movement of individual bodily parts into a unified whole.

The consideration of force that follows is divided into two parts: *internal force,* with its neuromuscular and emotional tension; and *external force,* or the physical, or natural, forces of physics acting on the body.

Internal Force. The internal forces which cause the body to move are produced by the energy released as the result of muscular tension. This involves two aspects:

Muscular tension is achieved by making the muscles, or groups of muscles, look and feel hard. Muscle and emotional tension affect each other.

Muscular relaxation is achieved by making the muscle look and feel relatively soft; this is attained by releasing the tension. Muscle and emotional relaxation affect each other.

Movement occurs during the interval between complete muscular tension and complete muscular relaxation. (The term *complete* is used as a relative term, as complete muscular tension, or relaxation, cannot normally exist.) (See muscle tone, p. 50.) Physically each body is constructed differently; therefore it is necessary for each child to experience and experiment consciously with movement to discover for himself the amount of muscular tension required and the correct timing for application of force to perform a given movement. Consider the following factors.

MOVEMENT QUALITY—The amount of and the method for muscular energy release give movement its distinguishing characteristics, or *quality considerations*. Such quality may be described in terms related to the muscular tension and relaxation of a movement, or its feeling relating to emotional and psychological factors associated with the movement.

A verbal description of movement is an account of its observable distinguishing characteristics. Much depends on the "eye" of the viewer—his past experience, his impressions, and his expertise in viewing movement.

When a child expresses a feeling or an idea through movement, the amount of energy he uses and the way in which he releases this energy depend very much on his past experience, impressions, and ability to express himself through movement.

Psychological factors also play a part in determining the quality of a movement. These factors and their associated feeling-states may be related to the temperature, light, sound, smell, color, space limitations, clothing, rhythm, and timing, to mention but a few possibilities.

Quality characteristics for the most common movements, are discussed in the section on the nonlocomotion of bodily movement (pp. 39–40). They are the swing, sway, rock, shake, push, pull, vibration, strike, dodge, and sequential movements. It is important to note that not all movement can be described verbally. This is especially true when viewing dance as an art form. The feeling inherent in a movement is sometimes lost by the over-intellectualization of the movement through verbalization of descriptive terms.

Making the muscles look and feel hard.

MUSCLE TONE—produced by the constant flow of energy to maintain balance between the parts of the body, and supports the body against gravity not only when it is in action, but when it is sitting or standing still. Muscle tone is an inherent balance of tension between opposing muscles. Muscles that are often used are likely to have more tone than those used less.

POSTURE—the manner in which one stands, sits, or carries out any number of ordinary activities. Highly individualistic, this manner should be considered from the standpoint of the child's body and the use he makes of it. This is to say that there is no correct posture for all individuals. The teacher should be very careful not to attempt to correct a child's posture, as this may be the kind of posture which is best suited for the child during this period of his life—or maybe a lifetime. Rather, the teacher should provide the child with enough physical activity, balanced by periods of relaxation, to increase muscular tonus, and to build strength, flexibility, balance, and coordination of the child's body. In addition, the teacher should make available to each child suggestions for a healthy diet. Moreover, the children should become thoroughly familiar with muscular tension and relaxation, as well as the need for its practice and use in the development of the kinesthetic sense.

COORDINATION—the synchronization of muscular tension and relaxation in movement or in balance.

MOMENT OF EXECUTION—that exact instant in time when the perfect amount of muscular force is applied in order to execute the desired movement.

KINESTHETIC SENSE—that sense through which movement of body parts can be perceived and directed in space. Sometimes kinesthetic sense is referred to as muscle sense, because the apparent sensation is due to muscle action which is conveyed to the central nervous system by nerve fibers. Through awareness, practice, and use of the kinesthetic sense, the child becomes consciously aware of movement; he is able to feel it and direct it. And through the use of the kinesthetic sense, movement becomes a personal tool used to discover and express oneself and to relate to one's environment. Terms which closely relate to the use of the kinesthetic sense are movement sense, movement awareness, and body awareness.

Progressive Relaxation (for Children). This is a conscious method for releasing the tension from one part of the body at a time, successively, until the whole body is relaxed.

Why present a method for relaxing the body to elementary school children?

Life is full of complexities, distractions, pressures of competition, and the continual race against time. Although many modern educators have made every attempt to lessen these tension-producing situations in the educational climate, such efforts will not remove the tension producing situations that abound in varying degrees outside the class-room. Each child copes with tension-producing situations in a manner which depends upon his own heredity and environmental makeup. It seems plausible, then, that the greater the degree to which a child reaches a state of self-awareness, especially with regard to concepts of tension and relaxation, the more apt he will be to react positively toward tension-producing situations that he will encounter during any of his life activities. The earlier this self-awareness takes place in the life of a child the better, since the tension-producing situations are ever present; for some children they are very prevalent and distressing even at an early age.

Tension states are produced when children are constantly pressured by peers, educators, and parents to do better, bigger, more, etc. (what-ever) . . . fear, worry, or are insecure . . . engage in excessive mental or physical activity . . . do not use their body correctly to move them-selves or another object . . . do not get enough sleep, or food.

Facts About Tension:

- The term *tension* refers to a general condition of activity throughout the body. Tensions are necessary in order to be alert and awake.
- When muscular tension exists, tension subsists in the nervous system and some hormonal glands.
- Individuals require varying degrees of tension to engage in normal daily activity. The amount differs within and among individuals.
- Since tension involves activity of the body, it uses up energy. The greater the tension the greater the expenditure of energy.
- The store of energy must be replenished through food, rest, and sleep.
- When tension is not reduced—when an individual cannot relax or

rest adequately—a state of increased muscular and emotional tension results. This can greatly interfere with the ability to live successfully with oneself, one's peers, one's family, or society in general.

What Can Be Done to Prevent Tension in School? The teacher can do any or all of the following:

- Since fatigue produces tension, balance the periods of work and rest through proper planning, and keep an alert, discerning eye on the child.
- Present creative activities which afford the children opportunity to use their own abilities in a variety of ways. These activities should be so presented as to reduce or eliminate competition with others or themselves and to incite their curiosity.
- Present to the children opportunities for learning about his body and how it can move efficiently, preventing the unnecessary expenditure of energy and thus reducing tension.
- Present a technique of relaxation for children to learn, practice, and use in school or before going to sleep at night.
- Relate the technique of progressive relaxation to daily life activities.

Starting Position for Progressive Relaxation
- Lie down in the back lying position.
- Rest arms on the floor, next to the sides. Flex the arms slightly at the elbows.
- Flex the knees slightly and permit the feet to flop outward, away from the midline; the small toes should be closer to the floor than the large toes.
- Put a small pillow, about two inches high, under the knees, to help support the above position. It should be a comfortable position; slight adjustments and practice will help to make it so.
- Close the eyes, although some children may prefer to keep them open the first few times.

Action for Progressive Relaxation
- Focus attention on *breathing* without interference with its normal rhythm. The breathing should be *easy and comfortable.*
- *Increase the duration of each exhalation* by giving in to gravity, releasing the muscular tonus of the body, especially the throat and chest muscles. Each bodily part is attended to during the exhalation. There is no movement. Each child thinks of, or is aware of, each bodily part as he releases the tension in that area. Awareness is enhanced when the child's eyes are closed and there is silence.

- Attend to the *pause* before beginning the *inhalation* again.

  Note: The teacher of elementary school children may find that this is as far as she can proceed without interjecting some activity. Since relaxation cannot occur without prior tension, the teacher will find that the children will more readily understand the concepts of relaxation if previous experience in body awareness and body tension has occurred. (See lesson plans 2 and 3 for rope movement, bodily tension and relaxation, and the quick change from activity, to relaxation, and back to activity again.)

- Attention is now turned to the *arms*. They are imagined as being very *heavy*. The teacher may go around the class and lift an arm of each child to test its heaviness. If the arm drops toward the floor, the child has been successful in releasing the tension in these muscles.
- The attention is now turned to the *shoulders* which *sink back*, while the *upper back* becomes *broad*, in an effort to spread *flat*.
- The *neck* feels *long* and the *head heavy*.
- Now think of the *upper body* as a *whole heavy unit*.
- Progress to the lower body. The *legs* become *heavy* and the hips spread out.
- Exhalation becomes very heavy, and the *abdominal* area, and the *lower back*, *sink* into the floor.
- The child is now encouraged to think of the *whole body* as one which has *given in to gravity*. The child should feel his body heavy against the floor, and feel the floor pushing up against his body.
- The release of the throat and facial muscles comes last. The *throat* is thought of as being *hollow and wide*, the *jaw drops*, and the *lips lie loose* and *slightly apart*. Imagine the *upper face spreading wide*. Some children will have difficulty becoming aware of the facial muscles, while other children will easily relax this area along with the rest of the body. Becoming aware of facial muscles may first be done by attending to the movements of the face and throat as the child vocalizes words and sounds to initiate movement. During vocalization, the child may put his hands on his own face and throat or on the facial muscles of another child. (See the section on *words* in chapter 5, pp. 221–24.)

Teaching Procedure:

The complete process of progressive relaxation should not exceed twenty minutes (the time should be reduced for children by only going part way through the procedure). Repeat the process often before progressing further. For teaching purposes, one may divide the progressive relaxation procedure into four parts.

1. The position and breathing.
2. Add the upper body, attending to each area at a time. Review.
3. Add the lower body, attending to each area at a time. Review.
4. Add the facial area. Constantly review all of the above.

The whole relaxation process can be introduced by having the children stretch, then progressively relax from the top down by collapsing each bodily part in succession until they are seated—ultimately lying down. (See lesson plan 2, in chapter 4.) Progressive relaxation should always conclude with stretches and deep breathing before activity resumes.

External Force. Although many of the external forces which act upon the body while at rest or during movement are difficult to define in children's terms, they are not difficult for children to experience, either through the movement of their own bodies or by the observation of other bodies. In addition, external forces can be experienced through the manipulation of objects and mechanical devices. It is through the act of doing that the realization eventually comes to each child that gravity, for instance, is a force which acts upon his body and all other bodies that exist in his surrounding world. A great deal of talk about gravity will not bring him to this realization as poignantly and as clearly as when he discovers it for himself. (Refer to motor learning teaching ideas, p. 000.) The external forces related to movement education for children are:

1. GRAVITY: The attraction of the earth for other objects. Newton's Law of Gravitation states that all objects attract one other. The force of their attraction depends on the mass of each object and on the distance between them.

   Center of Gravity. A body's center of gravity is that point at which the weight of the body seems to be concentrated. Gravity pulls on the body along a line straight down from its center of gravity. If the body leans too far to one side it will fall over if this line falls outside the body's base of support.

   Balance. The maintenance of the center of gravity over the base of support. The following concepts relate to balance:

   • The body will balance easier over a large base of support than over a small base of support.

- During movement and nonmovement, balance is influenced by the placement position of one's weight in relation to one's base of support. The body will balance more easily on a stationary base than on a moving base, and more easily when one's weight is centered over the base of movement than when it is off center.
- Imbalance is corrected by trying to recenter one's weight over the base of support, or by lowering one's center of gravity.
- Parts of the body may be moved to correct imbalance. This is called *compensatory movement.*
- Balance is easier when there is sufficient friction at the base of support.

2. FRICTION: A form of resistance to movement. The basic law of friction states that when the weight of a body pulled across the floor is doubled, the force necessary to pull it must be doubled. Three kinds of friction relate to bodily movement:

- Sliding, or kinetic friction, is produced when two surfaces slide across each other. The existence of friction between our feet and the earth or floor enables us to walk. The smoother the two surfaces are, the less friction between them, and the more difficult it is to walk.
- Rolling friction is the resistance produced when a rolling body moves over a surface.
- Fluid friction, or viscosity, is the friction between moving fluids or between fluids and a solid.

Air is a common ingredient of friction affecting bodily movement. The amount of friction between the body in motion and the air can be reduced by streamlining the shape of the body. This is accomplished by reducing the amount of body surface which pushes against the air in its flight through space, so as to increase its efficiency of movement. The *resistance of an object to the air* is called the *drag.* The less drag present, the greater the speed of the moving body, or the less effort required to move the body at the desired speed. The shape of the body can largely determine the amount of drag that will be present. Children enjoy experimenting with different bodily shapes in order to reduce the amount of drag and so to increase their speed. Children enjoy relating the principles of friction, drag, and streamlined bodily shapes in movement to the building of model rockets, airplanes, and cars.

3. SPEED: The average speed at which a child moves may be computed by measuring the linear distance he has gone, and dividing

this distance by the time which has elapsed while moving this distance. If a child runs 100 yards in 10 seconds, his speed will definitely exceed that of a child who runs the same distance in 15 seconds. The rate of speed for executing a movement is a factor which each child should realize, explore, and experience. It is especially important in understanding tempo. By consciously experimenting with speed through movement, the child gains a better perception of the relationship between fast, medium, and slow, and the amount of energy necessary to move in these tempos. The child will also be aware of what adjustments need to be made in his movements in order to go faster, or go slower, and how his movement is affected by these changes in speed.

4. VELOCITY: The average velocity with which a child moves is computed as a vector quantity, as it must include a statement pertaining to the direction of movement; this is a difficult mathematical computation for the elementary school child.

5. ACCELERATION: The rate at which a change in velocity occurs. It is easy for elementary school children to experience acceleration in movement, but it is not easy for them to compute this rate mathematically. A child may readily experience acceleration through any of the locomotor movements. He may begin walking slowly, and accelerate by walking faster and faster until he is running as fast as he can. As he accelerates, he may notice that the range of his movement becomes smaller as he goes faster, and that he must use more energy to go faster. He may also discover that the movement of those parts of the body which were used for balance has decreased in range, but are more necessary, as his speed increases. (See "streamlining the body" under Friction, p. 55.)

6. MOMENTUM

7. MOTION—*Newton's Laws:*
   a. Newton's First Law: A body remains in a state of rest or uniform motion unless it is acted upon by some other body. *Inertia* is that property of matter that tends to keep a body in motion when in motion, or at rest when at rest. A body is in a state of *equilibrium* or rest when the outcome of all forces acting upon it is zero. A body in *dynamic equilibrium* is constantly changing, and there are relatively few, if any momentary positions in which the conditions of stable equilibrium, as defined above, are met. The *flow of movement* is that movement which is in a state of

dynamic equilibrium. It is movement which grows sequentially like a chain reaction, one segment evolving from the preceding one. It is a principle of movement of prime importance in the development of movement patterns, phrases, and compositions, because the individual movements are made in relation to the whole. The awareness of the flow principle of movement can, and should, begin as early as possible in the child's movement education.

b. Newton's Third Law: Whenever one body acts upon another, the second exerts an equal and opposite reaction on the first. *Action and reaction.* For every bodily movement there occurs a reactive movement which is equal and opposite. The theory of action and reaction is important in oppositional movement and in attaining greater heights during leaping and jumping. (See motor learning teaching ideas, p. 246.)

8. CENTRIPETAL AND CENTRIFUGAL FORCES: Centripetal force produces radial acceleration and appears as a tension which pulls the object toward the center of rotation. Centrifugal force occurs at the same time, and with the same amount of force, but impels the object outward from the center of rotation. Children can feel the effects of these forces by rotating one or both arms horizontally, while positioned on a moving and rotating base of support.

Space

A body exists in and moves within and throughout space. The illusion of more or less space can be created by changing direction, level, range, and focus of the movement. A child's concept of himself and his relation to other objects in his environment increases with his awareness of space and his body of movable parts which exist and move within and throughout space. These concepts are important to his sense or reality and security.

There are three areas of space involved in achieving spatial awareness. They are *near space, far space,* and *extended space.* Creative rhythmic movement is mostly concerned with near and far space, although an awareness of all three areas and their relationships to one another strengthens spatial perception.

Near space is that area of space which immediately surrounds the body. It is the child's personal area of space; he can touch, punch, grasp, and feel it, without having to move to it.

Touching the near space.

Locomoting to the far space.

Far space is that observable space which lies beyond the child's grasp. In order to touch it, he must remove himself from his near space and locomote to the far space.

Extended space is that area of space which also lies beyond the child's grasp, but, in addition, exists beyond the child's vision. It is out-of-sight, out-of-touch space. However, it may be possible to hear and smell objects in the extended space.

The child's awareness of space begins while he is first becoming acquainted with his own body and how it exists and moves in near space. He then proceeds from what he has learned to what he wants to know. He should be aware of his body as a whole, its contour, its weight, the shapes it can make, and the possibilities and limitations of its movement. He should also be aware of his body as a system of movable parts. The child gains body awareness by looking at himself and others, touching himself and others, and consciously moving himself and others. (See lesson plans 1, 3, and 6, pp. 123, 142, 173.)

The child becomes aware of his near and far space in a similar manner. First he looks at it, then he touches it, and finally he moves within or through it. Employment of all the senses, especially the kinesthetic, visual, and tactile senses, is helpful for acquiring spatial perception during this process. The auditory sense is most advantageous in knowing extended space. (For examples on how to use the look, touch, and go method for spatial awareness see lesson plans 1, 3, 5, 8, and 9, pp. 121, 142, 165, 188, 196.) Now let us take a closer look at the extremely vital kinesthetic sense as it pertains to the child's development in acquiring special perception.

Kinesthetic sense (*in relation to space*). That ability of a person to be aware of the positioning and/or movement of his body or bodily parts in space.

Various aspects of space have terms that the child should learn so that he can refer to them and use them as tools for constructing patterns and compositions in movement. The following several such terms and their definitions follow. But unless the child actually experiences them (their meanings) through movement and explores all of their movement possibilities they will be meaningless. For instance it is very important that the child be aware of directionality and laterality in order to keep himself oriented in his surrounding world. Recognizing directional movement by name, as well as experiencing it through bodily movement, strengthens this awareness, and helps to give a sense of direction.

Focus is a place
upon which
movement is
concentrated.

DIRECTION—the path the body takes during movement. The most frequently used directional paths are: forward, backward, sideways, curvy, circular, diagonally, and zigzag. Movement can be made in any of the above directions by doing any one, or any combination of the following. For example, a child may move forward, backward, sideways, or diagonally.

>   . . . with the front of the body leading.
>   . . . executing any locomotor form of the feet or body mass.
>   . . . focusing forward; or to the side, above, or below.
>   . . . leaning forward, backward, or sideways.
>   . . . in the low, medium, high, or highest level.

FOCUS—a place upon which movement is concentrated. It may be a place lying in the near, far, or extended space of the child. Or, it may be a combination of any of the above, whereby the focus changes from one place to another. Focusing is most often done with the eyes. When the eyes stare at an imaginary spot, the individual is said to be spotting, or attending to a focal point. Use of the focal point helps the body remain on course or in balance when locomoting. It also emphasizes the movement, and helps to give a movement its quality characteristics.

BODY FACINGS—the facing of a body is the length of any one of the four aspects of the body from the top of the head to the toes. The body facings are front, sides, and back. They are important for the child to be aware of, and they play an essential part in directional movement.

RANGE—range of movement is the amount of space the body occupies while moving and pertains to the dimensions of the movement, conditioned mainly by the amount of joint action, the distance covered, and spacial limitations. The range of a movement is simply described as being small, medium, or large.

LEVELS—horizontal layers in space where the body mass positions itself, or within which it moves or through which it passes vertically. This space may be described to children as the up and down near-space which surrounds the body. The levels are as follows:

Low: the body mass occupies and moves throughout the space closest to the floor.

Middle: the body mass occupies and moves throughout a stratum of space midway between the low and high levels.

High: the body mass exists and moves as high above the floor as it can rise, while the weight of the body remains on one or both feet.

Highest: the body mass exists and moves as high above the floor as it can rise while the body is suspended in the space above. In order to stay at this level for any length of time, one must get a lift from another object or person. A fall moves one from the high or highest level through the medium, to the low.

SHAPES—contours which the body makes in the course of moving within and throughout space. As the body shapes the space while locomoting, it produces a *design in space*. (See lesson plans 5 and 6, pp. 165, 173, and the game, *statues*.)

FLOOR PATTERN—that imaginary design created on the floor or surface by the locomotor movements of the feet or the body mass. A floor pattern may resemble a straight line, a square, a circle, an arc, a zigzag, a snake, or any combination of these. (See lesson plans 6, 7, and 8, pp. 173, 180, 188, and for teaching ideas on directionality, shadows, and shapes refer to pp. 240–46.)

RHYTHM

Rhythm is an organizing force, manifested through repetition. In movement, rhythm is the relationship between time and force factors, and is manifested through repetition by the kinesthetic sense. The following statements apply to rhythmic movement:

- Rhythm develops from the repetition of movement.
- Time and force factors of rhythm are determined in the brain through the kinesthetic sense.
- Since the human body is the most accessible instrument of movement, one of the easiest and most obvious ways to become aware of rhythm is through bodily movement.
- Every person has the capacity for some rhythmic awareness.
- Rhythmic awareness improves with practice.
- The learning of a new movement can be facilitated by the analysis of its rhythmic organization.

This brings us, then, to an analysis of the two components needed to produce a movement's rhythmic structure.

Time and Force Factors

Time and force, as factors required to produce a movement's rythmic structure, are in themselves distinct and separate components of movement. Time relates to distance, tempo, repetition, regularity, size, and duration of movement, while force is concerned with gravity, buoyancy, resistance, friction, muscle power, energy output and accents of movement. The converging of these two components to produce a movement's rhythmic structure is accomplished in the brain. When bodily movement occurs, the proprioceptors, or sensory nerve endings which are embedded in the muscles, tendons and joints are stimulated. These sensations travel to the brain where they are registered, correlated, and compared with other sensations which have occurred previously, or are occurring simultaneously. It is from this sorting, sifting and comparison in the brain that one forms decisions as to the time and force aspects of movement. Through the action of the kinesthetic sense, or movement sense, the brain is constantly making decisions as to how much or how little time and force are involved in a given movement, and exactly when the greatest or least amount of effort is to be expended during the movement in order to execute it with the greatest amount of efficiency and satisfaction.

Rhythmic Factors of Time

Beat: the basic unit measure of time in bodily movement. That beat which underlies all bodily movement and measures the duration and steadiness of the movement is called the *underlying beat*. How many beats does it take to do two steps? It may take any number of beats depending on the tempo, speed of execution, and size of the steps. However, when two steps are taken about as fast as the tick of a clock, or as fast as a soldier usually marches, one can say that each step takes one underlying beat of medium tempo. The underlying beat, or steady, pulsating beat, which underlies bodily movement may be represented by a horizontal line. One underlying beat looks like this ―――― . Two underlying beats look like this ―――― ―――― .

Tempo: the rate of speed of successive recurring beats. In movement, the tempos may be designated as slow, medium (moderate) or fast. The sensing of tempo is relative and depends very much on a person's own physiological and psychological sense of rhythm. What is fast to one person may very well be moderate, or even slow, to another.

Rhythmic Factors of Force

Accent, Metrical Accent, and Measure. Rhythmic sensations are felt (perceived) as groupings of beats. These beat groupings are formed as the result of stresses or accents within the chain of recurring, underlying beats. *An accented beat* is a stronger or more determined beat, and occurs every two or three beats. *The metrical accent* is the strongest perceived beat in a chain of recurring beats. It is the positioning of the metrical accent which groups beats into a unit called the *measure*. The metrical accent is represented by the following sign >. If a strongly accented beat, such as the metrical accent, is perceived on every third beat, a measure is formed of two beats, and can be represented as follows; the number of beats in each measure is always indicated at the beginning:

$$2 \quad \overset{>}{\underline{}} \quad \underline{} \quad \Big|$$
$$ \quad 1 \qquad 2$$

Two measures with two beats occurring in each measure appears as follows:

$$2 \quad \overset{>}{\underline{}} \quad \underline{} \quad \Big| \quad \overset{>}{\underline{}} \quad \underline{} \quad \Big|$$
$$ \quad 1 \qquad 2 \qquad 1 \qquad 2$$

Three measures with three beats occurring in each measure appears as follows:

$$3 \quad \overset{>}{\underline{}} \quad \underline{} \quad \underline{} \quad \Big| \quad \overset{>}{\underline{}} \quad \underline{} \quad \underline{} \quad \Big| \quad \overset{>}{\underline{}} \quad \underline{} \quad \underline{} \quad \Big|$$
$$ \quad 1 \qquad 2 \qquad 3 \qquad 1 \qquad 2 \qquad 3 \qquad 1 \qquad 2 \qquad 3$$

Because the brain tends to group beats in units of two or three, a measure which contains more than three beats also has a *minor accent*. The minor accent is not felt nearly as strongly as the metrical accent.

The following shows the most common groupings of underlying beats into measures on the basis of the natural placement of metrical accents. Understanding the construction of these measures, and experience with its concepts through movement, music, and/or a percussion instrument, is fundamental to the teaching of creative rhythmic movement, and for further comprehension of this book.

```
2  >  ___  |
   1   2
3  >  ___  ___  |
   1   2   3
4  >  ___  >  ___  |
   1   2   3   4
6  >  ___  ___  >  ___  ___  |
   1   2   3   4   5   6
```

Suggested Teaching Procedure:

It is essential to repeat each measure fifteen to twenty times to get the feeling of the rhythm. One may practice the previous measures rhythmically by:

—hitting or tapping the beats on a table top or other solid object.
—clapping the beats with the hands.
—hitting a percussion instrument.
—moving any part, or parts, of the body.
—vocalizing a number on each beat; For example: *One*, two, *one*, two; or *one*, two, three, *one*, two, three. Remember, rhythmic awareness improves with practice. Repeat often!

Rhythmic Pattern and Accent of Execution. Although one finds underlying each bodily movement a steady, pulsating, underlying beat, a movement is better described rhythmically by its rhythmic pattern. The rhythmic pattern of bodily movement is formed by the natural positioning of the *accent of execution* which lies within the total movement experience. The accent of execution is found at the point of application of the greatest force within a movement. Sometimes it appears in the form of the largest of a series of movements. The accent of execution brings life to the movements, and usually can be readily detected by another person, since it has a determined or directed quality. These accents of execution divide or combine underlying beats to produce a rhythmic pattern.

The rhythmic pattern is written above the underlying beat as follows:

```
   >          >
4  ___  ___  ___ _ ___  ⟵ rhythmic
   1    2    3    4        pattern
```

Usually, the accents of execution occur on the metrical and/or minor accent of a measure. When this marriage of accents occurs, the movement and its underlying beat enhance or strengthen one another, resulting in a strong rhythmic experience. This would occur if a jump, leap, or stamp was executed on the first beat of the previous rhythmic pattern.

Rhythmic Analysis

Rhythm is perceived as unit groupings in the brain. In order to more readily perceive, strengthen, and recall these units the following suggestions may be used.

Vocalize. Say something on each beat.
Strike or beat. Produce a sound on each beat.
Move. Move one or more bodily parts on each beat.
Produce a tone on each beat.

Vocalizing on each beat by the use of numbers is a common way of helping one to perceive and strengthen awareness of rhythm. For instance, a measure which contains four underlying beats in each measure is numbered and vocalized as follows:

4   ——— ——— ——— ———   **or one, two, three, four**
     1   **2**   **3**   **4**

The accents are recognized by saying the numbers "one" and "three" louder.

Coincidental Beats: If the beats of the rhythmic pattern and the underlying beat coincide, they are counted exactly the same and may be illustrated as follows:

4   ——— ——— ——— ———   ← **rhythmic pattern**
     1   **2**   **3**   **4**
   ——— ——— ——— ———   ← **underlying beat**
     1   **2**   **3**   **4**

Combination of Beats: If the rhythmic pattern combines any or all of the beats expressed in the underlying pattern, the rhythmic pattern is counted and illustrated as follows:

4 ————————   ——   —— | ←—— **rhythmic pattern**
    1   ②   3   4
   ——— ——— ——— ——— | ←—— **underlying beat**
    1   2   3   4

3 ———————————— | ←—— **rhythmic pattern**
    1   ②   ③
   ——— ——— ——— | ←—— **underlying beat**
    1   2   3

Note: The numbers used to vocalize the underlying beat appear below the underlying beat while the numbers used to vocalize the rhythmic pattern lie below the rhythmic pattern. The accented underlying beat is indicated by a darker line. The encircled numbers are said to oneself, or whispered.

For Practice and Teaching

1. Vocalize on each beat of the underlying beat until the entire body has a feeling for the underlying beat as a unit. Be sure to emphasize the accents.
2. Beat the underlying beats on the floor, a table, or some other solid object with the left hand.
3. Vocalize and beat the underlying beats with the left hand. Repeat fifteen to twenty times.
4. Examine the written rhythmic pattern, and count it. Determine the coincidental accents and locate the coincidental beats. Vocalize on each beat.
5. Beat the rhythmic pattern with the right hand. Do not forget the tempo of the underlying beat. Since there is a definite relationship between the intervals of the rhythmic pattern and those of the underlying beat, the rhythmic pattern should fit into that same tempo. Repeat the rhythmic pattern often.
6. Vocalize and beat the rhythmic pattern with the right hand. Let the rhythm move throughout the whole body. This is especially true for the encircled numbers that are not audibly vocalized. Allow these silent beats to be an integral part of the total pattern.
7. Beat the underlying beats and the rhythmic pattern simultaneously. To commence, beat two measures of the underlying beats with the left hand, and then, on the first count of the third measure, start beating the rhythmic pattern with the right hand. This procedure should prove helpful in synchronizing the beat of the underlying

beats with the beat of the rhythmic pattern. Place the written patterns in front of you for easy referral.

8. If a whole class beats rhythmic patterns together, the teacher should have a start and a stop signal. The following starting signals are suggested:

- When using two or four beats to a measure, the teacher may say "*One*, two, ready, go!" Be sure to accent the number one. Also, be sure to say, "*One*, two, ready go!" in the tempo at which you desire the following beats to proceed.
- When using three or six beats to a measure, the teacher may say "*One*, two, three, *Ready*, and, go!" Be sure to accent *one* and *ready*.
- The stop signal may be indicated by the same procedure, simply by substituting the word "stop" for "go". Also, the teacher may raise her arm on the count of one, during the last measure, and lower it when she says stop. Repeat this often to get the feeling of it. If there is difficulty, begin again, try slower, but keep trying until everyone gets into the swing of it.

Following is a list of all the possibilities which can occur by combining one or more underlying beats to form a rhythmic pattern. Again, only those measures which contain two, three, four, and six beats to a measure are listed.

2	1	②		
	1	2		

3	1	②	③	
	1	2	3	

3	1	②	3	
	1	2	3	

3	1	2	③	
	1	2	3	

4	1	②	③	④
	1	2	3	4

4   1   ②   3   ④
     1   2   3   4

4   1   ②   ③   4
     1   2   3   4

4   1   2   ③   ④
     1   2   3   4

4   1   2   ③   4
     1   2   3   4

6   1   ②   ③   ④   ⑤   ⑥
     1   2   3   4   5   6

6   1   ②   ③   4   ⑤   ⑥
     1   2   3   4   5   6

6   1   ②   3   ④   5   ⑥
     1   2   3   4   5   6

6   1   ②   ③   ④   ⑤   6
     1   2   3   4   5   6

6   1   2   ③   ④   ⑤   ⑥
     1   2   3   4   5   6

6   1   ②   ③   ④   5   ⑥
     1   2   3   4   5   6

6   1   ②   3   ④   ⑤   ⑥

    1   2   3   4   5   6

The Division of Beats

A rhythmic pattern may also be formed by dividing the underlying beat. The division may be binary or tertiary. The *binary division* of a beat is formed by dividing it into halves or fourths. The *tertiary division* of a beat is formed by dividing it into thirds. Perceiving these divisions can be facilitated by vocalzing on each beat by using either numbers, nonsense syllables, or words.

Division of the beat into *halves:*

2   1 +   2 +   or   this way   that way

      1   2   1   2

Division of the beat into *thirds:*

or

2   1 + ah   2 + ah | sat ur day

      1   2   1   2

Combining *two-thirds* after the division into *thirds:*

2   long   short   >   ← note the rhythmic accent

Division of the beat into *fourths:*

2   1 + ah-ah | wat-er-mel-on   Feb-ru-ar-y

Following are some of the most common rhythmic patterns which may exist in measures containing two, three, four or six beats each. All the possibilities are not presented here. Developing competence with these patterns through practice in vocalizing, striking and/or moving on each beat, will greatly aid the teacher in presenting a program in creative rhythmic movement. Refer to pages 69–72 for suggestions on how to practice.

2	1		2 +	
	1		2 >	
2	1 +		2	
	1		2	
2	1		2 + ah	
	1		2	

3	1	②	③
	1	2	3
3	1	②	3
	1	2	3
3	1	②	3 +
	1	2	3
3	1	②	3 + ah
	1	2	3
3	1	2	③
	1	2	3
3	1	2	3 + ah
	1	2	3

4   1   ②   3   ④ |
    1   2   3   4 |

4   1   ②   ③   4 |
    1   2   3   4 |

4   1   ②   ③   4 + |
    1   2   3   4 |

4   1   ②   3 +   4 + |
    1   2   3   4 |

4   1   2 +   3   4 + |
    1   2   3   4 |

4   1   ②   ③   4 + ah |
    1   2   3   4 |

4   1   2 + ah   3   4 + ah |
    1   2   3   4 |

4   1   ②   3 + ah 4 + ah |
    1   2   3   4 |

6   1   ②   ③   4   ⑤   ⑥ |
    1   2   3   4   5   6 |

6   1   ②   3   4   ⑤   6 |
    1   2   3   4   5   6 |

6	1	②	③	④	⑤	6
	1	2	3	4	5	6
6	1	2 +	3	4	5 +	6
	1	2	3	4	5	6
6	1	②	③	4 +	5 +	6 +
	1	2	3	4	5	6
6	1	②	3 +	4	⑤	6 +
	1	2	3	4	5	6

The Rhythmic Analysis of Movement

Within every movement there exists an internal organization of time and intensity values that governs its form. While there are no absolute patterns to which movements must conform, every activity entails measurable periods of preparation, accomplishment, and recovery. It is by teaching the common elements found in movement, and their general functionings that learning is made possible. Through the analysis of the rhythmic structure of a movement into phases of stress and time one can improve his execution of a movement and consequently his ability to teach it. It is this kind of movement awareness that is valuable for the teaching of goal-oriented skills.

The rhythmic structure of a movement is characterized by the following:

- *Duration or time consumed by a movement.* Underlying all movement is an even, steady beat called the underlying beat. How many underlying beats are required to execute a particular movement? This determines the total number of beats it takes to do a movement.
- *Grouping the beats.* Movement is perceived as having a certain number of parts which have a definite time relationship to one another. Where are the metrical accents? This determines the number of measures it takes to do a movement and how many underlying beats occur in each.
- *Determination of the accents of execution.* Where are the points of greatest force? This determines the rhythmic pattern of the movement.

Teaching Suggestions for Practice in Determining the Rhythmic Structure of a Movement (for upper elementary grades only):

1. The teacher briefly demonstrates or describes one simple movement which can easily be performed by the children and repeated often. The children do it several times.
2. The children are asked to clap on the first beat of the movement and again on the last beat. They are told that each one may end his movement at a slightly different time.
3. The children are asked to count silently the number of steady, pulsating beats which it takes to execute the complete movement, including the first and last clap. Again, they are told that each one may have a different number.
4. The teacher settles on a total number of beats to perform the movement, which is an average of the different number of beats the children have selected. The children are then asked to adjust their movement to conform to this and practice executing the movement to these number of beats.
5. The children are now asked to determine where the accents of execution are in the total movement. In a simple movement, there is usually only one accent of execution, and it most often lies at the beginning of the movement, on the count of one, precisely on the metrical accent. When the children have determined all of the above, they should be able to represent this information in writing. They should be able to write the following: the underlying beats, the measures, the number of beats in the measures, the metrical accent, and the rhythmic pattern of the movement. Here are two examples of how this may appear:

Example One:

		push	with	two	hands		
6	1	②	③	④	⑤	⑥	
	1	2	3	4	5	6	

Example Two:

		swing	leg	forward		swing	leg	back	
3	1	②	③		1	②	③	
	1	2	3		1	2	3	

Further analysis of the rhythmic structure of a movement should proceed as follows:

1. Analyze the rhythmic patterns of locomotor forms and their combinations.
2. Look for simple movement patterns which the children themselves have composed; analyze them with the children in class.
3. Encourage the children to write the rhythmic structures of their movement compositions, so that they can compose a percussion or musical accompaniment. Start with short compositions, or a portion of a composition.

Additional Information Which Relates to Rhythm.

- *Rhythmic Accent.* That stress which occurs on a beat other than the metrical accent. Its usage is derived from a rhythmic law which states that when an undivided interval follows a short interval of a divided beat, the undivided interval is given emphasis. Analysis of rhythmic patterns containing rhythmic accents should be avoided in the first four grades of the elementary school, as it may be confusing.

- *Movement Phrase.* Comprises several movements which are related and grouped together to form one complete movement expression. It is comparable to a phrase of words within a sentence, or a phrase of music within a musical composition.
- *Movement Composition.* A complete movement theme fabricated by the synthesis of many movement phrases.
- *Syncopated Movement.* A sudden, surprising accented act which breaks the regularity of the metrical accent by occurring at an unexpected phase of the movement sequence. A syncopated accent may be taught along with the rhythmic accent in the fifth or sixth grade, provided that the children have had considerable previous rhythmic experience.

⟵ syncopated accent

3   1 +   ② +   ③

　　　1   　2   　3

Lesson plans which emphasize rhythm are as follows: 5, 6, 7, and 8, pages 165, 173, 180, 188.

More Difficult Rhythmic Patterns:

2   1 + ah   2 ⊕ ah

　　　1   　　2

3   1   2 + ah   3 + ah

　　1   　2   　3

4   1 + ah ah   2   3 +   4

　　　1   　2   　3   　4

4   1   ②   ③   ④ ⊕ ah

　　1   2   3   4

6   1   ② +   3 +   4   5   6

　　1   2   3   4   5   6

MUSIC AND OTHER ACCOMPANIMENT FOR TEACHING CREATIVE RHYTHMIC MOVEMENT

The basic concepts of creative rhythmic movement and music are very closely related. The most obvious concept—rhythm with its factors of time and force—is an especially important one to develop in the elementary school years. Other concepts shared by music and creative rhythmic movement which can be explored by children are the expression and communication of feelings and ideas brought about by tonality, harmony, and rhythm.

The following remarks are included to help the teacher judge when, how, and what type of music should be used for teaching creative rhythmic movement. However, this is of necessity only a superficial study of the music—CRM relationship, inasmuch as it would require volumes to cover the subject in its entirety.

Music is composed of rhythm, melody, and harmony, and as an art form expresses and communicates feelings and ideas. In movement, the underlying beat relates to the rhythm of music. The rhythm of the movement pattern relates to the melody; and two or three rhythmic movement patterns performed simultaneously relate to the harmony.

Children should *never* be encouraged to create movements to fit music—unless the intent of the exercise is to foster an awareness of similar elements in music and creative rhythmic movement. Composing movement to fit musical composition tends to inhibit self-awareness, creativity, and spontaneity in children—rather, children should be permitted the time, space and encouragement to explore, discover, and pattern movement by themselves, without relating to any other art form. They should experience the freedom of being themselves and knowing themselves. Then, by means of guided explorations and dis-coveries through CRM they should attain a level of readiness for first developing a form on their own and then working on it in conjunction with another form, such as music.

Does this mean then that each expressive activity should develop separately, independently from each other? Indeed not! It does mean, however, that children's movement should not be channeled before they are emotionally ready to absorb another art form concurrently with CRM. (Refer to Expression and Communication, pp. 90–95.)

When will the children be ready to combine creative rhythmic movement and music? Unless the unit is aimed at studying the relation-ship between concepts in music and creative rhythmic movement, music should only be included for the following reasons:

- Because awareness of a concept of creative rhythmic movement is enhanced by it.
- For fun, exhilaration, and the release of tension.
- For enhancing the expression of a feeling or idea.

In determining the appropriate time when music can be combined with creative rhythmic movement, the first question the teacher should ask herself is, "How can music or percussion accompaniment aid the child in perceiving a concept related to CRM? If there are no positive reasons, don't use accompaniment. However, rhythm with it's time and force factors is found both in music and creative rhythmic movement, so it follows that rhythmic accompaniment should not only enhance the expression and awareness of CRM but that the two should become dependent on one another.

Thus we see that the combining of music with creative rhythmic movement (after the child has been exposed to CRM by itself) is quite different from encouraging children to explore movement and form movement patterns to be set to an already formed piece of music. How can music and creative rhythmic movement be combined so that these activities enhance each other and become an interdependent unit?

The children may begin by developing rhythm and movement together. In fact, rhythm and movement, done creatively or not, may begin on the very first day, or may even begin at the preschool level. (See lesson plan 1, p. 123.) The initial introduction to rhythmic movement should be based on the child's own tempo of movement. Later the teacher may impose various other tempos upon the class which the children may follow; however, it should be made clear to the children that each member of the class has his own inherent tempo of movement which he will use as a basis of comparison against those imposed upon him.

Rhythmic patterns should first be created by the children themselves, and initially should relate to the simple patterns formed by words, names, and elementary forms of locomotion and nonlocomotion. Only after they have thoroughly explored the composition of their own rhythmic patterns should they be introduced to melody. This exploration period may take as much as twenty to thirty exposure hours, or may only take a few hours. (Refer to lesson plans 7 and 8 and the sections on rhythm, pp. 64 and 210.)

The introduction of melody and harmony should also first occur through the creative efforts of the children themselves. In order for the teacher to present problems to solve in relation to the development of melody and harmony as it pertains to creative rhythmic movement, more knowledge about music is required than you will find in this book. (Refer to Additional Reading Material for Teachers.)

What are the qualities of music the teacher should look for to enhance the creative rhythmic movements of children?

- The feeling quality or mood of the music should be the same as the movement quality.
- The rhythm. The underlying beat of the movement and music should coincide, but the rhythm of the music should not be too forceful, and should be subdominant to the rhythm of the movement.

Percussion instruments.

Moving with a percussion instrument.

- The accents and phrasing of the music and movement should be related or the same.
- The music should have large spaces void of melody, harmony and rhythm, wherein movement can occur. If the music is too full of melody, harmony and rhythm it is too complete in itself to be used to enhance creative rhythmic movement. The music is then better if it exists by itself—as a complete art form.

The above qualities should be predetermined by the teacher and if music is used, it should be a planned part of the lesson. It is seldom that a teacher will have a record or a piece of music at her beckoning that will be just right to enhance the spontaneous and exploratory movements of children. For this reason alone, recorded music should not be used to accompany the creative rhythmic movement explorations of children. However, after the exploration period, the teacher may find a recorded or written piece of music which enhances a pattern of movement which the class is doing. At this time, using it to accompany the movement pattern may augment the movement. (Refer to Orff-Schulwerk in the bibliography for more information on the development and use of rhythm, tonality, movement, and percussion instruments by children.)

Percussion instruments emphasize rhythm, and serve as the best accompaniment for creative rhythmic movement. Since playing them requires relatively little skill—children can create their own sounds and move to them. They may move to the dynamics, pitch, or duration of the sound. When moving to the timbre—the quality given to the sound —of a percussion instrument, it is best to begin with only one sound from only one instrument. Then proceed with a contrasting sound on another percussion instrument, and a third sound on a third instrument. (See lesson plan 2, p. 130.)

The teacher, herself, may desire to play the percussion instruments for accompanying the creative rhythmic movement of children. A small drum having good tone quality when played with the hand or fingers is especially useful, since it will allow her to focus her attention on the children as she plays it. In addition the teacher can carry it with her as she proceeds through the classroom. A small autoharp, ukulele, guitar, and castanets are suitable for these same reasons.

The teacher presenting lessons in creative rhythmic movement for the first time should practice using the drum often before attempting to use it in class. If the teacher has difficulty keeping a steady beat on the drum, she should not use it. Instead, she should allow the children to explore the use of the percussion instruments, and select one child who can provide a steady beat to accompany the class; that is, if there is a need for accompaniment.

The teacher may also provide a variety of sounds for the accompaniment of the movement patterns which children create, by selecting three or four percussion instruments and hanging or securing them in a place close to her home base. This will afford her the opportunity of providing an interesting and varied accompaniment spontaneously, as needed.

The teacher may purchase percussion instruments at music stores; some cities even have special music stores for children. Percussion instruments especially suited for children's creative rhythmic movement are: drums of various shapes and sizes; cymbals; bells and gongs; wood blocks; sandpaper blocks; dowels or other forms of hitting objects. (See additional ideas on rhythm, pp. 77–78 and the bibliography.)

The piano may also be used as a percussion instrument; and the teacher need not have any knowledge or skill in playing it in order to use it percussively. The piano may be pounded, tapped, or fingered just as a drum. However, the range of movement on a piano, and the accompanying sounds which occur are far greater than those created on any other percussive instrument.

Following are a few suggestions for using the piano as a percussion instrument:

- Determine the quality of the children's movement. If it is heavy, use the lower third of the piano, the bass; if it is medium, use the middle of the piano; and if it is light and airy, use the upper third of the piano. But if the quality of the movement is variable, use a combination, the left hand using one part of the piano and the right hand using another part, either alternately or simultaneously.
- Place the hand, or hands, on the piano in the desired location and strike, stroke, tap or finger the piano, making an effort to produce the same quality expressed in the movement. Disregard the composition of a melody. Try to enhance the feeling of the movement with the sound and rhythm of the piano.
- Enhance the rhythm and feeling of the movement. Do not compete with it. Sometimes let the rhythmic movement prevail, other times enhance the rhythm—accentuate it at exactly the same time the movement is accented.
- It is better to use less accompaniment than one might expect is needed. Exercise the art of silence.
- When using the piano or any other instrument percussively or music-

ally, begin and end with a definite, calculated movement, which is not necessarily loud, but has strength.
- The shape of the hand, or the distance between each finger determines the tones which will be stroked. If the same shape is maintained, one can move the hands anywhere on the piano keyboard and hit approximately the same tones. Only the frequency will be changed.
- Some of the most appropriate piano accompaniment can be played with two fingers, spaced a variety of distances apart from each other. The easiest and most effective distance is three keys apart.

CREATIVITY

Creativity involves a process whereby a state of uncertainty or chaos develops into one of order. It is nurtured by the anticipation of what might be. This creative process draws its beginnings from an initial impulse called an inspiration, which moves forward in a series of irregular steps. It is further spurred on by memory, imagination, the mystique which surrounds people and their activities, truth of expression, and devotion to a task. When creativity results there is an intense physical and emotional excitement, a sense of release and ecstasy from expressing that which must be expressed in a way which is satisfying, or just right for the creator.

Creativity, in the study of creative rhythmic movement, is manifested and practiced through a method of education known as heuristics. According to this method, the child is trained to find out things for himself. In the study of CRM, the child is encouraged to move his body creatively and rhythmically in order to:

—explore, search, investigate, and discover movement
—have fun
—seek a movement inspiration or some insight which leads to further movement
—call upon his powers of imagination and memory
—express his feelings and ideas
—further his awareness of his body, movement, rhythm, space, force, and creativity
—develop his movement into a pattern
—discard, reshape, select, and emphasize, his previous endeavors
—make a form which is a necessary expression of his first inspiration and which is satisfying to him.

The teacher of creative rhythmic movement nourishes the creative process by whetting the child's curiosity through the introduction of movement problems for the child to solve. She accomplishes this by presenting questions, hypotheses, speculations, challenges, commands, clarifications, and a general attitude of acceptance and enthusiasm. Through all this, the child gains further insight into himself, and his relationship with his world of objects and people. In addition, the process of creativity instills further creativity.

The creative process, as manifested and practiced through the exploration and discovery of movement, very often does not develop beyond the act of enjoyment, a flash of inspiration every now and then, or simply an awareness of how the body flexes and extends. However, even these attainments may necessitate a breakaway from old associations and the acquisition of new connections between ideas, feelings, and movement. Even if a child has fun through movement in a way he has never before experienced, this too is the creative process in action, for this newfound fun is a creative endeavor of one's own, and results in a further glimpse of oneself.

A form implies the general structure or shape of something. It is the end product of creativity, although very often this structuring incites additional creativity. If through the exploration and discovery of movement a child develops a form, what kind of structure can one expect to see? Even the simplest movement forms exist as patterns or designs.

Patterns of Movement

- Rhythmic pattern: *the description of a movement pattern—in rhythmic terms* through its division or combination of underlying beats resulting from the natural positioning of the accents of execution. (Refer to the section on rhythm, pp. 64–84.)
- Step pattern: describes a movement pattern in terms of locomotor and nonlocomotor foot movement. Example: Heel, toe, slide.
- Floor pattern: describes *the path taken by locomotor movement.* Example: A zigzag floor pattern.
- Movement pattern: *a combination of bodily movements which have one focal point,* or one point of interest. The point of interest may be in the direction, intensity, rhythm, range, or feeling, of the movement. This point of interest holds the movements together and forms a pattern. Examples: three hops and a jump constitute a step pattern, but if done in one continuous direction is also a movement pattern.

Fun through movement!

Three hops and a jump will create a floor pattern. A short series of nonlocomotor bodily movements all expressing the same feeling is a movement pattern but, in addition, creates a spatial pattern.
- Spatial pattern or design in space: a pattern appearing in one's immediate surrounding space and is formed by *shaping the space with the movements of the body.*
- Movement phrase: comprises several movements which are related and grouped together to form one complete movement expression. It is comparable to a phrase of words within a sentence, or a phrase of music within a musical composition.

Compositional Forms

The more complicated movement forms exist as compositions. *A movement composition is a combination of movements which begin, proceed, end, and contrast.* The movement composition is usually longer than the movement phrase, and contains several of the previous patterns. (Refer to lesson plans 2 and 3 for the development of the following two movement compositions: run, stop, and push; walk, dive, and swim. See pp. 130–50.)

Movement compositions are referred to by their letter labels or by name. They bear the same labels as are found in most art forms, especially those in music. Although each contains several movement patterns, the movements are interwoven by the flow, the momentum, of the preceding movement. Some of the easiest compositional forms of movement for children to experience and develop are described.

AB—a form composed of *two movements* which have contrast. Example: Push arms away, pull arms close.

ABA—a form composed of *three movements*. The first and last movements are alike, or similar. The middle movement provides the contrast. Both AB and ABA compositional forms are excellent for the early elementary grades and for introduction to composition in the upper grades.

ABCA—a form composed of *four movements* with the first and last alike, or very similar. The two middle movements provide the contrast, and develop from one to the other.

ABCBA—a form composed of *five movements* and is no more complicated than the preceding ABCA form. Since the two A's and B's are alike or very similar, the C provides the point of interest, or contrast, and the composition somewhat resembles a three-part pattern, except that it is longer.

Question and Answer—a compositional form composed of two rhythmic movement patterns. The first pattern is in the form of a question, and is directed toward an imaginary outside focal point, or another child. The answer may be done by the original child, another child or many children, but must entail enough contrast in movement or rhythm to extend the original pattern into a satisfying whole. This question and answer compositional form can be initiated in the early elementary years, and is best done by questioning and responding vocally, and then using the same question and answer in rhythmic movement. The response is mostly a rhythmic one, but the quality of the movement also tends to dictate the kind of response which develops. When words are used, their meanings often direct the movement response. The echo displays a similar form, except that the answering movement closely imitates the original.

Opposites—This compositional form of movement is also composed of two patterns, and gains its greatest strength for unity by its emphasis on the opposite—the contrast. In fact, the contrast may be so great that the movement composition appears comical, curious, strange or distorted. In this compositional form, one child executes a short movement pattern of four to eight underlying beats. One or more other children, move in the *opposite* direction, tempo, intensity, space, and feeling. This form may develop into a very interesting composition, or can be used as a game. It might also incite more movement exploration. In the early elementary years it may be used in its simplest form, if preceded by experience in such compositional forms as the round, and the group rondo.

Rondo or ABACADA: For the rondo compositional form the principal movement pattern is repeated many times within the unit, and is interposed with subordinate movement patterns. This form may be done by groups of children, or even by one child. However, it becomes an advanced compositional form when done by one child alone, and as such should not be attempted by one child alone who has not reached the fourth grade. The rondo form works very well to initiate group composition in the early elementary school and can also be used in early childhood education. The rondo is best presented in a circle where the children can see each other and have a feeling for the group as a whole. Discovering group compositional movement via the rondo should be preceded by adequate exploration in mirrored movement, and other imitational movement experiences. See the review between lesson plans 4 and 5, pp. 159–64, for directions on how to play the game of "Simon Says" in movement. Suggestions for presenting the rondo form are as follows:

1. Children sit in a circle.
2. The teacher points to one child and asks her name. The child may reply as follows: My name is Ann; or I am Robert. Or, the child might say: Who me? I am Melanie. The teacher may also start by using her own name.
3. Whatever the name is, it will have a rhythmic pattern.
4. This rhythmic pattern is repeated often vocally. The children are asked not to forget it.
5. The teacher now asks the child who sits to one side of the first child to say his name rhythmically. If the first child preceded her name with I am, or my name is, the second child is encouraged to do the same. The rhythmic composition will now be as follows: My name is Ann, my name is Robert.
6. The teacher now asks the children if they remember the first rhythmic pattern. They now return to it. The composition will now be as follows: My name is Ann, my name is Robert, my name is Ann.
7. The teacher now asks the child sitting next to Robert to say his name, preceded by the words, my name is. After some practice, the composition now appears as follows: My name is Ann; my name is Robert; my name is Ann; my name is Claudia; my name is Ann; go to a new name; my name is Ann. . .
   The same as above may be done with movement or a simple rhythmic pattern. The first few times, the teacher should be the first to move. Clarity of movement and rhythm should be encouraged. Moreover, both movement and rhythm should be kept extremely simple.

The rondo gives the child a good opportunity to be an individual within a group, and points out how freedom of movement occurs within a structure. Since in this form the child always returns to pattern A, it is an excellent method of being repetitive without chancing boredom.

Cannon or Round: a compositional form in which a short movement phrase is exactly imitated in the subsequent section or sections. The round is a common compositional form used in music and is usually moved to just the way it is sung. *Row, Row, Row Your Boat* is a classic example of the round form in music.

Suggested Teaching Procedure:

1. The teacher selects one movement phrase which has been composed by a child, or herself, and teaches everyone in the class to do it exactly the same. If the teacher plans to divide the class into two groups, she chooses a movement phrase composed of two movement patterns. If the teacher plans to divide the class into three groups, she chooses a three part phrase.
2. If the teacher chooses a two-part phrase, the first group begins the phrase and does it two complete times.
3. The second group begins the movement phrase when the first group begins the phrase for the second time.
4. The two part round may be diagrammed as follows:

	1st time Phrase	2d time Phrase	3d time Phrase	4th time Phrase
Group I or Child I	X	X	X	
Group II or Child II		X	X	X

Thus, group I and II each have a chance to move alone, *and* simultaneously. The round form may be done with two or three individuals also.

EXPRESSION AND COMMUNICATION THROUGH CREATIVE RHYTHMIC MOVEMENT

Our culture has emphasized verbal communication and repressed nonverbal communication for so many years that most adults find difficulty expressing themselves in any way other than through the written or verbal word. However, during the late sixties and early seventies, more scientists and educators have come to realize the value of nonverbal expression upon communication. What value does nonverbal expression and communication have and what are the implications of these values for the child of elementary school age? Nonverbal expression and communication may involve any or all of the senses, and prevails in all arts, crafts, recreational activities, and hobbies. The expression and communication of one's feelings and ideas is especially satisfying through movement, that is, nongoal-oriented movement. Each movement or gesture a person makes suggests his innermost feelings and ideas. Therefore, if a person wants to express himself fully and adequately, movement must become a tool of his language. As a result each person develops a vocabulary of movement for and relative to himself. This movement vocabulary starts with an awareness of his body structure, its movement possibilities, its limitations, and the forces which act upon it. He continues to build a vocabulary of movement through an awareness of his mental, emotional, psychological, and social self.

Obviously, one objective of education is to get the child to more adequately express and communicate verbally so that he will be able to meet the challenges of society. However, since expression and communication also exist on a nonverbal level, it also seems important that the child learn to express himself fully by communicating through movement and by other nonverbal means. Indeed, many feelings and ideas cannot be expressed adequately in words, and many children do not ever have the physical or mental ability to completely express themselves verbally. These children very often find other ways to express and communicate, and many of these ways are dangerous to the individuals and to society.

A young child's most immediate source of nonverbal expression and communication is through movement. This is true because his body, consisting of movable parts, is ever-present, which provides him with the immediate equipment for reacting reflexively and spontaneously to his surroundings.

The following list pertains to a child's expression of feelings and ideas through movement. (Also refer to imagination in children, p. 217.) Children will:

—express only what has impressed them
—express themselves on the physical, psychological, emotional and social level of children, not adults
—usually express themselves nonverbally more readily than do adults
—express themselves through movement more spontaneously than do adults
—have had less time to learn universal gestures and symbols of movement expression, and therefore express themselves in a more spontaneous way, free from constraint
—not have a large enough verbal vocabulary at their immediate command to be able to adequately express themselves verbally.

Expression—The expressive act implies that something is revealed through a personal and intuitive exploration of the material at hand.

Nonverbal expression!

In movement, children express their personal feelings and ideas in hopping, skipping, flexing, rolling, crawling, etc. It is a spontaneous release of energy, spurred on by curiosity to find out what might happen if. . . . Each child will express himself differently each time, and this expression will be individualistic.

Communication—Communication implies that a point has been reached at which children can call upon their experience and order it; through their growing awareness and expertise they will show their power of selection and memory. At this point, not only do the children know what their intent is, but the observers will also be able to recognize elements in the child's movements which are common to all, and which will permit them to share the idea, image, or the feeling that the child is expressing.

As previously stated, a young child's movement expressions are spontaneous and child-like. As the child matures he will begin to learn the gestures and idiomatic movements of his culture. Through an understanding of movement communication the growing child will become sensitive to the exact meanings of communications emanating from others. By accurately interpreting the movement cues of others, he increases his perception of the feelings, needs, meanings, and desires of others. Failure to properly interpret the movement cues of others may result in serious interpersonal misunderstandings.

Since the physical self is observable and touchable, it is the most obvious self which can be presented to the child. The presentation of problems to solve pertaining to movement expression and communication for children should begin with the self; it should begin with the physical self, and it should begin early in life.

Suggested Teaching Procedure for Presenting the Developmental Process of Communication Via CRM

This involves: knowledge of the physical body through *body awareness* techniques; use of sensory perception for body awareness, especially visual, tactile, and kinesthetic. The gradual building of body awareness has several purposes:

- to expand the children's movement experiences by enabling them to realize what body parts are available—their possibilities and limitations of movement.
- to enable the teacher to refer to any part of the body which is not responding to the movement problem as presented efficiently and effectively.
- to stimulate the awareness and use of the kinesthetic sense.
- To sharpen awareness and appreciation of the movements of one's self and those of others.

Exploration of movement. Present movement problems for children to explore, make discoveries, and develop a movement vocabulary. Through the exploration of movement, children discover the nature and mechanics of movement as related to them individually, and as outlined previously in this chapter. Through this knowledge they will discover how to express themselves in movement. Though the expression of feelings and ideas is an extremely important phase in the developmental process of a child's ability to communicate through creative rhythmic movement, it should be considered as a step, perhaps a giant step, in a progression. Indeed, most children and teachers never get beyond this point in the progression. However, the children should be stimulated and encouraged to go on.

Selection and repetition of a movement which is especially self-satisfying to them. This phase of the development must not be forced, but must be encouraged through the introduction of movement problems which stimulate the child to repeat in order to be self-satisfied and in order to begin building a movement pattern. (See lesson plans.) If the child can remember a movement so he can repeat it exactly, spatially, rhythmically, and emotionally, he is ready to begin to compose movement patterns. Through the use of *movement memory* he is now able to call upon his feelings and ideas and express them in the form of movement. This is *communication*. The teacher plays a very important role in this phase of movement communication. If a child is forced to repeat and memorize movements before he really wants to, he may lose all the fresh spontaneity which most children possess while moving, and the teacher may find that she may have to forget about CRM education with that particular child for a while. If this happens, the introduction of films or other media at this point may help. (Refer to the bibliography.) When the child discovers a movement which he seems to enjoy, he will show it in his facial or movement expressions, or he may even shout out: "This is my movement! I discovered it, and I like it because it is my very own!" Then the teacher will know that the child can be encouraged to repeat and proceed.

Formation of a movement pattern. After the natural development of the movement memory, the children are now ready to consider and explore ways of developing it. (See the discussion of patterns of movement, page 85.) However, it is most important for the teacher not to encourage them to shape or form their movement too soon. Nor should she expect them to use any of the forms which have been previously discussed. Rather, the pattern of movement, or composition, should evolve and grow naturally and organically. The teacher will now have to keep a watchful eye on the children and endeavor to interject a suggestion or idea for consideration or for exploration at just the right time. Remember, a movement pattern can be simple, containing only two parts, but if these two parts are two unrelated movements which are forced together simply to form a movement pattern, the whole idea of communication through movement has been lost.

The following steps are suggested for the formation of a simple ABA movement pattern. This progression may be seen in the two

films produced by the author entitled, *You Can Compose A Dance.*
(See bibliography.)

1. Explore movement.
2. Discover a good beginning movement.
3. Repeat it often until it leads you into a second movement. The second movement may differ considerably from the first, but it should be an outgrowth of the first movement—should flow directly from it.
4. Repeat the first and second movements often. Discover a final movement which is similar and relates to the first movement.
5. Compose a rhythmic or musical pattern to enhance the movement pattern.

Developing the above pattern may begin as early as second or third grade *if the children have developed a memory for movement.* It may take a child anywhere from twenty minutes to three class periods of twenty minutes each to develop a movement pattern. If a child has not done so by the end of three twenty-minute periods, leave it and return to it later.

The development of a movement pattern may be considered as related to the development of a short story or an English composition. The teacher may also relate it to the creative process involved in composing any other art form.

DANCE AND SPORTS AS CREATIVE RHYTHMIC MOVEMENT

The basic concepts of creative rhythmic movement and dance are very similar. In fact, they are so close when a comparison is made, that the two terms are often used interchangeably. However, there are substantial differences. The teacher and children should recognize these differences, and know each activity for what it is.

Creative rhythmic movement becomes a dance, as an art form, when it is done as an expression of one's feelings and/or ideas which are *artistically formed.* The dancer, as a performing artist, has a well-coordinated and sensitive body which expresses and communicates through movement, at a very high level, all that is embodied in the dance. In addition, dance, as an art form, shares all the basic ingredients which are found in all art forms such as: contrast, balance, a point of interest or climax, repetition, flow or growth, imagination, and a certain magic quality which makes it special.

The various arts differ in their outward form, but they all share a common need to reveal the creator's inner self through an external pattern. A simple comparison of three art forms is as follows:

	Instrument of Expression	*Medium*
Dance	Body—strong, agile, and well-coordinated	Rhythmic Movement
Painting	Brushes	Color and Shape
Music	Instruments	Tone and Rhythm

The main difference between dance and all other art forms is that the instrument of expression, the body of movable parts, is constantly present. Therefore, it behooves a dancer, as an artist, to keep his body physically strong and flexible in order to increase his range of expression. Seldom is so high a degree of training or knowledge necessary for, or even pertinent to, the goals and objectives for the child in the elementary school. However, since dance is composed of movement, done rhythmically and often creatively, the study of creative rhythmic movement is an excellent introduction to every type of dance.

Dance I

Dance II

Just as dance is closely related to CRM, so also are sports. Because CRM and sports share some of the same elements, a child who engages in a sport's activity moves rhythmically in order to *learn and develop skills which will achieve a goal or win the game*. However, this rhythmic movement is not done creatively and is not primarily done to express a feeling or an idea. A sports activity is rhythmic movement done spatially and is highly formed—or structured. It is through the awareness of the elements of this structure and its analysis rhythmically, spatially, and with motor impulse that children are able to learn a sport's activity more readily. (Refer to the rhythmic analysis of a movement on page 75.)

Since sports activities and creative rhythmic movement share two elements, movement and rhythm, the study of CRM is an excellent preparatory activity for all sports, in fact, probably the best, because

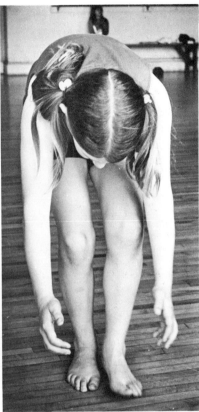

the child need only attend to his body of movable parts and how it moves in space, in time, and with force. The child need not be concerned with how fast, how perfect, or how effective his movements are in order to achieve a goal. The child also need not be concerned about the manipulation of any other object except his own body, as an instrument of movement. His reward is simple self-satisfaction and pleasure through the awareness he develops of his own movement and those of others and being able to direct his movement in order to express and communicate his feelings and ideas in a nonverbal way.

three

Teaching
Creative Rhythmic Movement

Creative rhythmic movement, as its name implies, has three main aspects or considerations. They are, in reverse order: bodily movement, with its concentration on the anatomical body, and its factors of space, time, force, and expressiveness; rhythm, with its factors of time, force, and communicative powers; and creativity with its factors of exploration, discovery, synthesization, and imagination.

If the teacher will attend to these three aspects of CRM and their component factors, and consider them as concepts to be presented to the children, she can then introduce problems for the children to solve which will bring about the clarification of these concepts relative to each child's individual physical, social, mental, and emotional needs.

The teacher should be aware of the fact that problem-solving acts in creative rhythmic movement are part of an endless maturational process which very personally involves both the teacher and the children. The process which concerns us here is mostly one of developing

100

self-awareness instigated and nurtured through the medium of bodily movement. It is also a process which includes the awareness of one's immediate environment and those other things and persons which coexist in one's milieu.

Development of the awareness process, through the medium of creative rhythmic movement, is most effective and self-satisfying when self-imposed. Therefore, the teacher takes on the role of an arranger or instigator of movement problems, and she incites the children to discover within themselves, and for themselves, the solution to the problem, and an awareness of the total concept. This is done by the children's actively exploring and discovering bodily movement, rhythmically and creatively. This kind of activity takes time and patience on the part of both teacher and child. Gaining self-awareness through creative rhythmic movement cannot be rushed. The teacher should be prepared to be patient and accepting, and to stand aside and let the whole process evolve, assisting the children with only a few well-placed questions and cues when needed.

In order for most children to have the optimum chance to achieve self-awareness through CRM, the problem-solving method of developing this awareness is the most ideal one to use. However, it is not always feasible or practical. In reality, elementary school classes are often large and crowded, and elementary school teachers are often too busy to allow the time needed for a child to mature and grow aware. For this reason, the ten model lesson plans in this book use and suggest a variety of approaches to the teaching of creative rhythmic movement in addition to the problem-solving technique. A brief description of these various approaches follows.

THE VARIOUS PROBLEM-SOLVING APPROACHES

Problem-Solving Method

The problem-solving method, as used in the teaching of CRM, is one whereby the teacher instigates an awareness of a concept by arranging or setting up one or more movement situations in the form of a question, riddle, puzzle, or problem. The children then proceed to become progressively aware of this concept by solving the problem or series of problems through the exploration and discovery of bodily movement by themselves and for themselves.

In most cases there are several solutions to one problem, and there are many problems which the teacher may think of in order to help a child become aware of a single concept. The solution of the problem depends in part on the child's individual physical, mental, and emotional makeup. Or the solution depends partly on where, when, and how the child is situated in his physical environment. Because each child discovers a solution to the problem which is related to himself, as a human being in a living world, there is no right or wrong solution, and the threat of a child failing is eliminated. Everyone in the class is right so long as he is exploring movement in an effort to solve the problem and thereby to initiate an awareness of its incipient concept. This type of learning process allows the child a great amount of freedom, yet requires self-direction.

The teacher's role in the problem-solving method is to first present the problem, keeping the concept in mind, and then to gently nudge and encourage the children toward a state of awareness of the concept. Most of the problem-solving method is proposed verbally by the teacher in the form of questions, postulations, invitations, and challenges which incite the child to begin and continue his seeking and finding activities. The children may continue to explore all the possibilities in seeking the presence of a concept for the entire lesson period. Or the teacher may choose to change the pace of the class completely by presenting another problem which is related to the same concept, or to an entirely different concept. If the class time is longer than a half hour, it is good for the children to work on two or three concepts in order to prevent boredom, and to enable them to put some unused groups of muscles to work while other muscle groups rest.

The teacher may also choose to sit down with the children and discuss some of their movement findings. This procedure provides an excellent rest period. The teacher should remember however, that the children will become much more aware of themselves as related to the basic concepts of CRM by moving rather than by talking about it. With this view in mind, the teacher should be ever-mindful of the balance between movement and discussion in a class of creative rhythmic movement.

During the course of solving a problem pertaining to creative rhythmic movement, the children may encounter a movement or a pattern of movements which they may find especially pleasing to do. Should the teacher permit the children to continue to do the same thing over and over again, and enjoy it just for the sake of enjoyment? Yes. Very often, as the children enjoy the movement and begin to do it better, they also gain insight into the concept behind it all. Having fun through movement is already a purpose seemingly inherent in most children; it is upon this basic quality that the teacher structures her whole strategy on how to help the child become physically, mentally, socially, and emotionally aware of himself and others through creative rhythmic movement. It is imperative that the teacher capitalize on any and every hint of enjoyment through movement, and build, emphasize, and embellish it in the hope that through fun in movement there will grow a better understanding and an awareness of self.

There are many adaptations of the problem-solving approach which can be used to teach CRM. They can be seen in the ten model lesson plans in chapter 5.

Partial Problem-Solving Method

By use of this method the teacher may choose to present a movement problem in a manner which limits the children to seeking only one or two solutions. In so doing, the teacher elects to emphasize these solutions by limiting the amount of exploration in which the children would normally engage themselves in order to seek all the other solutions to the problem. The awareness of the concept then is brought about by focusing on only one or two solutions to the movement problem, and activity in the exploration and discovery of further solutions is postponed to a future time.

In the partial problem-solving approach, the teacher not only presents the problem, but also quickly indicates all the solutions to the problem, except the one or two which she wants the children to seek and find. The teacher then encourages the children, again through related questions, to solve the one or two aspects of the movement problem which remain in question.

The partial problem-solving method is a good procedure to use to introduce the problem-solving method, and it has two advantages. First guidelines are set, allowing the student to attend to one or two facets of the problem. A limited amount of exploration is especially advantageous when children have not previously experienced a great amount of freedom through self-direction. After the children have had several opportunities to discover one or two solutions to various movement problems, the teacher may progressively present problems in such a way that more and more solutions are left to be explored and discovered. She can thus arrange more opportunities each time for the children to be self-directed. This partial problem-solving method is also valuable because it allows the child to experience faster and more immediate success. Unlike most adults, the child rarely has the patience to explore and seek the solution to a problem with continuing motivating zest. It is a wise teacher who can anticipate the psychological climate of the class and determine how far she can go with any one teaching method.

Alteration of Problem Solving

This method utilizes the creative powers of the child and further inspires him toward self-direction. After the child has discovered a solution to the movement problem which has been presented to him, he is encouraged to change it by altering one or more of its space, time, force, or quality characteristics. In so doing, the movement solution changes either slightly or drastically and either reinforces his concept awareness, or initiates the awareness of another movement concept. In both cases, self-awareness initiated by self-direction is very much emphasized, and the creative process is enhanced.

Extended Problem Solving

By this method, the teacher presents a movement problem and solution. She then uses the solution as a model to apply to the discovery of all other possible solutions to the problem. The extended problem-solving method is also a good approach for introducing the problem-solving method as it progresses from a teacher-directed situation to one which is child-directed.

Group Problem Solving

Using this method, the teacher and students discuss a concept of creative rhythmic bodily movement which they are already familiar with. They then, collectively, set up a related problem, and choose one or more strategies which they will use to further the awareness of the concept or relate it to the awareness of another. Each person in the group endeavors to solve the movement problem and bring to the group his discoveries, questions, criticisms, and suggestions.

This method is especially effective in helping each child understand the needs of others, but very often it takes a mature group of children supervised by a prudent teacher to make it work successfully. It is the duty of the teacher, in this case, to intervene diplomatically every time democratic action within the group is threatened, and it is most important for her to intervene if she feels the movement solution appears to lose its creativity, spontaneity, and fun. This often happens when children work with one another and tend to try to effect an awareness of a movement concept through the discussion of ideas, rather than through bodily movement.

Simple Examples of the Use of the Problem-Solving Approaches

Concept: The concept of creative rhythmic movement which is emphasized in the problem-solving examples that follow involve bodily movement, brought about through the awareness of the anatomical parts of the body and how they move. It deals specifically with circumduction.

Problem Solving (Example):

Teacher: How many ways can you (children) move your head? Try it! (Pause) Move your head in as many ways as you can think of. (Pause)

Partial Problem Solving:

Teacher: You have discovered (or, we all know) that you can move your head forward, sideways, backwards, and up and down. Can you combine all of these head movements into one movement? What kind of movement can we call this?

Children: Circumduction. (The teacher will probably have to tell them this.)

Alternation of Problem Solving:

Teacher: Close your eyes and think of the movement of your head as it makes its circumducting movement. Think of your head as it goes from front, to side, to back, to side, and front again. (Pause) Can you do this circumducting head movement in different tempos? Try it! (Pause) Can you change the size, or range, of your circumducting head movement? Try it! (Pause)

Extended Problem Solving:

Teacher: What other parts of your body can you move in circumduction? Can your shoulders circumduct? Try it! (Pause) Can your hands circumduct? Try it!

Group Problem Solving:

Teacher: We have seen that several parts of your body can move in a circular space pattern which is called circumduction. Can you (the group) state a movement problem which has to do with drawing a circular pattern in space, and also involves bodily movement? She states a movement problem which relates to the above.

Teacher: How can we draw a circular pattern in the space in this room with our whole body?

The group now explores all the possible solutions to the above problem through bodily movement. They then discuss and share the solutions, and either choose to do the same one at the same time or they interweave all or some of their solutions spatially and/or rhythmically and execute them at the same time.

There are many other methods which the teacher may use in helping the child become aware of the concepts of creative rhythmic bodily movement. These methods, most successful when they are combined with the problem-solving approaches, help to expedite the awareness process. They are the directive, labeling, relativity and comparison, and kinesthetic methods. However, it is important to note that if the concepts of creative rhythmic bodily movement are presented through the medium of the above mentioned methods alone, without combining them with one of the various problem-solving experiences, self-awareness and self-direction will be sidetracked, and whatever awareness results will be teacher-oriented and teacher-imposed.

DIRECTIVE

When using this approach, the teacher gives directions verbally and explicitly. The children react or respond verbally or with bodily movement. While it may be less creative, this approach results in immediate action. The approach may be reversed. That is, the teacher may direct the class by using a movement, and the class responds either verbally or also with bodily movement.

Example 1:

The teacher will use the following directive approach to quickly warm up the muscles of the children's bodies, to initiate an awareness of the various bodily parts, to engender an enthusiasm for getting started, and to relieve boredom by rapidly changing the pace.

Teacher: Touch your fingers to your toes. (Pause) Touch your knees. (Pause) Touch your shoulders. (Pause) Touch the space as high above you as you can. (Pause) We will now repeat each touching movement four times, and then progress to the next. Ready to touch your fingers to your toes four times? Begin. (The teacher says and counts the following while the children do it.) Touch toes—two, three, four; touch knees—two, three, four; touch shoulders—two, three, four; touch space —two, three, four.

Example 2:

The teacher now builds on what the children have learned through the directive method. She introduces a problem which the children can easily solve because it closely relates to what they have previously done.

Teacher: Can you discover three other parts of your body to touch, plus one other area in space to touch? (Pause) Be aware of these bodily parts as you touch them and remember them so you can repeat. Try it! (Pause) Touch each newly discovered part of your body four times and progress to the next. Then touch the near space four times. Do it the same each time. Don't watch anyone else, as each one of you will be doing something different. Be aware of what bodily and spatial areas you are touching. Ready to touch a particular part of your body? Begin. (The teacher says and counts the following while the children do it.) Touch—two, three, four; touch—two, three, four; touch—two, three, four; space—two, three, four.

Example 3:

    Teacher: Move exactly as I do. (Teacher hops.)
          (Children hop.)
    Teacher: Move exactly as I do. (Teacher swings arms.)
          (Children swing arms as teacher has done.)
             OR
    Teacher: What is the name of the part of my body which I am moving? (Teacher moves one part of her body and the children verbally inform the teacher what it is.)
    Teacher: Who can move that same bodily part (name it) the same way that I have moved it? (Pause) Who can move it differently?

LABELING

When this approach is used, the teacher and/or the students assign a name or label for what they are doing. This method is commonly used to impart a great amount of information in a short amount of time. Concepts of creative rhythmic bodily movement are more easily understood and remembered through the exploration and discovery of movement. However, if one wants to make reference to, compare, evaluate, or write about creative rhythmic bodily movement, one needs to know the names of everything associated with it. When the children learn the name or label or anything associated with this movement, make sure that it is the correct one. Even the youngest elementary school child can say a long word such as acceleration or locomotion, and once they associate their meanings with movement, the words are theirs forever.

(Please refer to the materials of creative rhythmic bodily movement in this book for a glossary of terms. See pp. 7–99.

RELATIVITY AND COMPARISON

The concepts of creative rhythmic bodily movement and their elements may be related to the many concepts which the children are pursuing in their other studies. The teacher may choose to capitalize on this relationship by stressing it and comparing it with the explorations and discoveries of creative rhythmic bodily movement. The double emphasis of the concept through relativity and comparison tends to reinforce the child's awareness of it, and makes it an especially exciting and meaningful approach.

Some of the following suggestions may be used to relate and compare creative rhythmic movement to other subject matter. (Refer to chapter 2, p. 7 and chapter 5, p. 210 for additional ideas on how to relate and compare.)

Relate and Compare

—The concepts of movement with the laws of physics: the forces of gravity, acceleration, action and reaction, momentum, and centrifugal and centripetal forces, etc. (Refer to the section on forces in the chapter on Additional Teaching Suggestions, p. 246.)
—The concepts of movement within and through space with reading, geographic, and architectural spatial concepts. (Refer to the section on space in the chapter on Additional Teaching Suggestions, p. 239.)
—The concepts of movement within and through space with the social and moral implications of humans existing, coexisting, and relating within and moving throughout space.
—The concepts of bodily movement—its expression and communication of feeling and ideas—with other art forms: painting, music, sculpture, poetry, drama, etc.
—The concepts of rhythm and mathematics with its orderliness, exactness, and reasoning.
—The concepts of movement with other activities which require movement such as: sports, industrial work, and movement in daily life.
—The concepts of creativity, as related to movement, with other creative ventures: fine arts, creative writing, crafts, cooking, sewing, architecture, design, and the like.
—The concepts of composition, as related to movement, with other

forms of activity requiring these same concepts (the same as for the concepts of creativity, above, plus many more).

KINESTHESIS

The use of kinesthetic awareness for the teaching of CRM is of prime importance. In this method, the children are constantly reminded to be aware of their body at rest and during movement. By constantly referring to it, especially during the process of exploration and discovery of movement, this method becomes an excellent avenue for effecting an awareness of one's self and a sensitivity for others, physically, mentally, emotionally, and socially. The children are constantly encouraged to be aware of their bodily position in space, the relationship of one's physical selves to others, and the movement of one's body (and parts thereof) within and through space. The teacher often admonishes them to slow down their movement in order to think more carefully about it. She sometimes asks the children to stop moving, close their eyes, and think of what they are about to do or what they have just done.

Developing kinesthetic awareness in the teaching of creative rhythmic movement is an excellent means of effecting self-awareness when used in conjunction with the problem-solving method. (The reader will find that the kinesthetic sense is stressed in several of the lesson plans which appear in chap. 4. Also refer to the section on progressive relaxation, **p. 51**.)

Suggestions for the Teacher

1. Think of a concept of CRM you would like to present, and of avenues for arousing or conveying awareness of this concept. Bear the concept in mind throughout the lesson; the children will help open avenues of awareness for you to urge upon them. The concepts associated with creative rhythmic movement are the same no matter what age level. It is only the avenues of approach that are different.
2. After the teacher has determined where she is going, what strategy should she use to effect an awareness of the concept? She should be keenly aware of the needs of each student, and use that strategy which best fits the child physically, mentally, socially, and emotionally. (See previous suggestions of various methods for helping the child become aware of himself through the medium of CRM, on p. 101.
3. The teacher should keep in mind that whatever works to help the

child in his effort to explore, discover, and synthesize his activities in creative rhythmic movement is valid. Each class and each child in the class is different. A lesson which works well in one class will not always work well in another. Though the concept pursued in each class may be the same, how it is arrived at differs for each child and class. Therefore the teacher should try different avenues of approach with each child and/or each class, thus assuring each child the optimum chance for self-awareness.

4. Allowing the child both opportunity and time to become aware of a concept of creative rhythmic movement is one step each teacher must take. However, constantly prompting the child toward an awareness of that concept is a conscious effort to be made by the teacher. If the teacher has the children's best interests in mind at all times, the children will know it, and respond by constantly indicating to the teacher what their needs are. Even though the teacher may never have had any previous training in CRM, if she is receptive to the students' cues she will be in a position to help them to help themselves learn about their physical, mental, emotional, and social selves.

5. It is necessary for the CRM teacher to establish and maintain a relationship with the class which, though short of familiarity, borders on the interrelationship of camaraderie. Every effort should be made by the teacher to know each child, physically, mentally, emotionally, and socially—to share in his movement experiences and delight in his movement discoveries. The teacher must have charisma. She must be kind and accepting of all verbal and movement suggestions made in class. She must have patience to pursue these ideas and suggestions, especially those in movement, knowing that the child and class will grow in their attempt to explore, discover, and solve problems.

6. The class proceedings should be conducted as democratically as possible, for it is in the nature of creative rhythmic movement to be friendly, informal, free and easy, and self-governing.

7. It is most important for the class to have privacy and freedom from interruptions. Since the expression of one's feelings and ideas through bodily movement is a very personal one, spectators should not be admitted until the teacher and children feel very comfortable working together, and a free-and-easy class atmosphere exists.

8. The class should be so structured by the teacher that each child can attain optimum freedom. The kind of structuring the teacher should endeavor to establish, and the kinds of freedom that should exist are suggested here.

Structuring Space. The room used to teach creative rhythmic movement should be large, but not so large that the teacher needs to strain her voice in order to be heard. The minimum amount of space for each child of the lower elementary school years is approximately forty-six square inches. The total room space will be utilized by the class largely in three different ways: (1) the whole class will move, at the same time, in a circular pattern around the room; (2) the children will move, one, two, or three at a time, across the room from one point to another point; or (3) when the entire class participates each child will occupy a particular space in the room which he claims as his own for exploring, discovering, and synthesizing movement. The teacher may find it necessary to draw a rectangle or square six feet by six feet, or seven by seven, within which each child will move. This procedure may be best for children who are new to the idea of exploring, or discovering movement, or, for the children who are first attempting to compose. After the children have learned to explore movement within a structured space, they may try moving to other parts of the room, continuing to be ever mindful of the space they have been using, and respectful of the rule that the same amount of space belongs to every other child moving in the room. Even though all the children are moving at once in what seems to be an unstructured and haphazard spatial arrangement, they will move comfortably and without collisions if they have first had ample opportunity to become spatially aware. This kind of class movement takes a large amount of self-direction and self-discipline on the part of the children—an atmosphere easily and quickly attained in some classes, while attained gradually in others.

If the room is too small, the children may be put into groups and each group may take turns. This method is not as good as having all children moving at the same time, because concentration and awareness are difficult when groups of children watch one another. If it is necessary for one group to move at a time, the teacher should rotate the groups often, or give the watching group something to do. Children who watch can do the following:

- Accompany the movement on percussion instruments. Be sure the children have had enough rhythmic practice before they do this. If there is a pianist accompanist, she may take charge of this.
- Each child may be given one or more rhythmic problems to solve for that day. The rhythmic patterns may be written on three by five cards and may be practiced very softly and very adequately by tapping the two index fingers together. (For more ideas on rhythmic activities refer to chapter 5.)

- Each child may write his feelings or ideas about a particular subject, later to be expressed by him in movement. (Refer to the discussion of imagination, words, stories and poems in chapter 5.)
- The teacher may set up a media center where each child may look, quietly, at pictures of other children engaging in some of the same activities they are experiencing in class. (See the bibliography.)

Structuring behavior: A class atmosphere free from the anticipation of failure should be developed and maintained by the teacher. The interaction of the students and teacher should be so free that any spontaneous response is accepted as a contribution to the creativity of the whole. How is this kind of freedom attained? Does it just happen, or does the teacher make a conscious effort to achieve this rapport with the class? The experienced teacher will, of course, recognize that there must be class rules in order to set up a structure within which freedom of learning can exist. The number and kind of rules which the teacher and children set for their CRM class depends on the number of children in the class, the size and physical setup of the room, the social and mental maturity of the students, and the behavioral structure of the school. If time permits, the children should help to set their own rules; it being most important for them to understand the need for such rules. Rules are mostly based on assuring the safety of every child, the guarantee that each child will have a space to occupy and space to move within and throughout, and that each child will be given the opportunity to get as much out of the class as each other child in the class. The following rules are suggested to help behaviorally structure a CRM class.

- Don't touch one another. Each child in the class is to occupy an empty space. This is the child's space to move within. Stay away from the space of another child in the class.
- When several children or the whole class move at the same time, move throughout the space in the classroom in the same direction. The teacher should demonstrate, and the children should practice this procedure until everyone understands it perfectly.
- One or more stop signals should be decided on and practiced until all children are thoroughly acquainted with them. Most often the stop signals are a loud beat on the drum, no sound, or simply the word *stop*. It is necessary for the children to be aware of all three signals of this type as each situation dictates the need for one signal or the other.
- Each child should respect the right of another, and the teacher, to express themselves verbally. The children should not talk while the

teacher or anyone else is talking. They should be encouraged to listen, watch, think, and be aware.

- The children should not talk while they are moving, but concentrate on what they are doing. It is impossible to become kinesthetically aware or develop any kind of sensitivity to oneself and to others if any of the children are talking while moving. Each child should ask himself the following questions (silently) while moving . . . Where is my body in relation to the space around me? How is each part of my body moving? Where is each part of my body in relation to the space around me? Where is each part of my body in relation to every other part of my body? Am I occupying the space of another person in class? Am I trying to solve the problem as set up by my classmates, myself, or my teacher? How do I feel about the movement I am doing? . . . The student should be so busy, mentally, answering the above questions that he will find no time to talk to others in the class. Stress self-concentration and behavioral problems will disappear.
- If there are many children in the class, each child should be encouraged to raise his hand when responding or making a verbal contribution. Remember, this is a movement class. Here the child learns about himself through the medium of creative rhythmic movement. Therefore, limit the amount of talk and stimulate the learning process to occur through movement. However, if and when a child asks a question or makes a contribution verbally, it should be heard by everyone in the class.

9. Children who have never experienced a creatively taught class may not know what to do with the freedom they have suddenly acquired. Such children may need to be taught how they can move freely and creatively. They may need to be urged to explore and discover. How can the teacher stimulate a child to be more inquisitive about his body and how it moves? How can a teacher incite children to move intent on curiosity, eager to discover movement concepts, and eager to use these basic fundamentals to learn more about themselves and their environment? Some of the following approaches can be tried:

   - The teacher may ask questions of the class or individuals in the class, and challenge them to discover the answer. . . . Why? When? Who? What? Where? What for? How? Can you? Are you able to? Examples: How many ways can you move your head? Try it. Move your hips in as many ways as you can. Can you move them back? Show me. Who can show me how to walk in a zigzag floor pattern? What is a step pattern? Show me. Billy, can you do that same step pattern using a diagonal floor pattern? Show me in as many ways as you can how different parts of your body can rotate?—can flex?—can extend? Where in your movement do you make the largest and strongest effort? What name can you give to your movement? How do you feel when you move this way? Show me, by moving your body, how you feel when you touch this ice cube. Do you know where you are going? How will you get there? What parts of your body will you move to get there?

- The teacher hypothesizes. For instance, she may say to a child . . . if you push your hips backward as far as they will go, what happens to your upper body? Try it. Now close your eyes and think carefully. Don't move. What would happen to your upper body if you pushed your hips forward? Think about it. Then try it and see what happens.
- Children will be encouraged to move more freely and creatively if the teacher reinforces their efforts positively. Creative rhythmic movement may be the first and only success experience for a child who has other learning difficulties. The teacher should ask herself . . . how can I make the child aware that he is doing well, and how can I make him aware that I know he is doing well? Furthermore, how can I make the class aware of a child's success experiences without causing embarrassment to the child? How will the success experiences of one child benefit the others? What can I do to reinforce positively each individual child in the class?

The teacher may try using words of encouragement and praise. Look for the good in a child and tell him about these points immediately. This method works very well in a CRM class, since the child is not always looking at the teacher, but while he is moving in the space throughout the room he is able to hear her voice. Examples are as follows: That's a good try! That's the way to do it! I like the way you are moving! Billy is a good listener, he knows how to follow directions. I like the way Jane is discovering new and different ways to locomote, etc.

The teacher may also reinforce learning(s) positively by allowing the child who is doing well to demonstrate. Example. . . Billy concentrated so well on his own movement, that I'd like the class to watch him. Do you see his eyes following his own movements? He does not watch anyone else's movement except his own. Can you do the same? Let's try it! . . . Make sure when you ask a child to share his experiences with the rest of the class that he will not be embarrassed by doing so.

The teacher may reinforce comprehension and learning positively by affording special privileges to those who do well in class. For instance, she may make a list of those children who take their shoes off first and are ready to go. She may allow these children the special privilege of playing the drum, handing out equipment, being the leader, or being excused first. Putting a child's name on a list very often demonstrates to the child that you are very much aware of his presence in class and are interested in him.

Each child is different and is positively reinforced in a different manner. Because of the very personal, creative, and individualistic nature of CRM, the teacher is afforded an excellent opportunity to really get to know the needs of each child physically, socially, emotionally, and mentally. As a result, she will know what type of positive reinforcement will work for each child.

10. Because CRM is really a process of self-awareness effected through the individual pupil's bodily movement, the teacher seldom demonstrates during the presentation of the unit. The children discover for themselves how their body moves in relation to the concepts of creative rhythmic bodily movement. In fact, awareness of a concept is most satisfying to the children if they discover it, or understand it, for themselves. Consequently the teacher need not be a dancer or an athlete, though it is helpful for her to be rhythmically aware.

11. The teacher should allow for two or three short two-minute rest or relaxation periods during the class lesson. She may use the rag doll method of having the children recline progressively lower and lower down to a sitting or lying position. Until the time that the children become accustomed to listening to the verbal directions of the teacher without looking at her, the teacher should avoid speaking to them while they are lying down.

12. The voice quality of the teacher is very important. While the children are moving, they are attending to their own movement, and are not looking at the teacher. Therefore, the CRM teacher depends on her voice to direct, incite, praise, and suggest without interfering with their concentration. She directs a class by what she says, but what is even more important is her ability to use the tone of her voice as a motivating force. Changing the tone and

dynamics of one's voice works especially well in the teaching of children. Once children discover that they can listen for the teacher's guidance without looking at her, the teacher will make great strides in helping them be more aware of their body in movement simply by using her voice to guide, thereby not diverting them from their self-awareness. The right word, perhaps with a dramatic touch, said at just the right instant, works wonders. On the other hand, sometimes the greatest amount of learning takes place when the teacher is silent. The teacher should learn when to allow the children space, time, and silence in order to become self-aware.

13. Repetition is very important in a CRM class. A movement is fun and self-satisfying when the child is fully aware that he is doing it efficiently and easily. Some children will be able to move efficiently and easily immediately. Other children will find that only through repetition, or by choosing a different avenue of approach in solving the problem will they achieve this self-satisfaction. The teacher should explain and demonstrate very early in the unit the importance of repetition with its rhythmic and emotional significance, and its importance in fulfilling the need for body awareness of each child in the class. Moments of repetition should be strategically placed and spaced throughout the lesson and unit to avoid boredom.

14. Boredom should not occur in a problem-solving class such as creative rhythmic movement. If the class does become bored, it may be for the following reasons:

- The teacher is inadequately prepared. Creative teaching, as described in this book, takes preparation. The teacher should be very familiar with the subject matter.
- The avenues for effecting the awareness of a concept, or the teaching strategy, are not right for the individual or the class. More often than not, if the child does not understand, it is not the child's fault—the teacher is leading the child down the wrong path for effecting a state of awareness.
- The children are tired. This is a common problem, but one often overlooked. CRM is an activity class and can be physically and emotionally exhausting. Better, then, to have several short periods a week than one or two long periods. The lower elementary school children will best benefit from a daily period fifteen to twenty minutes in length. The upper elementary school child will benefit most from a period of twenty to forty minutes in length given daily or three times per week. If the period is too

long for the students, and they are tired, try reading them a story, giving them a snack, or playing a quiet game. The teacher may find that this is a good time to listen to them talk about themselves, especially their feelings and ideas.

A child is sometimes tired because he is over-stimulated, either from his school experiences or as a result of parental eagerness to have their child succeed. This kind of child needs many moments of rest within the lesson. Because creative rhythmic movement is not goal-oriented and because the threat of failure is not a factor, the over-stimulated child may have his first real opportunity to learn about himself in a completely relaxed atmosphere. This is an excellent opportunity for the teacher to present basic concepts of movement as related to force, and how the body uses it in work, play, and rest. Examples . . . How do the muscles of your body look and feel when you try to push your living room sofa? How do your muscles look and feel when you try to push against the wall? Let's try it. Look at your muscles. Touch the muscles of one arm as it pushes hard against the wall. Are you able to move the wall? Would it be easier for you to push a balloon away from you? Show me how you would move your arms if you pushed a balloon up and away from you. How do your muscles look and feel now? Are your muscles more relaxed when pushing the wall or the balloon? How much muscle tension do you need to push a balloon up and away from you? How much muscle tension do you need to push the wall? How much muscle tension do you need to hold your body in an erect standing position? Try it. Get rid of all the muscle tension in your body. Will you fall down? Now try standing again and use only as much muscle tension as you need in your body to prevent you from falling. Could you say that your muscles now have a medium amount of tension? Do you think that it is best to live your life with a lot, medium, or no tension? Why? . . .

Children who are tired or over-stimulated can also be taught some basic movement concepts, not by moving their own bodies, but by watching the movement of other objects. The teacher may find many suggestions in beginning physics or mechanical books. Or, she may ask the children to bring a mechanical toy to class, or a kitchen gadget which needs to be moved in order to function. This method also works well with the child who is physically handicapped.

15. Boys enjoy moving their bodies. It is the boys in the class who will be able to move the highest, widest, fastest, and strongest. It is

a wise teacher who points out each boy's good movement qualities for motivational purposes, and uses them for demonstration. In order to motivate the boys in class who are athletically inclined, make frequent reference to how each movement they do in class is related to a particular sport. In order to motivate the boys who are mechanically or scientifically inclined, relate each movement to the physical laws of movement. (Refer to the materials on movement in this book or in an elementary book on physics. Also, refer to the bibliography for a book on movement education.)

Each child in class should know that many of the basic concepts of CRM are shared with dance and sports, and should understand the essence of this relationship. When boys become aware of this relationship, they will be much more comfortable with the dance and will have a much more positive attitude about dancing.

16. Sometimes children object to taking their shoes and socks off. The teacher should explain that the children will move better and more safely without their shoes and socks, and should demonstrate the flexibility of the feet and toes and how to grip the floor when the child locomotes. The room should be kept warm. If the room is cold, the children should be encouraged to rub their feet with their hands or rub their feet on the floor before moving and at various times during the class period.

17. If the class remains understimulated, the following suggestions may be applied:

- The teacher may move with the children.
- The children may be stopped while they are exploring movement, and asked by the teacher to look at their hands. This will help them concentrate on their own movement. She may then ask them to think about where their other bodily parts are in the space about them.
- Encourage the children to ask questions of themselves and their movement. . . . Why? When? What for? How? Where? . . .
- The teacher may act as a catalyst; that is, she may speed up or slow down the action of the students. Examples: if the children are having difficulty discovering new movement, the teacher may teach a lesson on falls to incite each child to explore and discover the possibilities of going from a high to a low level and encourage them to develop their own special fall. Or, the teacher may start a rhythmic pattern and incite the children to move each part of their body to this rhythmic pattern. If the class becomes boring or falls flat, a rhythmic pattern done with per-

cussion instruments, sounds, or words is bound to spark some interest. In fact, a whole new interest reaction may develop merely by changing the tempo of a rhythmic pattern on which the class has been working.

18. Children will not always be able to verbalize their understanding of a movement concept. Very often the teacher will know when the children understand a concept of creative rhythmic movement by the way they move their bodies and use the concept to explore, discover, and develop other movement. This is especially true of the five- and six-year-olds and is also true of the mentally retarded. Remember, too much talk in a movement class leads to nowhere! CRM is a doing, experiencing, try-it-out kind of class. Before talking about movement, experience it first.

19. How does the teacher help the children develop self-confidence in their own creative efforts? The teacher stresses individuality by helping the child concentrate on his own movement. She helps the child attain a respect for the efforts of each of the other children, but encourages him not to copy by helping him gain confidence and self-satisfaction in his own efforts. The teacher is patient, kind, truthful, and respectful. She shows this in her voice, her movements and her words. There should never be a need for the teacher to tell the child that his movement is wrong. A wrong movement just doesn't exist in the study of creative rhythmic movement. When each child realizes this, and realizes too that each child in the class expresses his feelings and ideas differently from all others in the class, the creative process will be nourished and will grow.

20. The CRM teacher does not command. She encourages learning to take place through acts of problem solving and guided discovery. She hypothesizes, postulates, reiterates, relates, clarifies, and focuses. She constantly nudges the child to participate by whetting his curiosity about his physical, mental, emotional, and social abilities and limitations by asking questions. . . . Can you? How can you? What can you do? Try it. Show us. Do everything you can think of doing. How many? Where? Experiment with that idea. How many? Compare. . . .

four

Ten Lesson Plans for the Teacher

Introductory

Each lesson plan is an example of the use of one or more concepts of creative rhythmic movement, employing various methods of presentation to demonstrate these concepts. There may exist many other methods of presentation for the development of this awareness, and the teacher is encouraged to use her own creative ability to think of them. The ten lesson plans which follow are by no means to be regarded as or used as a set formula for the presentation of CRM classes. There are too many variables involved in the teaching of children to present an exact pattern which will fit the needs of each teaching situation. However, these lesson plans should give the teacher pertinent teaching examples which relate to the philosophy of teaching creative rhythmic movement to children, and should encourage the elementary school instructor to try them out.

The teacher who is well acquainted with the problem-solving method and who has had some training in rhythmics, music, dance, art, and/or physical education, will probably find the lesson plans most valuable as examples of the kinds of movement problems that can be presented and what can be expected from the children. The teacher should tend to use the lesson plans as models only. Once she understands the idea of the techniques employed, it will be apparent to her that one can easily compose different lesson plans which will be more appropriate to the specific needs of the children in each class.

The teacher who has had little or no experience in teaching the creative arts, physical education, and/or using the problem-solving method will perhaps need to use the lesson plans, or parts thereof, as written. If CRM is a new subject area for the teacher, it would be best to limit the exposure time to fifteen or twenty minutes, and use only half the class each time. It is better to have the children begging for more exposure than begging for less. No matter how the plans are used, each teacher will bring to them her own personality, individuality, and special talents, which will make each lesson plan a special one for a special group of children.

Each of the lessons which follow is planned for a fifty- to sixty-minute period. The teacher may lengthen the lesson by allowing children more time to explore and discover more movement which will lead to a greater understanding of the concept. The teacher may also introduce more rest or discussion periods, or may choose to introduce a rhythmic pattern. There is no limit to the amount of time which can be used to work on rhythmic awareness, as practice leads to perfection.

It is not wise to try to condense a fifty-minute lesson plan into a thirty-minute period, as development of the self-awareness process through the exploration and discovery of the concepts of creative rhythmic movement takes time. The lesson plan may therefore be shortened by teaching only a segment of it. However, each lesson, no matter how short or long, should contain some, or all, of the following parts.

Each lesson should have a *warmup period.* This can usually be done quickly and effectively with children by performing several elementary forms of locomotion. Starting with locomotor forms not only quickly warms up most of the body, but rapidly tires the children, at least for a while, so that they are ready to move more slowly, purposefully, and with more insight. It also gives them the comfortable and secure feeling of starting the class with something they already know how to do. Another fast and exhausting warmup is the use of a simple rhythmic pattern which can be done in bodily movement. (Refer to Additional Ideas—Rhythm, chap. 5, p. 210.)

Each lesson should have at least one *movement problem* which the children will endeavor to solve and which will lead to an understanding of one of the basic concepts of CRM or its elements.

Each lesson should have at least one period of *relaxation*. This period may be no longer than a brief moment during which the children may stretch and then hang their heads low. Or the relaxation period may be long enough for the child to experience progressive relaxation throughout the entire body.

Each lesson should have a *satisfying movement ending*. This may be done by synthesizing some of the movements discovered during the lesson into a movement phrase or composition, sharing their movement experiences with each other and the teacher, or simply doing a skip to their place of dismissal.

In addition, the lesson may contain bodily movement, or physical exercises, specifically done to increase the child's strength, agility, balance, and coordination. However, children who engage in classes of creative rhythmic movement should attain these goals anyway, simply as the result of their activities in the exploration, discovery, and synthesis of movement. In other words, if the children are solving movement problems, they will, by so doing, be constantly building a stronger and more agile body as the result of their efforts. The reader will note that body-building exercises and dance techniques, are for these reasons, purposely omitted from the lesson plans. True self-awareness through the awareness of the body's physical possibilities and limitations learned through the medium of CRM and the problem-solving method, cannot be achieved by doing stretching, bending, bouncing, etc., exercises to the one—two—three—four command of the teacher. This does not mean that there is no place for these activities in a class of creative rhythmic movement for children. For instance, if the children are not leaping as high in space as they would like to, they may be encouraged to discover why they are not, and this may lead them to the discovery of some movements which will strengthen their bodies and assist them in attaining their aspirations. On the other hand, the teacher may be aware of several children in the class who need to build their strength and agility in order to solve the most elementary movement problems. These children may benefit from performing a daily series of physical exercises which will help to meet their specific needs. (Refer to the bibliography.)

The teacher will find that the greater the encouragement given to children to explore, discover, think, and be aware of their own movement, the less she will have to rely on set physical exercises to meet her teaching objectives.

LESSON PLAN 1

Teaching Objectives:

- To initiate a class environment both physically and behaviorally structured, but free from the threat of failure; to invite and encourage freedom of movement within this structure.
- To encourage the children to become relaxed and self-confident in their movement exploration by positively reinforcing each child's efforts at every opportunity.
- To introduce the drum as a controlling rhythmic force.
- To initiate kinesthetic awareness of the movement of various bodily parts by moving each bodily part, and thinking of each part as it moves.
- To guide the children toward rhythmic awareness through slow, medium, and fast bodily movements.
- To initiate an awareness of the rhythmic patterns of the following locomotor forms through bodily movement: the walk, run, and hop.
- To present the children with ample opportunity to explore their immediate surrounding space by way of bodily movement; and to initiate an awareness of spatial concepts by developing the ability to concentrate on their own bodily movements within and through space.
- As the teacher, to begin to become acquainted with each child in the class—identifying him by name; and to begin to become aware of each child's behavioral and movement patterns.

Equipment needed: (1) a room free from interruption, and having enough empty space to allow each child the liberty to move without touching anyone or anything else in the room; (2) a drum which the teacher can play while locomoting and moving around the room freely; (3) optional equipment—a blackboard and piano.

Words and Concepts Used:

creative rhythmic movement (CRM)
moving rhythmically
moving creatively   tempo
space   beat
explore   locomotor forms—run, walk, hop
discover   stay in rhythm
bodily movement   occupied space
parts of body—head, shoulders,   touch
   elbows, arms, hands, fingers,   feel
   hips, legs, feet, toes, nose   space surrounding you
                                     balance

Class setting at start of lesson: The children are seated on the floor in front of the teacher. The teacher is in front of either the blackboard, the piano, the phonograph, or at some point which can be considered home base, or a place to return to for rest and discussion.

The Lesson

Movement:

Teacher: This is a class in creative rhythmic movement. In this class, you will move your body rhythmically and creatively in the space surrounding you in order to discover some facts about bodily movement —particularly your own bodily movement. You will find these facts very useful in your everyday activities. You will also discover that as you get to know more about your own body and how it moves, you will begin to be better acquainted with yourself and others. Sometimes, I will help you by telling you exactly what to do. However, for the most part, I will ask you questions, propose problems for you to solve and make suggestions, which will lead you to the exploration and discovery of your very own bodily movement. Let's see how this works! Let's begin by moving your head. (*Pause*) . . .

Very good! I see some of you moving your head forward and back. Others moving their head side to side, and still others are moving their head in a big circle. Stop moving your head. (*Pause*) . . . Now, move your head another way. Discover a different way to move your head. Move! (*Pause*) . . .

If you have moved your head more than one way, you are exploring and discovering the many ways your head can move. I see Jim doing a different movement with his head than he did before. Ann's head movement is different than her first movement. Good, class! Stop moving your head. Now, let's try to discover the many ways your shoulders can move. Move your shoulders in as many ways as you can think of. I liked the way you moved your shoulders without watching anyone else's movement. After all, moving your shoulders in many different ways is simple for you to do. There is no need to copy each other's movement. (*Pause*) . . .

Move your elbows. Move your arms. Move your fingers. Move your legs. Move your feet in as many ways as you can think of. (*Pause*) . . .

Rhythmic Movement:

Teacher: We will use the beat of the drum to help you in your exploration of bodily movement. The drum will inform you when to begin, when to stop, how fast to go, and will sometimes even tell you how to move. Listen to the drum carefully, and become very familiar with its beat. Put your hands on the floor behind you and lean back on them so your feet are free to move. Move your feet in rhythim to this drum beat. Listen first, then move. . . . (*Teacher beats a fast drum beat. Children move their feet rapidly in time to the fast drum.*)

Teacher: Now, move your feet in rhythm to this drum beat. Listen first, then move. . . . (*Teacher plays a slow drum beat. Children move their feet slowly in time to the slow drum beat.*) *As they move their feet slowly, the teacher asks if they are moving fast or slow. The teacher also asks if the drum beat is fast or slow.*

Teacher: The rate of speed of the drum beat and of your movement is called tempo. The tempo tells you how fast or how slow to move. If I beat the drum in a fast tempo, and you move your feet in a fast tempo and go somewhere, what will your feet be doing?

Children: Running.

Teacher: (*Choose one child to run around and demonstrate to the rest of the class.*) Good running, Maria. And good stopping. I like the way Maria stopped running when the drum stopped beating. In this class, we will often move throughout the space in this room. You will be able to start, to stop, and to move best with your shoes off. . . . (*The teacher will now instruct the students as to how to take their shoes and socks off and where to put them. It is most important for the teacher to give explicit directions, and to repeat this procedure exactly each time, as the taking-off-shoes period can lead to many behavioral problems.*)

Teacher: I like the way Ken, Susan, John, and Mary took their shoes off, placed them carefully in their spot, and returned to their places in front of me. Can the four of you run in this room at the same time? Can you stay in time with the drum? If you start running here, near the piano, and go around the room this way (*teacher points*) you will each have enough space of your very own. Ready to run, go! . . . (*Four children run around the room demonstrating to the class the direction they will use when they get up and run.*)

Teacher: I liked the way the four of you stayed away from each other. That way, each of you had plenty of space to move in. Let's see if we can have eight children running around the room at the same time. . . . (*The teacher chooses eight children to run, and reinforces them positively for a good start, for a good stop, for staying away from each other, and for staying in rhythm with the drum.*)

Teacher: Class, take a look at all the space in this room. I think it's large enough for everyone in this class to run at the same time without touching each other. . . . (*Children run to fast beats of the drum.*)

Teacher: Good stopping, Tommy. Good stopping, Jane. Let's watch Tommy and Jane and see what they do with their body in order to make a good stop. Do you see how far apart Jane's legs are when she stops? Do you see how Tommy gets his body lower and closer to the floor when he stops? Where are their arms? Do you see how this kind of stop balances their bodies, and prevents them from falling? They are able to stop as fast as the drum tells them to. Can you run in rhythm with the drum, and stop exactly when the beat stops, without falling? . . . (*Teacher gives them several chances to start and stop, and to run to the fast tempo of the drum beat.*)

Teacher: When the drum beats a medium tempo, it is the tempo and rhythm of a walk. Ready to walk in rhythm, go! . . . (*The teacher beats fast and medium beats while the children do runs and walks, until she feels they have gained an awareness of tempo, fast, medium, and slow, through locomotion. The children should by then be tired enough to listen and try the next part of the lesson. If some of the children are not walking in rhythm to the drum beat, the teacher might point this out now by urging them to take a step on each sound. Better, however, not to dwell on this, as most rhythmic problems will be resolved by repeating the movement in future lessons.*)

Teacher: The run and the walk are forms of locomotion. The run and the walk locomote you, or get you from one place to another. There are other locomotor forms which I'm sure you are familiar with. Listen to the rhythmic pattern of the hop. . . . (*The teacher beats the rhythmic pattern of the hop on the side of the drum. This produces a different sound, which the children can easily recognize as the rhythmic pattern and sound of a hop, and will prevent them from confusing it with a fast walk.*) Hopping is done by lifting one foot off the floor and landing on the same foot. Ready to hop? Go! . . . (*The teacher asks the children to hop on each foot several times. The children should now be tired enough to sit still and listen to the next explanation.*)

Creative Movement:

Teacher: Let's take a good look at this room. Take a good look at the floor, the walls, and the ceiling. Let's take a look at the objects that are in this room. Can you name them? (*Pause*) . . . Let's take a look at the group of people in this room, our class. Now let's look at the space in this room: the space, which is not occupied by things or people. . . . (*At this point, children might suggest that space is occupied by air, etc. A discussion of outer space might ensue. It is up to the teacher to decide on the amount of time she wants to devote to a discussion of space. Bear in mind, however, that since the children learn about space by moving within and throughout it, a detailed discussion of the subject might be more appropriate at a later time.)*

Teacher: We have been moving throughout this almost empty space. Is it a lot of space? . . . (*Don't wait for verbal answers—continue quickly, and allow the children to discover the answers to the teacher's questions through movement.*) Now take a look at the space right in front of you, the space between you and the person in front of you. Can you touch the person in front of you? If you can, move a little bit away from this person. (*Pause*) . . . Again, look at the space in front of you. Is it a lot of space? Touch it with your hands. (*Pause*) . . . Look at your hands touching the space in front of you. (*Pause*) . . . Now look at the space above you. Is it a lot of space? Touch the space above you. (*Pause*) . . . Look at the space next to you. Touch the space next to you. (*Pause*) . . . Look at the space on the other side of you. Touch the space that you are looking at. Look at your hands. Look at the space. Look at your hands touching and feeling the space. Don't look at me. You can hear me—just use your ears. Look at the space you are touching, and get well-acquainted with it. Feel all the space that surrounds you. Stop. (*Pause*) . . . Are you looking at your hands touching the space around you? Stand up and touch the space which surrounds you now. (*Pause*) . . . Stop. (*Pause*) . . . Are your eyes looking at your hands touching the space around you? Can you touch the space surrounding you with other parts of your body? Try it! Touch the space surrounding you with your elbow. (*Pause*) . . . Touch the space surrounding you with your head. (*Pause*) . . . Feel the space around you by touching it with your hips. . . . (*The teacher then encourages each child to concentrate on what he is doing. Since the movement is so simple, every child in the class should be able to succeed on the first or second try. Individualization and self-esteem is stressed throughout all the lessons in an effort to encourage a maximum amount of creativity. If a child is having difficulty watching and concentrating on his own movement, the teacher might choose several children who have succeeded in concentrating on their movements to demonstrate. Or she might demonstrate by focusing her eyes on an object, and then releasing that focus. The children will easily see the eyes move away from the object.)*

Creative Rhythmic Movement:
Teacher: I will now beat the drum at a fast tempo. The drum tells you to run. When the drum stops, you will stop running and look at the

Look at your hands touching and feeling the space!

128

Look and touch!

space around you. Each time you stop I will tell you what part of
your body you're to use to touch the space surrounding you. Ready to
run, go! (*Teacher sets her own rhythmic pattern as to how fast the
children will run, and how long, and with which part of the body they
will touch the space surrounding them.*) *Children do the following:*

Run   ———   Stop   ———   Look And Touch

(*The teacher will stop the touching movement in midair whenever she
feels that the children are not concentrating on what they are doing.
That would be a good time to introduce music or sound accompaniment. The teacher may elect to use one of the following depending on
what equipment is available: (1) Percussion: Snare drum for runs, large
gong sounds for look and touch. (2) Piano: Glissando or trill for runs,
chords with broad intervals played with both hands for look and touch.*

(3) Voice. Create a wind-like sound for the run by cupping the hands and blowing into the hands strongly. The look-and-touch movements may be accompanied by vocalizing the words move, look, touch, *or* space. *Repeat the words several times, and change the tone and timbre of the voice.)*

Dismissal:

Teacher: I'm going to beat the rhythmic pattern of a hop. All boys get ready to hop to your shoes in rhythm with the drum beat, put them on, and sit and wait for dismissal. Go! (*Pause*) . . . I'm going to beat the rhythmic pattern of a walk. All girls get ready to walk to your shoes in rhythm, put them on, and sit and wait for dismissal. Go! . . .

LESSON PLAN 2

Teaching Objectives:

- To continue encouraging the children to become relaxed and self-confident in their movement explorations.
- To guide the students toward rhythmic awareness by way of a review of slow, medium, and fast movement.
- To instill further awareness of the rhythmic patterns of the following locomotor forms by means of bodily movement: the walk, run, hop, and leap.
- To further initiate conscious awareness of the movement of various bodily parts.
- To increase familiarity with the drum as a controlling rhythmic support.
- To provide the children with the opportunity to continue the exploration of their immediate surrounding space through bodily movement; specifically, through push-and-pull movements.
- To initiate an awareness of muscular tension and relaxation through push-and-pull movements.
- To initiate an awareness of the bodily movement of other children within the group by observing their muscular tension and relaxation.
- To provide the children with their second opportunity to experience the freedom involved in moving creatively, while remaining within a structured pattern of movement.
- To familiarize yourself with each child in the class by learning his name; and to become aware of each child's behavioral and movement patterns.

Equipment needed: (1) A room free from interruption, and having sufficient empty space to allow each child the liberty of moving without touching anyone or anything else in the room; (2) a drum which the teacher can play while freely moving around the room; (3) nine to ten yards of rope, the ends of which should be tied together so that a circle can be formed with it; (4) a blackboard.

Words and Concepts Used:

(These words may be listed on the blackboard for the children to view before the class begins.)

leap	stretch
tension	push and pull
relaxation	muscles
progressive relaxation	pretend
droop	imagine
flop	be aware
let-go	

Class setting at start of lesson: The children are seated on the floor in front of the teacher. The teacher will first review with the children the procedure for taking off their shoes, placing them in a particular location, and returning to their place in front of the teacher. Since the children will take varying amounts of time to take their shoes off, the teacher might prod them to hurry along the procedure by writing something relevant and interesting on the board each day. She may also write a movement problem on the board for them to solve, or play a review game. (See the section on review following lesson plan 4.) The children should be instructed to proceed as follows each day, and soon it will become a habit executed efficiently and rapidly: take their shoes and socks off as soon as they enter the activity room, seat themselves in front of the blackboard, teacher, and/or piano, a movement distant apart, then read silently whatever is written on the blackboard and react accordingly while waiting for the class to begin. (The amount of time and effort spent on this procedure will vary tremendously with each class.)

The Lesson

Locomotor Movement:

Teacher: Do you remember the rhythmic pattern of the run? . . . (*Teacher beats a fast run on the drum*). Who can show me a run in time to the drum beat? . . . (*Teacher chooses two or three children who have raised their hands. These children run in rhythm to a fast drum beat.*)

Teacher: Good stopping! These children moved very well in time with the drum beat and also stopped without losing their balance. Let's all try it! Be sure you all move in this direction (*teacher demonstrates*) around the room. Stay away from each other so that each one of you has space to move in. (*Children run to fast, slow, and medium running beats.*)

Teacher: What happens to your run when you take larger steps? . . . (*The teacher may expect one of the following answers from the children*):

—Some children take high steps, while other children take broad steps.
—The beats are slower. (*Someone may remember the word* tempo *and respond by noting that the tempo is slower.*)
—The arms swing more fully in order to help the body balance.

Teacher: Let's all try doing very big running steps, and see if you think of the name of this new locomotor form which develops from the run. Ready, go! (*Pause*) . . . What name do we know this locomotor form by?

Children: A leap.

Teacher: Very good. A leap is a run done with larger steps which take us up and off the floor. Let's all try leaping. Swinging your arms as your leap helps you to get your legs further apart. Ready to leap? Begin. . . . (*Children do leaps.*) The kind of leap most of you have just done is the kind you might use to leap across something, such as a puddle or a small stream. Who can show me a leap you might use in order to get over something, such as a fence? . . . (*One child is chosen to demonstrate a high leap.*) What are some of the things you need to do with your body in order to leap high off the floor? Let's all try leaping as high as we can. Try it several times and discover the answer for yourself. (*Children try high leaps.*) . . .

(*Teacher looks for several children who can do high leaps very well. She then asks those children what they did in order to get so high off the floor, and expects one of the following suggestions*):

—Swinging your arms higher helps to get your body higher.
—Stopping the swing of your arms going up just as you reach the highest point of your leap helps you to stay off the floor longer.
—Pushing one foot down into the floor harder helps to elevate your body higher.

Teacher: Now, use all these ideas to help you do the highest leaps you can possibly do. (*Pause*) . . .

From Tension to Progressive Relaxation:

(The teacher may find it expedient to do the following along with the children.)

What happens to your run when you take larger steps?

Teacher: Stretch your bodies by reaching as high as you can. Reach for the ceiling. I know you can't touch the ceiling, but try. Look at the space you're reaching for. Don't look at me. Reach up, look up. Stay up there. (*Pause*) . . . Now let your hands droop. Look at your hands drooping. Let your arms relax and your head flop. Allow your shoulders to droop. Let go in your upper back and bend your lower back so your head falls forward and hangs low. Stay there with your head hanging low and your whole body relaxed, except your legs. (*Pause*) . . . Stretch up again. Try stretching as high as you can again. (*Teacher repeats the points for the stretch, and goes through the same directions for progressive relaxation.*) . . . Now let your knees relax and sit down. Keep your head hanging low and relaxed. Keep your whole body relaxed. (*Pause*)

Look at the space you're reaching for.

How high can you reach?

. . . Now, let your whole body go, and lie down. Close your eyes and rest.
. . . (*The resting period should be no longer than one to one-and-a-half
minutes, and the students should be encouraged to keep their eyes and
mouth closed during this time. The teacher should make the students
aware of the fact that the resting period is a no-movement, no-non-
sense period which is essential in the regaining of strength for a movement period to follow.* If the movement periods are kept at a vigorous
pace, the resting period will be a welcomed relief.)

Locomotor Review:
Teacher: (*while the children's eyes are still closed.*) Today, you have
done two locomotor forms. They are the run and the leap. (*As soon as
the teacher begins talking, some children will open their eyes and look*

Let your head hang low.

at the teacher, who should emphasize the fact that one does not have to look in order to hear, and encourage all the children to keep their eyes closed while listening. It is advantageous for the children, early in the unit, to develop the skill of listening without looking at the teacher, as many times later on they must confine themselves to moving and listening [at the same time], but will not be able to look at the speaker.)

Teacher: During the last lesson you also did two other locomotor forms. Listen to the drum beating these previous locomotor rhythmic patterns. Can you recognize them? If you recognize them, do not tell anyone, do not locomote, but keep your eyes closed and think about it. Here's number one. (*She beats the rhythmic pattern of the hop.*) Can you picture in your brain, what you would do to that drum beat? Here's number two. (*She beats a walk.*) Can you imagine what locomotor form is done to that rhythmic pattern? Now let's see if you can do them. Open your eyes, stand up, and get ready to locomote in rhythm to the drum. (*Children enact number one and number two as above.*) Very well done! I can see that you're beginning to know the rhythmic patterns of several locomotor forms very well. Let's sit here in front of the blackboard and list the names of all the locomotor forms which we have learned so far. Who can give me the name of one locomotor form? (*The teacher then proceeds to call on each child as they raise*

Heavy, heavy head.

their hand to suggest one of the following: walk, run, hop, leap. The teacher writes them on the blackboard and asks each child to describe the identifying characteristic of each locomotor form. [See pp. 11–19.])

Tension and Relaxation:

Teacher: (The children continue to sit on the floor in front of the blackboard.) Put your hands in front of your eyes where you can see them easily. If you were pushing a balloon away from you, how would you move your hands and arms? *(The teacher may suggest to the children that in order to push something away from the body, the palms of the hands are facing away from the body. Allow the children time to experiment with this movement many times.)* . . . As you move, look at the muscles in your arms and your hands. Are they soft or hard?

Children: Soft.

Teacher: How do you know they are soft?

Children: When we touch our muscles they are soft. When we look at our muscles they look soft.

Teacher: Show me how you would move your hands and arms if you were pushing an elephant or a piano away from you. . . . (Children do so several times.)

Teacher: What are your muscles like in this movement? Are they soft or hard?

Children: Hard. We can see it and we can feel it.

Teacher: Let's try both pushes again, and look and think about the muscles in your hands and arms. Ready to push the balloon away? . . . Pu - - sh! *(Teacher says softly.)* When our muscles are soft and do very little work, we say that they are relaxed. Ready to push the elephant away? . . . Pu - - sh! *(Teacher's voice has an incisive quality.)* When our muscles stretch and get hard in order to work hard, we say that our muscles are tense. Show me again, your tense arm and hand muscles. *(Pause)* . . . Relax, or let go of those muscles. *(Pause)* . . . Can you show me tense leg and feet muscles? Relax, or let go of them. Can you show me tense face muscles? Relax. Show me tense back muscles? Let go. Show me tense stomach muscles? Relax. Show me a whole body of tense muscles? Relax your whole body.

Teacher: Can you follow the beat of the drum and my voice by first locomoting, and then by using tension and relaxation? First, run in rhythm to the drum. It will sound like this. . . . *(Teacher beats a medium fast running beat.)* Second, stop when the drum stops. Third, push your

Pu—sh—sh!

arms and hands anywhere in the space surrounding you with a lot of tension. Remember, first you will run; then, stop! Then, do one big push. Ready to run, go! (*Teacher beats the following pattern.*)

Run!	**Stop!**	**Pu—sh—sh—sh!**
Any number of beats —	**One beat** —	**Beat a fast roll on the drum and say push.**

The above pattern is the children's first opportunity to do a movement composition. It should be repeated several times to allow each child to have a success experience. Since the only creative part of the movement composition lies in the children's choice of what direction they direct their push, the teacher should encourage a change of direction each time they do it. When children have done the last push the teacher says: Stay there! Look at your arms and hands. Don't look at me. Don't move! *Freezing your movement at the end of a series of movements makes it feel final, like a period at the end of a sentence.*

Tense!
Relax!
Pull!
Let go!

Teacher: (Choose eight children, at random, to sit in a circle while the rest of the class sits and watches. The teacher has a nine- or ten-yard rope which has been tied securely at the ends and, when placed on the floor, may be used to form a circle. She places the circle of rope in front of and on the inside of the circle of children.) Take the rope gently with both hands. Do not pull on the rope, now. Be sure both of your hands are on the rope. The muscles of your arms and hands are relaxed as you hold the rope. Now tighten your grip on the rope and pull as hard as you can. Hold on. *(Pause)* . . . Relax! . . . *(Teacher asks the other members of the class.)* Did you see how the muscles of their hands, arms, shoulders, and then the rest of their body tensed when they pulled? Did you see how their muscles relaxed when they stopped pulling? I have some more rope. You can all form more circles and feel your muscles tense and relax as you pull. *(If there are many behavioral problems in class it is best to use only one rope while the others watch. Give the children several chances to pull and relax. Then, alternate the children. Encourage more pull from the stronger ones. This will pull the circle out of shape but will allow these children an even greater opportunity to explore and discover tension and relaxation through movement. Be sure to stop the pulling action before there are any behavioral problems.)* Now, I'm going to take the rope away. This time, pretend that you are holding the rope again with both hands, and pull and relax when I tell you to. Be sure to get that same amount of tension and lack of tension as you did when you were really holding on to the rope. Ready, pull! *(Pause)* . . . Relax! . . . Be sure to continue to work as a group. Be aware of the other children in your circle. You can see the other children in your circle out of the corner of your eyes, and at the same time look at your arms as you pull and as you relax. Ready, pull! *(Pause)* . . . Relax! . . . Be aware of the tension you are creating in your muscles, and the tension of the whole circle. Notice how your muscles let go of the tension when they relax. Ready to pull, go! *(Pause)* . . . Relax! . . . *(At this point, the teacher may encourage questions or a discussion about tension and relaxation,* but a discussion concerning this particular concept of movement education, should not be forced. *There will be plenty of opportunity in the ensuing lessons. If, however, the children seem eager, and time permits, the teacher might look for some of the following points to be made)* :

- Movement occurs somewhere between a completely relaxed muscle and a completely tense muscle.
- It is necessary to tense a muscle in order for it to move.

- It is necessary to relax a muscle in order for it to tense again and move again.
- If one tenses a muscle, many other muscles tense along with it. (Although this lesson does not stress the states of feeling evoked by muscular tension, some children might discover and discuss it.)
- When a person tenses his muscles, he gets a feeling about what he is doing. Sometimes, this feeling makes him even more tense and gets him emotionally involved.
- In order to avoid too much tension in life, one must learn to relax and become tense at appropriate times.

Dismissal:

(The teacher plays one of the previously presented locomotor forms, i.e. walk, run, hop, or leap on the drum to each circular group. They perform the appropriate locomotor form to their shoes and are dismissed.)

LESSON PLAN 3

Teaching Objectives:

- To continue encouraging the children to become relaxed and self-confident in their movement explorations.
- To instill further awareness of the rhythmic patterns of the following locomotor forms through bodily movement: the walk, run, hop, leap, and jump.
- To continue a familiarity with the drum as a controlling rhythmic support.
- To give the children the opportunity to continue the exploration of their immediate surrounding space by using bodily movement; specifically touching, pushing, and swimming movements.
- To continue an awareness of tension and relaxation of the muscles of the body.
- To initiate an awareness of the step pattern and movement pattern, and present the opportunity for practice in each.
- To initiate an awareness of the movement composition and how it is formed.
- To familiarize yourself with each child in the class by learning his name, and to become aware of each child's behavioral and movement patterns.

Equipment Needed: (1) A room free from interruption, and with sufficient empty space to allow each child the liberty of moving without touching anyone or anything in the room; (2) a drum which the teacher can play while freely moving around the room; (3) a blackboard; (4) one or two cymbals, a guitar, or an autoharp.

Words And Concepts Used

approach	movement composition
swimming movements	roll
touching movements	concentrate
step pattern	motionless
movement pattern	

Class setting at start of lesson: The children are seated on the floor in front of the teacher looking at the blackboard which contains a list of the names of the even locomotor forms: walk, run, hop, leap, and jump. Their shoes and socks have already been taken off.

Elementary Forms of Locomotion:

Teacher: Let's see how well you can recognize and do these locomotor forms when I beat the rhythmic pattern of each one on the drum. (*The teacher points to the blackboard, and beats the rhythmic pattern of all the even locomotor forms, one at a time:* run, walk, hop, leap, *and* jump. *The children listen to each rhythmic pattern, and do the appropriate locomotor form as soon as they recognize it. The teacher makes comments about the execution of the even elementary forms of locomotion. She positively reinforces the children who do well. She makes general suggestions to the whole class for improvement, and repeats those locomotor forms which the children do not do well. At this time, the teacher should expect the children to execute even elementary locomotor forms quite well. However, if there is a child having difficulty, she does not single that child out. She waits to see how that child will do later in the unit; since locomotor forms are repeated almost every lesson, the child has every opportunity to improve on his own.*)

Step Patterns:

Teacher: Very often these locomotor forms are combined to form step patterns. Step patterns are found in all sport events and in dances too. Do you know what the step pattern is for doing a dive? What step pattern do you do on the diving board before diving in?

Children: Two or three walks and a jump. (*If the teacher has a picture of a person executing a dive it is helpful.*) What is the rhythmic pattern of three walks and a jump when it is used as a step pattern for an approach to diving? Does it sound like this? (*Children who are in the fourth through sixth grades will discover the rhythmic pattern and tempo on their own. Teacher says it one time and pauses.)*

walk	w	w		j u m p			
3	1	2	3	1	②	③	pause
	1	2	3	1	2	3	

(When the Teacher repeats the above, she begins to beat it on the drum, also.)
Let's say the step pattern in rhythm to the drum.

Children: Walk, walk, walk, jump. *(Repeat often with the drum to enable the children to get the feeling of the rhythm.)*

Teacher: How many children can do it in rhythm to the drum? Don't forget to wait after each rhythmic pattern. *(All the children get up and do three walks and a jump . . . pause. Children remain standing in their own self-space in the room.)*

Movement Pattern:

Teacher: If you were using this step pattern on the diving board, how many patterns would you use to make one dive?

Children: One step pattern for each dive.

Teacher: Very good! What would you be doing after the jump off the diving board?

Children: Diving into the water and swimming.

Teacher: Let's do diving and swimming movements by moving our bodies in the space surrounding us instead of in the water. *(Pause for movement) . . .*

Teacher: What kind of forward dive do you like to do best? You need to do a forward dive with this type of approach. Try several forward dives. Choose one that you like the best, and repeat it often enough so that you will remember it. *(Pause for movement) . . .*

Teacher: What kind of swimming stroke would you like to do? You can do any kind you want in the space surrounding you. Choose one swimming stroke that you like the best, and repeat it often enough so that you will remember it. *(Pause for movement) . . .*

Teacher: Now, let's create a three part movement composition. First, do the diving approach, and second the jump and dive. Remember, it sounds like this. . . . (*Teacher plays and says the following rhythmic pattern of* walk, walk, walk, jump.) Third, do swimming movements in the space surrounding you. The swimming movements sound like this: (*Teacher plays on the cymbal, guitar strings and/or the autoharp.*) Ready to put it all together—begin!

The teacher does not write any of the following rhythmic patterns on the board, as it is too early in the unit for the children to be concerned with the mechanics of constructing a rhythmic pattern. The rhythmic patterns are shown here to aid the teacher in presenting and accompanying this part of the lesson.

	walk	w	w	jump and dive		
3	1	2	3	1	②	③
	1	2	3	1	2	3

		swim			swim	
3	1	②	③	1	②	③
	1	2	3	1	2	3

		swim			swim	
	1	②	③	1	②	③
	1	2	3	1	2	3

drum

	walk	w	w	jump and dive		
3	1	2	3	1	2	3

cymbal

		swim			swim	
	1	2	3	1	2	3

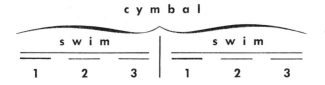

(*The teacher makes appropriate comments and then repeats the entire pattern several times to give the children a feeling of success and enjoyment. She asks the children to freeze on the last move, and then invites them again to sit in front of the blackboard, where she writes the following*):

- walk, walk, walk, jump
- dive
- swim, swim, swim, swim

Teacher: If you call part number one a step pattern, what name can we give to part numbers two and three?

Children: A movement pattern. The dive is a movement pattern and the swims are another movement pattern.

Teacher: So we see that when we combine elementary forms of locomotion, we compose a step pattern. And, when we combine movements, we compose a movement pattern. And, when they are all put together, a movement composition is formed. Let's try another step pattern. Listen to it on the drum. It will be a combination of two of the forms listed on the blackboard. Look at the list of elementary forms of locomotion, and see if you can recognize this step pattern? (*The teacher plays the following*):

	hop	h	h	h	jump		i	
4	1	2	3	4	1	②	3	④
	1	2	3	4	1	2	3	4

(*One child answers and demonstrates. The teacher invites the children to say it and then try it. Children execute the above step pattern while the teacher plays it on the drum and says it. The teacher writes the step pattern shown above, on the blackboard, as : hop, hop, hop, hop, jump, jump.*

The teacher again disregards the rhythmic value of each beat in order to stress the fact that step patterns are composed by combining loco-

motor forms; and to present ample opportunity for the children to structure and practice these step patterns. Again, the teacher may ask half the class to get up and execute the above step pattern while the other half of the class claps. The children may further practice the step patterns by saying exactly what they do with their feet. For example, the above step pattern may be said in rhythm as: hop, hop, hop, hop, jump, jump.)

Teacher: Can you do this step pattern twice and then add a movement pattern? The step pattern done twice sounds like this. (*Teacher beats the following on the drum, two times.*)

hop	h	h	h	j u m p		i	
4 1	2	3	4	1	②	3	④
1	2	3	4	1	2	3	4	repeat

Teacher: Ready to do it, begin. (*Pause*) . . . The rhythmic pattern of the movement sounds exactly the same. Now, however, you will move another part of your body. Let's touch the space surrounding us with our hands and arms to this same rhythmic pattern. Ready to touch! Are you looking at the space you are going to touch? Go. (*Teacher beats the following as the children touch the space.*)

touch	t	t	t	t o u c h		t	
4 1	2	3	4	1	②	3	④
1	2	3	4	1	2	3	4	repeat

Teacher: Now let's put them both together. Ready to do the step pattern twice, and ready to do the movement pattern twice with touching movements. Begin. (*Pause for movement*) . . . You have now created another movement composition.

Tension and Relaxation:

(*Repeat the instructions for progressive relaxation as described in lesson plan 2. The teacher starts out by asking the children to stretch their bodies by reaching as high as they can. These instructions should be repeated until they make every effort to reach high and to look up and not at the teacher or anyone else in the class. The progressive relaxation should now be taken down to the low level; that is, the children should be lying down relaxed and listening to the teacher.*)

Teacher: During the last lesson, you practiced tensing and relaxing some and then all of the muscles in your body. Do you remember that you created muscle tension by making your muscles hard? Do you remember that you produced a relaxed muscle by letting go of that tension? Keep your eyes closed and only tense and relax those muscles of your body which I will name. Ready? Tense the muscles in your arms. (*Pause*) . . . Relax the tension in your arms. (*Pause*) . . . Tense the muscles in your face. (*Pause*) . . . Relax your facial muscles. (*Pause*) . . . Tense the muscles of your legs. (*Pause*) . . . Relax the muscles of your legs. Tense all the muscles in your body. (*Pause*) . . . Relax all the muscles in your body. (*Pause*) . . .

Teacher: Now tense all the muscles of your body by making your body very thin and tall. Keeping your body quite tense, roll your tall, thin body. Stop. Roll back. Stop. Relax. (*Pause*) . . .

Teacher: Open your eyes and sit up. (*holds up a pencil*) The pencil is one straight long, thin, piece of wood. By lying down on the floor and stretching your body, and tensing the muscles of your body, your body can roll in one piece just as this pencil rolls. (*The teacher rolls the pencil on the floor.*) Let's try again to tense all the muscles of our body, and make our body tall and thin. Now roll your body in one piece, just as the pencil did. (*The children do so. The teacher then asks them to roll several times in each direction, but carefully reminds them to stay away from each other.*)

Teacher: Relax all the muscles of your body. Lie on the floor quietly and motionless while I count five counts. As soon as you hear the number five, stand up and get ready to run. (*The teacher slowly counts to five. When the children have all stood up, she continues*): Look for an empty space to run. Stop, and push your arms into the space surrounding you, using a lot of muscle tension. Ready to run? Go. . . . (*The teacher beats the following rhythmic pattern on the drum*)

Run	**Push**

(*Children carry out the instruction.* This is a review, and each child should be familiar enough with the procedure to attend to his own movement. *The children should be showing a great deal of muscle tension in their arms and hands, and their eyes should be focused on their arm and hand movements. Each child should be running toward an empty space, occupying that space, and not touching anyone or anything else in the room.*)

Teacher: Now, let's try pushing in all the space that immediately surrounds us. Look at the space way above you. Push your hands and your arms with a lot of tension into that space above you. Ready? Push! (*Pause*) . . .

Teacher: Look at the space which surrounds your feet. Ready to push in that direction? Push! (*Pause*) . . . Look at the space behind you. Ready to push in the space behind you? Push! Look at the space next to you; next to your hips. Ready to push next to you with a great deal of tension in your arms? Push! Push on the other side of you. Ready to push? Push!

Teacher: What part of the surrounding space do you like to push against best? Some of you will choose to push in the space above you. Others, will choose to push in the space behind you, or next to you, or in front of you. Try it out now. Discover which space is best for you to push in. Go ahead, and try it. (*Teacher pauses.*) Many of you will do something different. This is good. Remember, concentrate on your own movement. Do the push that is best for you. (*Pause*) . . .

Teacher: Have you discovered a good push? Show me. Ready? Begin. (*Teacher beats a roll on the drum and says,* push, *with a great deal of tension in her voice. Pauses*) . . . Very well done. I like the way each one of you has discovered his own best push. Show me that same push again. Begin! (*Pause*) . . . Stop right at the end of the push and freeze your movement. We will call this push number one. Discover another push in the space surrounding you. Try it out! Don't forget push number one. (*Pause*) . . . Show me push number two. Ready, go!

Teacher: Now, can you do push number one and then push number two? Let's try it together. Ready to do push number one. (*Teacher says* push *with a lot of emphasis in her tone.*) Ready to do push number two? (*Teacher again says* push *with tension in her voice. Pause*) . . .

Teacher: Let's add a run before the two pushes. Run when the drum beats a run. Stop when the drum stops. Then, do push number one, followed by push number two. Ready to run? Go! (Following this, teacher tells the children to stretch and progressively relax to the sitting position and then look at the blackboard.)

Movement Composition:

Teacher: Today, you have done several movement compositions. (*She points to the first composition which was the walk, walk, jump, swim,*

swim, swim, swim.) Remember the first movement composition, with its step pattern and movement pattern? A movement composition like an English or musical composition has many parts. When you write an English composition, you combine words, sentences, and paragraphs. In order to form a movement composition, you combine locomotor forms into a step pattern and movements into a movement pattern. When they are all added together a movement composition is formed. Look at the second composition which we did today. (*Teacher points to the following pattern*):

hop	h	h	h	j u m p	i	Repeat from
4	= =	= =	= =	= = = =	= = = =	Beginning

touch	t	t	t	t o u c h	t
4	= =	= =	= =	= = = =	= =

Teacher: Does it also contain a step pattern and a movement pattern? (*Pause*) . . . Who can point to the step pattern? (*Pause*) . . . Who can point to the movement pattern? (*Pause*) . . . When two or more patterns are put together, it is called a movement composition. The movement composition we just did has 4 parts to it. First, there's the run. Second, there's the stop and look. Third, there's push one. And fourth there's push two. The teacher illustrates the above on the blackboard as follows:

R u n	Stop And Look	←——Step Pattern
Push #1	Push #2	←—— Movement Pattern

Teacher: Before leaving today, let's see if you can repeat your push composition three times. Hold the last push and stay motionless—it is the end of the composition. Ready to run? Go! (*Children repeat the above composition three times, and are then dismissed.*)

LESSON PLAN 4

Teaching Objectives:

- To continue encouraging the children to become relaxed and self-confident in their movement explorations.
- To instill further awareness of the rhythmic patterns, of the following locomotor forms through bodily movement: walk, run, hop, leap, and jump.

Freeze your movement!

- To continue increasing familiarity with the drum as a controlling rhythmic support.
- To continue an awareness of tension and relaxation of the muscles of the body.
- To continue initiating an awareness of the step pattern and movement pattern, and present the opportunity for practice in each.
- To initiate an awareness of the movement composition and how it is formed.
- To familiarize yourself with each child in the class by learning his name, and to become aware of each child's behavioral and movement patterns.
- To initiate in each child an awareness of the vertical space surrounding him, through the exploration of that space, using bodily movement.
- To instill in each child a conscious awareness of his contribution to the group through the medium of bodily movement and how it functions to create a design in space.
- To develop a sense of group awareness through bodily movement and its role in creating a design in space.

Equipment needed: (1) a room free from interruption, with sufficient empty space to allow each child the liberty of moving without touching anyone or anything in the room; (2) a drum which the teacher can play while freely moving around the room; (3) nine to ten yards of rope, the ends of which should be tied together so that a circle can be formed with it; (4) a blackboard.

Words and Concepts Used:

tall	levels
small	slow motion
vertical space or up	design in space
and down space	awareness, be aware

Class setting at start of lesson: The children are seated on the floor in front of the teacher, looking at the blackboard which contains a list of the names of the *even* locomotor forms. The following is also written on the blackboard: step pattern, movement pattern, and movement composition. The movement begins immediately.

The Lesson

Movement: (Elementary Forms of Locomotion—Review)

Teacher: Listen and locomote as the drum beats tell you what to do. (*Beats the rhythmic patterns of the following: walk, run, hop,*

jump, and leap. By this time the children should be able to recognize and execute these even locomotor forms readily.)

Note: The teacher should constantly check for the following:

1. Each locomotor form should be done in rhythm or in time to the
   drum beat. That is, each time a sound is heard, a movement is made.
2. Each locomotor form should be executed with exactness and pre-
   cision. Explain that these elementary forms of locomotion are used
   as building blocks to create a step pattern.
3. Each child should be using the other parts of his body, especially
   his arms, to assist him in maintaining his balance while executing a
   locomotor form. (Attention should be called to the easy swing of
   the arms to assist the body in balance while moving. However, too
   much reference to opposition at this time very often confuses the
   child. Opposition is a difficult concept for a child of the early elementary years to grasp. It is better to stress using the arms naturally,
   and how they will usually swing in opposition to the movement of
   the rest of the body. The theory of opposition is best introduced to
   children of the upper elementary years or later in the unit.)

Teacher: When locomotor forms are combined, a step pattern is formed.
Can you remember this step pattern from the last time? Listen to it on
the drum. (*Beats the following rhythmic pattern*)

hop	h	h	h	j u m p		i	
4							
1	2	3	4	1	2	3	4

When you can say the step pattern with the drum beat, raise your hand.
(*The teacher calls on one child to say:* hop, hop, hop, hop, jump, jump.)

Teacher: Who can do the step pattern in time with the drum beat?
(*Calls on several children to do it, while the other class members clap
and watch.*)

Teacher: Let's have everyone try it! (*Children do four hops and two
jumps.*)

Teacher: Here's another step pattern from last time. How many of you
can do it? (*Beats the following:*)

walk	w	w	j u m p		
3	1	2	3	1	②	③
	1	2	3	1	2	3

(*Everyone tries it.*)

Teacher: How many walks are there in this step pattern? Who can say the step pattern in rhythm to the drum? Let's all say it and do it together. (*Pause*) . . .

Teacher: Listen to the drum beating this new step pattern. (*Pause*) . . .

	run r	r r	r r	r r		j u m p		
4	1 +	2 +	3 +	4 +	1	②	③	④
	1	2	3	4	1	2	3	4

We have not had this step pattern before. Listen again. (*Pause*) . . . Clap in time to the drum beat. (*Pause*) . . . Who can say the step pattern in time to the drum beat? (*Teacher chooses Paul to say* run, run, run, run, run, run, run, run, jump.)

Teacher: Let's see if the rest of the class can clap the rhythmic pattern while you, Paul, say the step pattern. Remember, there are eight runs. (*Pause*) . . . Who can do the step pattern in time to the drum beat? (*Teacher selects several children to demonstrate first. Then permits the whole class to do it together after the demonstration.*)

Levels:

Teacher: Stretch all the way up and make yourself as tall as you can. (*Pause*) . . . Slowly relax every part of your body until you are as small as you can get. Make your body as small as it would be if you were in a box with the lid closed. (*Pause*) . . . Now, when you hear the drum beat, get small fast. Ready, go! (*Teacher beats the drum once when she says* go *and the children move from a tall position to a small position very rapidly.*)

Teacher: When you hear the drum beat again stretch tall very rapidly. Ready, go! (*Pause*) . . . Follow the drum and my voice. Small! (*Teacher beats the drum once and repeats the word. Children move small. Teacher beats the drum once and says* tall. *Children move tall. Teacher repeats several times:* small, tall, small, tall. *Children sit down.*)

Teacher: Can you do tall, small three times to this rhythmic pattern? (*Teacher says* tall, small *as she beats the following rhythmic pattern. Notice that the word* tall *is said much more rapidly than the word* small.)

Tall	**Small**	**Tall**	**S**		**T**	**S**		**T**
3	**1**	**2**	**3**	**1**	**2**	**3**	**1**	**2**	**3**

Teacher: Can you say tall, small in time with the drum beat? Which word do you say fast, tall or small? (*Pause*) . . . Let's say tall, small together in time with the drum. (*Pause*) . . . Can you do tall, small in time with the drum beat? Let's do it together. Since your body is going to move to the tall position first, in what position will it be when you begin?

Children: We will be in the small position. (*The children do the tall small movement pattern several times, with the teacher encouraging them to go as tall as they can. Several children will discover that movement to an extremely tall bodily position elevates them from the floor, forming a jump. These children can be used to demonstrate. After the class has tried it several times, the teacher asks the following questions and encourages the children to discover the answers for themselves through their own bodily movement.*)

Teacher: How high in the space above you can you reach by jumping? (*Pause*) . . . How can you move your arms to get your body higher? (*Pause*) . . . What do you do to the muscles of your arms to get your body higher in the space above you? (*Children experiment and answer.*)

Children: The muscles in the arms go from relaxation, as they start to swing up, to tension at the highest point of the jump.

Teacher: Look at all the space above you. Is there any way your body could get higher in the space above you than by jumping up there?

Children: (*may answer as follows*) using ropes, stilts, an airplane, a balloon, etc.

Teacher: Is there any way your body could get higher in the space above you without using any other objects for assistance?

Children: We could leap high or hop high.

Teacher: How high in the space above you can you get by leaping? Try it now. (*Pause*) . . . How high in the space above you can you get by hopping? Try it. (*Pause*) . . . Now try jumping again as high as you can go. (*Pause*) . . .

Teacher: We can readily see that there are three elementary forms of locomotion that lift our body up in the space above us. They are the leap, hop, and jump. Let us divide the vertical space, or the up and

How can you move your arms to get your body higher?

down space surrounding us, into levels. You have just jumped, leaped, or hopped as high as you can: you have just moved into the highest level. (*Points to the highest level*) We can then call the standing level the high level, and the lying down level the low level. Put your body in the high level. (*Pause*) . . . Put your body in the low level, go! (*Pause*) . . . There is a level between low and high in which our bodies frequently move. Show me that level. Right now, put your body in that in-between level, go! Stay there. (*Pause*) . . . Take a look at all the other children in the class. (*Pause*) . . . As you can see, there are many positions that your body can take while being in this level. Some children are sitting one way or another, while others are kneeling in many different ways. What can we call this level?

Children: The medium level.

(*Teacher writes the names of the levels on the board: highest, high, medium, and low. She reviews the levels now by pointing to them one at a time, and asking the children to put their bodies in the appropriate level.*)

Teacher: Let's see if we can move our bodies in slow motion. Go slowly from the high level, through the medium level, and on to the low level. Now slowly move from the low to the medium to the high level again. (*Pause*) . . . Now, go to the highest level! (*Pause*) . . . Now, go to the highest level, again! (*Pause*) . . . Notice that you can't go to the highest level in slow motion because the force of gravity pulls you down. (*Pause*) . . .

Teacher: Let's move through the levels again in slow motion. This time, explore the space surrounding you by touching it with your hands, arms, and elbows. I'll call out the levels. Move in slow motion and touch the space sourrounding you as you go from one level to another. (*She calls out one of the three levels, and allows time for the students to explore the space surrounding them in each level by touching that space with their hands, arms, and/or elbows*)

Teacher: Now we're going to add a part. Every time I call the high level, I will also call out one of the locomotor forms. Ready to move through the levels? Ready to touch the surrounding space while going through the levels? Ready to locomote while in the high level? Go! . . . (An example detailing the method and sequence the teacher may use for directing the children to move through the various levels follows.)

Teacher: Medium level. (*The children go to the medium level in slow motion while they touch the surrounding space with their hands, arms, and/or elbows.*)

Teacher: High level and walk. (*The children slowly go to the high level where they begin to slowly walk and continue to touch their surrounding space.*)

Teacher: Low level. (*The children slowly go to low level where they continue to touch their surrounding space.*)

Teacher: High level and run. (*The children slowly go to the high level where they begin to run slowly or quickly, for a change of pace. They continue to touch the space.*)

Teacher: If we could take a moving picture of your body moving, you would see your body making many designs in space. If you keep your eyes on your own movement, you will be able to see some of the designs in space which you are creating. However, in order to see each other's designs in space let's take turns moving and watching. (*The teacher now divides the class in groups of eight children each. The eight children in each group share the spatial designs which they create while moving through levels, touching their surrounding space, and locomoting: in the meantime, the other groups in the class watch. Since it is the first time in the unit that the children are asked to present their movement experiences to the rest of the class, the teacher should take this opportunity to emphasize the fact that the children are sharing with the class some of the movements which they have discovered for themselves. The emphasis should be on sharing each other's experiences, and not on showing them off. The teacher may go on to point out the uniqueness of each child's design in space and positively reinforce the class members for their effort to be original in their movement.*)

Group Awareness:

(*Teacher assigns a space on the floor for each group of eight children.*)

Teacher: Take one step closer to the person next to you. You will now do the same creative movement through levels; however, you will now move together as a group. Let's go through the levels again with each of you being very aware of every person in your group, and especially of the one closest to you. Continue to be original in your movement, but move slowly as a group. Don't locomote when you are in the high level. Concentrate on your own movement, but also be aware of the movements of the other children around you. You will be able to see them out of the corners of your eyes. You will also be able to feel, sense, or be aware of them moving near you, even though no one will be touching each other. Move slowly! Be aware of each other! Move as a group, but also be aware of yourself moving within the group.

Begin. Do not locomote. (*The teacher calls out each level and each group of eight children move together. It is best to go from high to low and back to high again, thus leaving the highest level out.*)

Teacher: Very well done. I like the way each of you is relating not only to your own design in space, but also to the structure or shaping of the group design. Let's watch group one and two make their design in space. Let's watch carefully to see if each person within the group is aware not only of the total group, but each member within the group as well. (*Alternate groups.*)

Teacher: Stay in your groups and I'll pass out the ropes. Hold the rope with both hands. When I ask you to begin, pull again as hard as you can on the rope. As you pull, watch your own movement, but out of the corners of your eyes watch the movement of each child in your group. Be aware of each other while moving. Ready to pull, begin. Be aware of the tension in the muscles of your hands, arms, and your whole body. Also, be aware of the tension created by the whole group. Let's try it again. Watch your own movement, but feel the tension of the group. Think of yourself, not alone, but as a member of the group. Ready to pull, begin. (*The teacher asks the children to do the same as above without the rope. See lesson plan 2. The children are asked to hold the last movement and are then dismissed.*)

Review

Before beginning the fifth lesson, many teachers may see a need to review some, or all, of the previous material. Since most children enjoy playing games, the following material is presented in game form. Most of the games presented require a child to move alone in front of his peers, and this might cause embarassment if there is a misunderstanding of the exact procedure of the game. For this reason it is suggested that the game be explained precisely, demonstrated, then practiced a few times before actually being played.

Rhythm: Game 1.

The teacher claps or beats a series of beats of even duration, making sure the first beat of each series is accented. The first child who correctly guesses the number of beats in the series, gets one point. It is best, at first, for the teacher to keep the series in multiples of two. This is a good game for those who have had little or no training rhythmically.

Rhythm: Game 2.

Game 1 (above) may be varied as follows. Instead of the child answering vocally, he moves the answer. For instance, if the teacher beats eight beats, and the child moves eight times, with no accompaniment and in the same rhythm with which the series of beats were presented, he has made a successful answer in movement. The teacher may find that beating the first beat along with his first movement in a series, facilitates the child's answer.

Rhythm: Game 3.

This game may also be played with a combination of beats of different duration. For instance, the teacher may beat the following:

———   ———   ———————

The child may answer in any of the following ways. (The teacher should insist on rhythmical exactness.)

- He may say: short, short, long. See lesson plan 5.
- He may diagram the movement on the board. See lesson plan 6.
- He may answer by clapping.
- He may move to the pattern. See lesson plan 5.

Step Patterns: Game 1.

The children may form their own step patterns by selecting several of the locomotor forms and combining them in any pattern they wish. The children should be encouraged to keep the pattern simple, so they may easily execute it, and possibly teach it to the rest of the class. The following chart may help them in their selection. This game is best suited for children of the upper elementary and older ages, as some of the chance combinations which may arise are not rhythmically easy to execute.

The game begins by drawing the following chart on the blackboard, and selecting one child to begin the game.

The chart is used as follows:

1. To choose a step pattern, a child, with eyes either closed or open, puts his fingers on one square and draws a cross within that square. This square is the location where the step pattern is determined. A second child is then selected to figure out the step pattern and do it.

2. The second child determines the step pattern by reading the top horizontal list of locomotor forms first, and counting down the number of squares, which are indicated on the right, to the cross. This step pattern will thus begin with two hops. Next the vertical list of locomotor forms is read. Since the cross is located on the jump line, the second part of the step pattern will consist of jumps. To determine the number of jumps, count three spaces over, as indicated on the bottom of the chart, back to the cross. The step pattern, as determined in the previous chart will be two hops, and three jumps.

3. Since the game is concerned principally with the formation of a step pattern, the importance of the rhythmic pattern is minimized. For example, a child has made a successful answer when he has determined that the above step pattern consists of two hops and three jumps and can do it, no matter what rhythmic pattern he uses.
4. If the second child has made a correct response, he then becomes the one who chooses the next step pattern. If he does not make a

correct response, he forfeits his right to try again, and another child is selected to take his place.

Step Patterns: Game 2.

Each child composes a step pattern and writes it on a three by five card. For instance, the child may write three walks, and three jumps; or two hops, two jumps, and four leaps. It is best to limit the pattern to two or three locomotor forms. The teacher collects the cards and shuffles them. She may then use one of the two following procedures: (a) Each child in the class selects one card, finds a space to work in, figures out the step pattern, and does it. (b) One child selects a card, reads it to the class, and the class tries to do it. When one child feels he can successfully execute it, he runs to the teacher, or leader, and demonstrates it. The one who first successfully executes the step pattern is the next leader.

Step Pattern: Game 3.

The teacher makes a list of ten to fifteen step patterns, which she writes on the board. The class practices all of them to near perfection. Then, the teacher chooses one child to execute any one of the fifteen step patterns he wishes, while the rest of the class watches and guesses the identification of the step patterns. The child who is identifying the step pattern either points to it on the board, or he says it. As soon as one child guesses it, that child gets to choose and execute another step pattern in front of the class, and the guessing procedure begins all over again. This activity may be varied as follows: One child may clap the rhythmic pattern of one of the above fifteen step patterns, while the rest of the class guesses which pattern it is. As soon as another child is able to guess and execute that step pattern, he becomes the leader who claps another step pattern.

Step Pattern: Game 4.

The teacher tells a simple step pattern. The first child to execute it perfectly shows the rest of the class, and, if it is correct, he receives one point. A running score is kept, and the child with the most points over a certain period of time, wins the game. This game may continue throughout the semester, the children accumulating points all the while.

Levels and Locomotion: Game 1—Simon Says.

"Simon Says," works very well with the locomotor forms and the four levels, and is also an excellent review. As with all "Simon Says" games, the children only move when Simon commands them to move. If they move to any other command, they are eliminated from the game. The children should be spaced at least eight feet apart to encourage originality of thought. The game proceeds as follows:

Teacher: Simon says, go to the lowest level and locomote. Stop. (*The children do as commanded.*) Simon Says, go to the middle level and stay motionless, or freeze. (*The children do this.*) Simon Says, go to the highest level. (*The children do so.*) Simon Says, go to the high level and hop. (*The children do as commanded.*) Simon Says, stop. (*The children do as commanded.*) Go to the lowest level. (*Pause*) . . . If the children go to the lowest level now, they are eliminated from the game because the command did not include "Simon Says." The game then continues with the remaining children, and so on.

The "Simon Says" game can be simplified for younger children by limiting the command to only one aspect of movement such as, levels without locomotion. The game may also be used as a review of directional movement. For instance, Simon Says walk forward, run backwards, hop in your own circle, jump to the right, etc.

Levels and Locomotion: Game 2.

This simple game for early elementary school children involves the pitch of a musical tone, chords, or melody and movement. The teacher uses any musical instrument which produces a tone. The children are asked to move into the high, medium or low spatial levels depending on the pitch of the tone played on the musical instrument. For example, when a tone or a melody is played in the upper third area of the piano keyboard, the child moves in the high level. The children move in the middle spatial level when the middle area of the keyboard is played, and in the low level when the lower third of the keyboard is played. The game may be played with the whole class eliminating each child as he fails to respond correctly in movement to the tone's pitch. Points, or another form of reward may be given to the individual child for successfully responding.

Since pitch has not been referred to in the previous lessons, the children should be allowed time to become thoroughly familiar with it before playing the above game.

Space: Game 1: Statues.

Statues is a very old game, but it has long been and continues to be one of the best means of imbuing the child with an awareness of the contour of the physical body, and how it can occupy and produce a design in space.

There are three categories of players in this game. First, there are the statues who are the children in the class. Second, there is the sculptor, who is the teacher, or one or several children. Third, there is the buyer, another child, who selects his favorite statue.

The sculptor begins the game by swinging each child into a statue-like pose. The swing is done by having the sculptor grasp one or both hands of the child, then pivot around on the balls of the feet while holding him. When the sculptor feels that the movement has accelerated to an almost dangerous speed, he releases his hold, and the child is swung into space. In order to stop, the child simultaneously tenses all the muscles of his body and shapes himself into a pose. He remains motionless, like a statue. The kind of pose is somewhat determined by the kind of swing he gets from the sculptor, and how he stops his momentum. The sculptor does this with each child in the class until there is a room full of statues, all in different shapes and poses. The buyer, then comes along and selects the statue which pleases him most. The statue then becomes the buyer; the buyer becomes the sculptor; and the sculptor becomes a statue.

This game may be varied as follows: (1) The teacher is always the sculptor. This is a particularly good idea if the children are very young, or have behaviorial problems. However, because it takes quite a while to swing each child, the game played with only one sculptor works better when the class is small; (2) Before or while the children are swung, the buyer calls out the kind of pose he is most interested in buying as a statue. For instance, the buyer may announce that he is looking for the ugliest, most beautiful, tiniest, most unique, most grotesque, spookiest, or largest statue that he can find. If he indicates his preference before the sculptor swings the children, they will form their poses more carefully; with less abandon and freedom of movement than they would if the call were to come during the swinging. However, the game has advantages if played either way. One classification the buyer might be interested in selecting presents a very unique challenge to the children: the most alive-and-moving statue! The question each child must answer for himself is, how do I keep my body looking alive and moving while remaining motionless? The answer is discovered as he becomes kinesthetically aware of each part of his body, its relation to the space it occupies, and the tension involved in creating and maintaining the pose.

LESSON PLAN 5

The Lesson

Rhythmic Bodily Movement:

Teacher: (*Teacher plays the following rhythmic pattern at a peppy tempo on the drum.*)

4	1	②	3	④	1	2	3	4
	1	2	3	4	1	2	3	4

Teacher: Every time you hear a sound, move your head any way you wish. Move, move, move, move, move, move. (*She beats the above rhythmic pattern, and the children move to it.*) Every time you hear a sound move your shoulders. (*Beats the above rhythmic pattern, and the children move to it.*) Move your elbows in time to the drum beat. (*Continues with the rhythmic pattern, and the children move to it.*)

Teacher: Stand up. Take a step each time you hear a drum beat. Step in place. Do not locomote throughout the space in this room. Ready to step in time with the drum? Go! (*The teacher continues to softly play the previous rhythmic pattern on the drum while she gives further directions. She does not stop the drum beat at any time, endeavoring thereby to set up a rhythmic condition which is infectious, hopeful that the children will be almost mesmerized by the beating drum and its invitation to move to its rhythm.*)

Teacher: Continue to move your feet in time to the drum beat. (*Pause*) . . . Now, move your head in time to the drum beat. Continue to move your feet and your head. (*Pause*) . . . Now, add your arms. (*The teacher keeps the drum beat going, continuing to invite the children to add the movement of different bodily parts to the above rhythmic pattern. The children should be given ample time to experience the movement of each part of their body to the rhythmic pattern before another part is added.*)

Teacher: Now, add your hips. Now, move your whole body in rhythm to the drum beat. (Moving the entire body is the climax of this part of the lesson. The experience can be electrifying and hypnotic for the viewer as well as for the moving children, and is an excellent fast warm-up for the beginning of a lesson. To simplify the above procedure, beat a simpler rhythmic pattern and do all of the bodily movements while lying on the floor. The teacher stops beating the drum—the children stop moving!)

Teacher: Stretch all the way up as high as you can. Look and stretch in the space above you. Now, let your head hang low and relax. Let your knees go, and sit down and relax. Close your eyes and listen carefully to the rhythmic pattern we have just moved to. (*She plays the above rhythmic pattern again.*) Open your eyes. How many beats are there in this rhythmic pattern? That is, how many sounds do you hear in this rhythmic pattern?

Children: Six beats, or six sounds.

Teacher: Do all the beats sound the same?

Children: No.

Teacher: How do the beats differ from each other?

Children: Some beats are faster, while other beats are slower. (*Or, some beats are longer while others are shorter.*)

Teacher: Let's draw a slow or long beat with a long horizontal line. It will look like this on the blackboard.

_____

Let's draw a fast beat with a short horizontal line. It will look like this.

_____

Now, listen to the rhythmic pattern again. Can you tell me where the long beats occur and where the short beats occur?

Children: The first two beats are long. The last four beats are short. (*The teacher calls on one child to draw the long and short beats on the blackboard. She then calls on another child to label each beat long or short.*)

    long   **long**   **s h o r t s**

_____   _____   ____ ____ ____ ____

Teacher: We can now say this rhythmic pattern as follows: long, long, short, short, short, short. Say the rhythmic pattern as I point to it. (*Pause*) . . . Clap the rhythmic pattern, and at the same time, say the rhythmic pattern in longs and shorts. (*Pause*) . . . Touch the space around you with your hands. At the same time say the rhythmic pattern in longs and shorts. Ready to touch the space around you? Are you looking at your hands? Begin. (*Pause*) . . .

Teacher: The more you learn about rhythm, and the more you practice it, the more aware of it you become. For instance, you may begin to discover rhythm in many different things. Can you think of something else that you have seen or heard that has a rhythmic pattern?

Children: We are aware of the rhythmic patterns of things like bird calls, rain dripping, a faucet dripping, repetitive designs in fabric and architecture, and other things. (*The teacher waits for the children to suggest the rhythm inherent in words, poems, and songs, and makes some suggestions.*)

Rhythmic Analysis of a Name:

Teacher: Billy, how do you say my name?

Billy: Mrs. Winters.

Teacher: Can you say each part, or each syllable, of my name?

Billy: Miss-es Win-ters.

Teacher: Very good, Billy. Nancy, can you say my name, so we can hear each syllable? (*Encourage the clear enunciation of each syllable.*)

Nancy: Miss-es Win-ters.

Teacher: Very good, Nancy. Repeat it many times. (*While Nancy repeats it, the teacher softly beats her name's rhythmic pattern on the drum. She then signals the rest of the class to clap the rhythmic pattern, as Nancy repeats the name over and over again.*)

Teacher: Each name, in fact, each word, when said, has its own rhythmic pattern. Most words and names have more than one rhythmic pattern, depending on how you say the name or how you use the word in a sentence. Let's say and clap my name the way Nancy said it, and see if we can discover where the long and short beats are in the rhythmic pattern of my name. (*Pause*) . . . Who has discovered what part of my name has the longest beat?

Children: The syllable, 'ters,' has the longest beat.

Teacher: Let's draw a long beat on the board and write, 'ters,' over that beat.

ters
_____

Are all of the other beats of the rhythmic pattern of my name shorter?

Children: Yes.

Teacher: Let's draw all the short beats on the blackboard. How many short beats should I draw for Mrs.?

Children: Two beats.

Miss -es
—   —

Teacher: How many short beats should I draw for the first part of my name, Win.

Children: One short beat.

Win
—

Teacher: (*The teacher will then have drawn the rhythmic pattern for her name on the blackboard.*)

Miss-es	Win	ters
— —	—	————
2 1 + ah		2
————		————
1		2

Teacher: Let's check and see if we have drawn the right rhythmic pattern for my name. We can check it by saying my name over and over again and looking at the long and short beats. (*The teacher and children repeat the name many times until they get such a strong rhythmic feeling for it that they will not forget it easily.*)

Teacher: Remember when I said previously that names, as well as other words, may have several different rhythmic patterns depending on how you accent each syllable, and how you use the name or words in a sentence? Here's another rhythmic pattern for my name. (*The teacher writes the rhythmic pattern for her name on the blackboard:*)

	Miss-	es	Win-	ters	
	—	—	—	—	
4	1	2	3	4	
	—	—	—	—	
	1	2	3	4	

Let's all say my name to this new rhythmic pattern. (*She points to the new rhythmic pattern for her name which she has written on the blackboard.*) Let's all clap and say this second rhythmic pattern for my name again. Good for you. (*This way the children are given ample opportunity to get a feeling for the new rhythmic pattern.*)

Teacher: How many syllables do we now find in this new rhythmic pattern of my name?

Children: Four syllables.

Teacher: How many syllables did we hear in my name when Nancy said it earlier in the lesson?

Children: Four syllables.

Teacher: Very good. The number of syllables do not change in a word or name. However, what may change, depending on its use?

Children: The rhythmic pattern.

Teacher: Now let's put both rhythmic patterns for my name together. Let's clap and say each rhythmic pattern four times. Ready, begin. (*She points to the rhythmic patterns which have been written on the blackboard as the children say and clap them.*)

2 Miss - es Win   ters

   — — —   ———   — — —   ———

   ————   ————   ————   ————

     1   2 | 1   2

Miss - es Win   ters

   — — —   ———   — — —   ———

   ————   ————   ————   ————

     1   2 | 1   2

Miss   es   Win   ters

4 ——   ——   ——   —— | ——   ——   ——   —— |

    1   2   3   4   1   2   3   4

Teacher: Very well done. Let's say these same rhythmic patterns again, but instead of clapping let's touch the space surrounding us. Ready, watch your hands, begin. (*Pause*) ...

Feeling and Movement:

Teacher: Can you see the tremendous difference in the two rhythmic patterns of my name? (*Points to the two rhythmic patterns, above, on the board.*) This time, touch the surrounding space again, in rhythm, to both patterns. However, do not say my name. Concentrate on, or think about the rhythmic movement you are doing, and how you feel about the movement when you do it. Let your feeling about the movement, and its rhythm, be revealed in your movement. Ready to move? Ready to show me your feelings through movement? (*Pause*) . . .

Teacher: How does each rhythmic pattern make you feel when you move? Are the movements different for each pattern? Which rhythmic pattern makes you move more vigorously or with greater strength? Which rhythmic pattern has more of a swing to it? Let's try moving to both rhythmic patterns of my name again just the same way we did before. See if you can discover, through movement, the answers to these questions. How do you feel when you move to each rhythmic pattern? Which movements are stronger; using more tension? Which movements have a swing to them? Ready, begin. (*Pause*) . . . Did you discover, through movement, the difference in feeling between the first and the second rhythmic pattern of my name?

(*The teacher and children discuss the movements and feelings evoked from the two previous rhythmic patterns. The teacher waits for, or encourages, the following observations to be vocalized.*) The first rhythmic pattern:

- Has more of a swing.
- Is less tense and requires less effort to do.
- The movement can be described by using any of the following words: Swingy, smooth, interesting, soft, flowing, moving.
- When we say your name and move to the first pattern, you seem to be a kind, friendly person.

The second rhythmic pattern:

- Is more measured and vigorous, like a soldier marching.
- Is more tense, but not real tense. Has strong percussive movements.
- The movement can be described by using the following words: Percussive, hitting, smacking, whacking, spanking, punching, and stiff.
- When we say Mrs. Winters and move to the second rhythmic pattern, you seem to be a mean and strict teacher. (*The teacher should encourage and emphasize the use of the word* percussive *and its synonyms, as the following part of the lesson relates to percussive movement.*)

Percussive Movement:

Teacher: We can readily see that movement and feelings go together. When we move, we get a feeling about what we are doing. Movement can be described by using words such as swingy, soft, percussive, hitting, punching, and many more. Can you think of any more words to describe how one moves? (*Pause*) . . . How about a lazy movement? Show me how you can lazily move to a spot on the floor, far enough from the person next to you so that you cannot touch that person. (*Pause*) . . . Look at any part of the space surrounding you that you wish. Can you punch a hole right through the empty space around you? Ready to give that space one good percussive punch? Look at it, ready, and punch! (*The teacher hits the drum or any other percussive instrument when she says punch.*)

Teacher: Use your other hand. Look at another piece of space surrounding you. Ready to punch it? Punch! Now, punch three different areas of space surrounding you. Be sure you look at the space at which you're punching. Ready to punch three times, begin. Punch-punch-punch. (*Do to a short, short, long rhythmic pattern.*) Stay there. Freeze! (*Pause*) . . . Let's try three punches again. Ready, begin. Punch-punch-punch. Freeze! (*Pause*) . . . Very well done. Can you punch the surrounding space with one knee? Ready. Look at it. Punch! Try punching with your elbow. Ready, look, punch! Make sure you're not just touching the space around you. Make sure that you are doing a percussive movement. A percussive movement is quite different from a touching movement. A percussive movement is quite different from a swinging movement. Show me where your hips are by putting your hands on them. Ready to punch the space around you with your hips? Ready, punch! (*Pause*) . . .

Teacher: Now compose a movement pattern with three different punches. You might want to use three different parts of your body. For instance, you might want to use your head for one punch, your elbow for another and your foot for still another. Or, you might want to use three different levels for your percussive punches. Perhaps you will want to punch high for the first punch, low for the second punch, and high again for the third punch. Compose a movement pattern now of three percussive punches. Use the same rhythmic pattern as above. That is, two shorts and one long. Try it. Try one punch, then add two, and then add three. Remember each punch before adding another. Remember, show your feelings about your movement. Ready to practice it? Go. (*Pause*) . . .

Teacher: I like the way each one of you is concentrating on his own movement. This is your own movement pattern. You will each have three percussive punches in your pattern. However, you decide what space you want to use, and you decide on what part of your body you want to punch with. Ready to practice again—go! (*She allows the children to practice their percussive movement pattern several times, most of the time she remains silent; now and then, however, she may encourage the children's efforts.*) Some of you are concentrating because you are watching your own movement. I like the way some of you are using all of the space surrounding you. Some of you have chosen three distinctly different pieces of space. I can see how you feel about what you are doing. You are letting your feelings show! It's quite obvious that some of you are really enjoying your movement. I like the way many of you are freezing on the last movement. This gives your movement pattern a nice ending. (*The teacher now encourages the children to try to finish composing their movement pattern within a specified time.*)

Teacher: You have discovered such excellent movement patterns that I'd like you to share them with each other. Let's divide the class in half right here. (*The teacher points to the middle of the room and indicates which half of the group will move first.*) This half of the room will show their movement pattern first. The rest of you will sit down right where you are and watch. First group—repeat your movement pattern three times so that we can get well acquainted with it. Ready, begin. (*Each group of children does its movement pattern three times.* The teacher may accompany these percussive movement patterns by using three different percussive instruments. The rhythmic pattern will be as follows:)

_____   _____   _____

____ ____   ____ ____   ____ ____   ____ ____

Teacher: Do you think that some children move more percussively than other children? Why were some children more successful in their percussive movement than others? What did they do with their body to make a percussive movement? Let's all get up again and try your very own movement pattern again. This time, let your feelings show even more than before. Show me your feeling through bodily movement. Ready, begin. (*Pause*) . . . Excellent, class. I can see that your percussive movement pattern becomes even more percussive when you allowed your feelings and movements to work together. Put a run in front of your movement pattern. We now have a movement composition which will look like this (*points to the following on the blackboard*) and will sound like this (*beats it on the drum*).

R u n ~~~~~~

4 ══ ══ ══ ══ │ ══ ══ ══ ══ │
    1   **2**   **3**   **4**   **1**   **2**   **3**   **4**

Punch   **Punch**   │   **P u n c h**

4 ── ── ── ── │ ── ── ── ── │
    1   **2**   **3**   **4**   **1**   **2**   **3**   **4**

Teacher: Say the movement pattern with me as I beat it on the drum. (*The teacher and children say the following many times in order to get the feeling rhythmically before locomoting.*) . . . Run, run, run, run, run, run, run, run, punch, punch, punch.

Teacher: Ready to move, begin. (*The children move to the above pattern for the enjoyment of it and not for exactness of execution, as it will be reviewed in subsequent lessons.*)

LESSON PLAN 6

The Lesson
Locomotor Review:

Teacher: Listen and locomote as the drum beats tell you to do. (*The teacher beats the rhythmic pattern for each of the even elementary forms of locomotion. At this time, the teacher may also review some, or all, of the rhythmic patterns which have previously been presented to the students. After the students have reviewed locomotor forms and step patterns, they are asked to stretch, relax, and sit down.*)

Rhythmic Analysis:

If you were to represent a walk by a short or long horizontal line, what kind of line would you draw on the blackboard? One child draws a horizontal line _____ to represent a walk. (Although the length of the line is relative and not too important at this point, the ensuing lesson will flow easier if the teacher encourages the child to draw a horizontal line which is somewhere between two and five inches long. Most children will do this naturally.)

Teacher: Let's draw four walks on the blackboard. (*draw*) __ __ __ __ (*Pause*) . . . Let's clap four walks. Ready, begin. (*Pause*) . . . Let's put a vertical line after the four horizontal lines and write a w above each line.

w	w	w	w
—	—	—	—
1	2	3	4

We will now draw four more horizontal lines which represent four more walks. Again, we will put a vertical line. We now have two measures, each containing four walks. Because there are four walks or four beats in each measure, I will write a number four at the beginning of the two measures. Now I don't have to count the number of beats in each measure. I'll simply look at this number, and it will immediately tell me that, in this case, there are four beats to each measure. (*Teacher points to the blackboard.*)

Teacher: Let's clap these two measures of walking beats. Ready, begin.

4 walk	w	w	w		w	w	w	w	
—	—	—	—		—	—	—	—	
1	2	3	4		1	2	3	4	

Is there a pause, or a wait in between each measure?

Children: No.

Teacher: If you heard someone clapping these two measures, without seeing them written on the blackboard, how would you know how many walks, or beats, there are in each measure? Before you answer this question, let me clap several measures with four beats, or walks, in each measure. (*She claps the above making sure to accent the first beat of each measure.*) Could you tell, by my clapping, how many beats or walks there are in each measure?

Children: There are four.

Teacher: How do you know?

Children: We can hear you clap the first beat of each measure louder than the rest of the beats in the measure.

Teacher: Good listening. We call this loud first beat, the accent—or the major accent. Let's all clap together. We will clap eight measures with four beats in each. Don't forget to accent the first beat in each measure. Ready, begin. (*Pause*) . . . Let's have each person in this class make a percussive movement with their arms every time they hear the major accent. I'll play the drum. (*The teacher plays eight measures of 4/4 time being sure to strongly accent the first beat of each measure. The children move their arms percussively on the accented beat.*)

Teacher: Good for you, class. I saw some very good individual percussive movements that were right on the major accented beat. Let's see if you can hear the major accent when I play the piano. Clap on the accented beat. (*She plays eight measures of 4/4 time on the piano, or any other musical instrument, making sure to strongly accent the first beat of each measure.*)

Teacher: Can you step hard and strong every time you hear me play the major accent? Try it. (*Pause*) . . . Alternate feet. Stamp on one foot for one accent, and stamp on your other foot for the next accent. Let's call this accented step or walk, a stamp step. Now, if you do a stamp step on the accented first beat of each measure, how many regular walks will you do to complete the measure?

Children: Three regular walks.

Teacher: Who can write this rhythmic and step pattern on the board? (*Select a child to write.*)

	stamp			
4	**step**	**walk**	**w**	**w**
	1	2	3	4

Let's do eight measures of stamp, walk, walk, walk anywhere in the space in this room. Be sure to accent the first beat in each measure by making a strong stamp. You will be stamping on the same foot all the time. (*Pause*)...

Teacher: You have just done a phrase of eight measures each containing four walking beats. Let's look at the eight-measure phrase on the board.

4	**stamp**	**walk**	**w**	**w**	**s**	**w**	**w**	**w**
	1	2	3	4	1	2	3	4
	s	**w**	**w**	**w**	**s**	**w**	**w**	**w**
	1	2	3	4	1	2	3	4
	s	**w**	**w**	**w**	**s**	**w**	**w**	**w**
	1	2	3	4	1	2	3	4
	s	**w**	**w**	**w**	**s**	**w**	**w**	**w**
	1	2	3	4	1	2	3	4

We call these eight measures a phrase of movement because they go well together. They are all alike and belong together. We are now ready to start another phrase of eight measures. However, this time let's have each measure contain running beats. I wonder how fast the running beats are in comparison to the walking beats? We know that the running beats are faster than the walking beats. But how much faster? Let's experiment with movement and sound and see if we can discover the answers to these questions. Let's have this half of the class clap the walking beats. Let's have the other half of the class clap the running beats. Before we begin, let's have the children clapping the walking beats, clap a two measure introduction. This way, we can hear and get the feeling of the tempo of these walking beats. Are you ready, walking beats? Begin.

Children: (Half of the class claps the following:)

4 ⎯⎯⎯ ⎯⎯⎯ ⎯⎯⎯ ⎯⎯⎯ | ⎯⎯⎯ ⎯⎯⎯ ⎯⎯⎯ ⎯⎯⎯ |

(After the above two introductory measures, and without hesitation, the other half of the class claps faster running beats. The children attempt to fit the faster running beats into the slower walking beats. If the children are fairly rhythmic-wise, the teacher simply waits until the running half of the class claps twice as fast as the walking half. However, she may have to help them by strongly clapping the two to one ratio until all the children get the feeling of it.)

Teacher: Take a good look at the horizontal line which represents the walk. What kind of line would you draw to represent the run?

Children: A short line like this —.

Teacher: How many short running lines would there be to every long walking line?

Children: Two.

Teacher: Suppose we call the walking beat, the underlying beat. The underlying beat is a steady, measured, walking beat of about marching tempo. How much faster is the running beat? Can you draw the running beat above the walking beat and show me by the length of the line how many running beats there are to each walking beat?

⎯⎯ ⎯⎯ ←⎯ **running beats**

⎯⎯⎯⎯⎯ ←⎯ **underlying—or walking beat**

Stand up and walk or run in place to these same beats. This half of the class will walk, in place, to the rhythm of the underlying beat. (*The teacher points to the underlying beats on the blackboard.*) Remember, let's give these beats two measures to get started so we can get the feeling of the tempo. The other half of the class will run, in place, to the rhythm of the running beat. You will move twice as fast as the underlying beat. Ready to walk in place, underlying beats? Begin.

	walk	**w**	**w**	**w**	**w**	**w**	**Ready**	**Run**
4	1	2	3	4	1	2	3	4

run								
walk	**w**	**w**	**w**	**walk**	**w**	**w**	**w**
1	2	3	4	1	2	3	4

(*Repeat as often as you feel it necessary.*)

Teacher: Very well done. You could hear, and feel the faster run fitting right in time with the slower walking beat. Let's change groups and have the walking group become the running group, and the running group become the walking group. Ready to move, after two introductory walking measures, begin. (*The teacher may want to repeat the walking and running beats, through movement, by utilizing one or both of the ideas that follow.*)

• Form partners. One child walks and the other runs alongside.
• Have the children move various bodily parts to the underlying beat and/or the running beat either in partner formation or with the class divided in half.

Teacher: Before going on to do some other movements, let's review some of the words that we have learned today. Who can point to a beat? Who can point to a measure? Who can point to a phrase? Who can point to an underlying beat? Who can point to the number which informs us about how many beats there are in each measure? Who can point to a running beat? Who can point to four walking beats? Who can point to an accented beat?

Progressive Relaxation and Body Awareness:

Teacher: Find a space on the floor and lie down. Be sure you are far enough from everyone else so that you cannot touch them if you stretch out any part of your body. Close your eyes and rest. (*Pause*) . . . Think of all the parts of your body. Think of your head. Do not move your head. Only think about where your head is in space, and where, and how, it is resting on the floor. (*Pause five seconds.*) . . . Think of your legs. Are they crossed? What part of your legs are resting on the floor? (*Pause five seconds.*) . . . Think of your toes. (*Pause five seconds.* . . . the teacher takes her time directing the children to be aware of each part of their body. She waits about five slow counts in between each bodily part, to allow the child to think, and think again, about his body.)

Space:

Teacher: Think of the many parts of your body working together to move your whole body. Keep your eyes closed. Slowly move your whole body now so it takes the shape of the letter O. Make a nice round O with the whole of your body. Very well done. Keep your eyes closed. Now, put your body in the shape of the letter P. (*Pause*) . . . Can you put your body in the shape of either your first initial or your last initial? (*Pause*)

Teacher: Good! I can see that Todd's body has formed the shape of the letter T. Cheryl's body is in the shape of the letter C, and I can see many other shapes on the floor in this room. Without thinking too much about it, let's quickly make three different shapes with our bodies; just any shape. Ready for number one, then two, and three. Begin. (*Teacher calls out the shape number one, two, and three.*) Now open your eyes and stand up. This time, instead of forming the shape of your body on the floor, you will form the shape in the space around you. Ready to do three shapes? Any three shapes will do. Begin. (*Teacher calls out shape one, shape two, and shape three. She waits about four counts between each shape.*)

Teacher: This time, when you do your three shapes, do them percussively. (*She again calls out shape one, shape two, and shape three.*) I can see by watching your movements, that many of you have remembered the meaning of percussive. Who can describe in words the meaning of a percussive movement?

Children: A percussive movement is a hitting or striking movement. It is done quickly and decisively.

Teacher: The drum is called a percussive instrument because in order to make a sound one must strike it. So it is with a percussive movement. Let's strike three percussive shapes in the space around us again. Ready,

begin. (She hits the drum three times for accompaniment.) Very good.
I see the whole class striking three percussive body shapes. Let's put
a run and stop before the three percussive shapes. It will sound like
this: (*Teacher speaks and beats the following rhythmic patterns.*)

4	r r	r r	r r	r r	r r	r r	r r	stop
	1 +	2 +	3 +	4 +	1 +	2 +	3 +	4
	1	2	3	4	1	2	3	4

	s h a p e	s h a p e		s h a p e	
1	②	3	④	1	②	③	④
1	2	3	4	1	2	3	4

(*The teacher may now introduce several percussive instruments, using
one for each percussive movement. Or she may use the piano as a percussive instrument. [Refer to the section on accompaniment, chap. 2,
pp. 78–84.] Or, better yet, this may be an excellent time to allow the
children to experiment with a percussion instrument. They may then
practice playing the above rhythmic pattern. Half of the class can
provide the accompaniment, while the other half moves.*)

Floor Pattern:

Teacher: Very often movements are done in a particular direction:
Sometimes forward, sometimes backwards. And, sometimes they are
done sideways and diagonally. If you put chalk on the bottom of your
feet and locomoted throughout the space in this room, you would
create a design or pattern on the floor. This is called a floor pattern.
Whenever you locomote, you create a floor pattern. Can you imagine
the fantastic floor pattern created during a basketball game? Square
dancers make a floor pattern which looks like a square. The most
simple floor pattern is a straight line. Can you see some straight-line
floor patterns already painted on the floor in this room? (*Pause*) . . . Let
us locomote on this red line which starts here and goes straight across
the floor and ends down here. (*Teacher walks on the red line to show
them the start of it, the complete floor pattern, and the end of the red*

line.) Todd, you will be the leader. Everyone else will line up behind Todd in this space right here. Todd is going to walk on the straight-line floor pattern. When he gets to the middle, Nancy will begin to walk on the red straight-line floor pattern. When Nancy gets to the middle of the red line, David will begin his straight-line floor pattern. When you get to the end of the straight-line floor pattern, you will sit down in a line, in this space, all behind the leader, Todd. (*It is important for the teacher to make her directions very clear when first presenting floor patterns, as the floor patterns get very complicated later on.*)

Teacher: Let's have Todd, Nancy, and David demonstrate a run on the red straight-line floor pattern. Ready to begin, Todd? Nancy, are you ready to begin when Todd is half-way finished with his floor pattern? Ready Todd, begin. (*Pause*) . . . Very well done, Todd, Nancy, and David—now please go directly back where you came from and we'll start the whole class running in a straight-line floor pattern. (*The teacher may now take as much time as she pleases to reinforce the concept of moving on a straight line and creating a straight-line floor pattern. The children will enjoy doing any, or all, of the locomotor forms and step patterns while creating a straight-line floor pattern. They will also enjoy moving backwards and sideways on this straight-line floor pattern. After they become well acquainted with one straight line, another one in another direction may be introduced, or the children may create their own. Also, several children may move at once in many directions, each creating their own straight-line floor pattern. Here, now, is an exciting and interesting climatic ending to this lesson which can be performed on the straight-line floor pattern.*)

Teacher: Run to the drum beat on the straight-line floor pattern. When the drum beats a loud percussive sound make a percussive shape with your whole body in the near-space surrounding you. The percussive shape may also be made in the space above you. (*If the children follow the above directions, they will be doing a run, a jump, and while their body is suspended in space, a shape.*)

LESSON PLAN 7

The Lesson

Rhythmic Names:

The teacher points to this rhythmic pattern, written on the blackboard.)

Miss- es Win-	ters	is the teach-	er
— — — _____	_____	— — — _____	_____
2 _____	_____	_____	_____
1	2	1	2

This pattern is presented for review, together with the suggested procedure that follows. Since it is a review, a lead-in to the main part of the
lesson plan, not too much time should be spent on it.

- The teacher says the above rhythmic pattern three or four times,
  and then signals the class to join her in saying it. Then, teacher and
  children together clap and say the pattern.
- While the teacher says the rhythmic pattern again, the students touch
  the surrounding space with their hands in rhythm to it.
- The teacher repeats the pattern, while each child touches the surrounding space with that particular part of his body which he or
  the teacher chooses.
- The teacher says the pattern again while the students step to each
  beat, and then while they walk (locomote or, go somewhere) on each
  beat.
- Finally, the teacher says the above rhythmic pattern while the children locomote on each beat *and* touch the space surrounding them.
  The children freeze on the last movement.

Teacher: All names have a rhythmic pattern. Let's see if we can discover the rhythmic pattern of some of the names of the children in this
class. (*She chooses the first and last name of one child in the class.*
[By this time, the teacher should know the children well enough so
that she can select a child who needs to be positively reinforced by
being chosen, but will not be embarrassed.] Here, then, is an example
of one method for discovering the rhythmic pattern of a child's name,
and moving to that rhythmic pattern.)

Teacher: Let's discover the rhythmic pattern of the name Johnny
Brown. Johnny, how do you say your name? (*Pause*) . . . Johnny, if you
say your name five or six times, maybe we can all hear and feel its
rhythmic pattern. (*Pause . . . Teacher and children say the name with*
Johnny Brown. Make sure that the others in the class do not impose
another rhythmic pattern for the name of Johnny Brown. Since the
name Johnny Brown can be said several different ways, allow Johnny
Brown himself to choose his own rhythmic pattern of his name.)

Teacher: Let's figure out the rhythmic pattern of Johnny Brown in long and short beats. As we clap and say Johnny Brown three or four times, let's think of which part of the name will have the longest beat. (*Pause*) . . . Who can tell us which part of the name will have the longest beat?

Children: Brown.

Teacher: Johnny, come up here and draw a long beat with the name Brown above it on the blackboard.

(*Johnny writes*)

Brown
———

Teacher: Who can draw the rhythm for the name Johnny?

(*Volunteer writes*)

John - ny
——— ———

Teacher: That's right. Johnny has two beats to his first name and they are faster than the one beat of his last name. Who can write the whole rhythmic pattern, writing in the number of beats to each measure, the underlying beats, and the rhythmic pattern of the name Johnny Brown? (*The following rhythmic pattern should be written on the blackboard:*)

	John - ny		**Brown**	
	——— ———		———	
2	1	+	2	
	———————		———	
	1		2	

(*The remainder of the procedure for exploring movement to the rhythmic pattern of Johnny Brown, is the same as followed for the name Mrs. Winters, as presented in the preceding lesson, p. 181. If time allows, the teacher may encourage the name Johnny Brown to be followed by a descriptive phrase which has the same or similar rhythmic pattern. Such as, Johnny Brown—lives in town.*)

John - ny	Brown	Lives In	Town
2 1 +	2	1 +	2
1	2	1	2

If the children are sharp rhythmically, the teacher may encourage them to compose other phrases after the name Johnny Brown which are a little more complicated rhythmically, such as: Johnny Brown— what a fine rhythmic sound. Or, Johnny Brown found a great big hound.)

Teacher: Maria, how do you say your first name? Repeat it over and over again. (*The teacher signals the class to join Maria. Since the rhythmic pattern of Maria begins on the up beat, and the children have not*

Ma	ree a Ma	
2 and	1 + ② +	
	1	2

yet been introduced to this type of rhythmic pattern, the teacher may skip the rhythmic analysis and go on, moving directly to the name, Maria. Or, she may find another child in the class whose name follows Maria's ear'ly, and makes the combination rhythmically interesting. Or perhaps the teacher may know of two friends in the class whose names sound interesting together. For instance: Maria and Adria are good friends, and have rhythmic patterns which follow one another easily.

ree - a and A – dree	– a Ma	ree – a and A –
2 1 + 2 +	1 + ② +	1 + 2 +
1 2	1 2	1 2

Since the above rhythmic pattern is quite complicated, the children may simply enjoy saying and moving to them rhythmically. However, the teacher should alternate the complicated rhythmic patterns with some easily analyzed patterns. She should look for several children whose names have simple rhythmic patterns, and can be readily analyzed and written on the blackboard, and capitalize on these names to demonstrate the analysis of a rhythmic pattern. For example; an interesting rhythmic combination, but difficult to write rhythmically is Juan García and Larry O'Toole. A combination easily analyzed rhythmically; Tom Hance and Gary O'Neill. If the teacher has had but a minimum of experience rhythmically, she should prepare herself for the name she will choose in class and practice it to perfection. She should start with the names which are easiest to say, move to, and analyze rhythmically. However, during the unit each child's name should be rhythmically uttered and moved to at least once. No one should be excluded because of a difficult rhythmic name.)

Patterns of Rhythm and Movement:

(The teacher has written the following on the board: step pattern, floor pattern, rhythmic pattern, and movement pattern. She then writes: run, jump, punch, punch, punch.)

Teacher: Do you remember what a floor pattern is?

Children: A floor pattern is an imaginary design which is made on the floor every time we locomote.

Teacher: Do you remember what a step pattern is?

Children: It is a combination of locomotor forms. *(The children have not as yet been introduced to nonlocomotion.)*

Teacher: Can you point to a step pattern which has been written on the board?

Children: Run, jump.

Teacher: Can you do a step pattern and make a floor pattern at the same time?

Children: Yes, we can.

Teacher: Can you point to a floor pattern which has been written on the board?

Children: No, we can't.

Teacher: Can you do a step pattern to a rhythmic pattern?

Children: Yes.

Teacher: Point to a rhythmic pattern which has been written on the board. *(The children point to the many rhythmic patterns which had been written on the board when they were saying names.)*

Teacher: Point to a movement pattern. *(Children point to punch, punch, punch.)*

Teacher: Can you do a step pattern, a movement pattern, and make a floor pattern, all at the same time?

Children: Yes, we can.

Teacher: Show me. Let's use the straight-line floor pattern. Susan will be the leader today. Let's do the run, jump, punch, punch, punch on a straight-line floor pattern. (*Pause*) . . . Everyone is lined up behind Susan, ready to go. Good. Begin. (*Teacher beats the following on the drum while the children do it on a straight-line floor pattern.*)

	r u n ∿∿∿∿∿∿∿∿∿∿ j u m p	punch	punch		punch	
4	1 + 2 + 3 + 4	1	2		3 ④	
	1 2 3 4	1	2		3 4	

Teacher: Very good, class. I see some very good percussive punches into which you have put a lot of feeling. Let's try another floor pattern. We will call this floor pattern the short diagonal. There is also a long diagonal which we will do later. Diagonal floor patterns move from corner to corner. The short diagonal floor pattern moves from this corner to here. (*She now walks diagonally from one corner of the room to a point located in the middle of the room, then continues diagonally to another corner at the far end of the room.*)

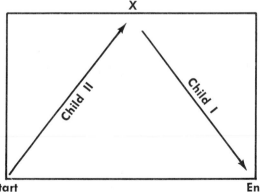

(*As she walks on the short diagonal, she verbally informs the children where they are to run, and where they are to do their three punches. The teacher will find that the children can understand the concept of moving on the diagonal floor pattern much more easily if she presents*

Free! Flying! Exciting! Different! Happy!

the short diagonal pattern before presenting the long diagonal pattern. After the children have done the movement composition on the short diagonal, as above, they may then try other locomotor forms, step patterns or other various combinations on this same floor pattern. Also, the teacher may augment this pattern by using four diagonal shapes instead of two. This allows four children to move at the same time and affords a challenging climax to this lesson for those children who are ready for it. See the following diagram.)

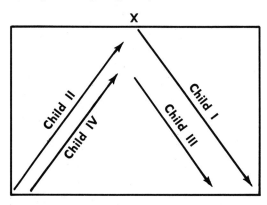

LESSON PLAN 8

The Lesson

Locomotion:

Teacher: Listen to the rhythmic pattern of a skip. (*Skips*) . . . Can you skip in time to the drum beat? Try it! (*Teacher beats a skipping beat, of medium tempo, while the children skip freely around the room.*)

Teacher: It looks to me like all of you know how to skip very well. Where did you learn to skip? (*Children may offer many answers to the above question. However, the teacher looks for the answer which explains that the child has known how to skip for a long time, and often does not remember where or when he started to skip.*)

Teacher: Because you have known how to skip for many years, and because it seems to be a natural thing to do, the skip is also called an elementary form of locomotion. Listen to the rhythmic pattern on the drum again. (*Pause*) . . . How many beats are there for one skip?

Children: Two beats for each skip.

Teacher: How many beats are there for one walk?

Children: One beat for each walk.

Teacher: How many beats are there for one jump, one hop, one leap, and one run?

Children: One beat for each.

Teacher: Right. The skip is the first locomotor form that you have done in this class which has two beats. Listen to the beats of the skip again. What would you draw for the skip—two long lines, two short lines, or a short and a long line?

Children: A short and a long line would be best for the rhythmic pattern of a skip.

Teacher: Do you mean to say that the skip consists of one short and one long beat?

Children: Yes, it does.

Teacher: Who can draw the rhythmic pattern of one skip on the board, with the words long and short above the appropriate lines? (*Pause*) . . .

long   **short**
_____   ____

Let's say the rhythmic pattern of the skip in longs and shorts as I beat the pattern on the drum. (*Pause*) . . .

Teacher: Now, let's see how well you remember the short diagonal floor pattern. Gary, you will lead the class in doing a skip on the short diagonal floor pattern, and Bobby, you will follow Gary, when he reaches the first corner of the short diagonal. (*See p. 185 for diagram*) Ready Gary, ready Bobby, ready class, begin. . . . Very well done, class. . . . Some of you have a skip that swings along easily. Pamela, will you show us your skip on the short diagonal? Katherine, will you show us your skip on the short diagonal also? Class, watch Pamela and Katherine. Can you discover how each one moves her body in order to make a smooth, swinging skip?

Children: We know what they did. Pamela and Katherine swung their arms to make their skip look more swingy. They also moved higher off the floor.

Teacher: Do you think that swinging their arms helped them to get higher off the floor?

Children: Yes, it must have.

Teacher: This time when we skip on the short diagonal, let's all try to swing our arms as easily and as high as we can. Let's see how high we can get our bodies off the floor while skipping. (*Pause*) . . . Now you are using your whole body to skip. Your skips look just great. Can you discover where in space you stop the swing of your arms on the way going up? Does stopping the swing at a certain place help you to go even higher? Try it. (*Children all skip around the room at the same time in one direction exploring the bodily movement of the skip in order to discover the above answers.*)

Long Diagonal Floor Pattern:

Teacher: I told you once before that one of the diagonal floor patterns we would move on is called the long diagonal. Who can find a long diagonal floor pattern in this room? Can you show it to us by walking on that long diagonal floor pattern? (*She calls on one or more children to walk on the imaginary long diagonal floor pattern, in order to develop for the class the concept of feeling, seeing, and moving diagonally in the room space. She insists on the exactness of each child's movement on the long diagonal.*)

Teacher: The long diagonal floor pattern starts here at one corner of the room and goes all the way across the floor to the directly opposite corner. (*She walks on the long diagonal floor pattern, which is an imaginary line created by locomoting from one corner of the room to the diagonally opposite corner.*)

Teacher: We are going to skip on this long diagonal floor pattern. David will lead. When David gets to the middle of the long diagonal, the next person will begin. When David gets to the end of the diagonal floor pattern, he will stop skipping. He will then walk to the other corner of the room which he has not used as yet. (*She walks this whole floor pattern out.*) David will sit down at this new corner of the room and everyone else will sit down behind him and wait.

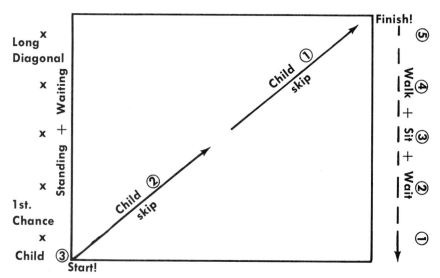

Let's have the first three children try skipping on the long diagonal. If everyone watches them carefully, you will be able to see the long diagonal floor pattern each child creates. Ready to skip, David? Begin.

Teacher: Very well done, David, Nancy, and Bobby. Let's have the next three children try skipping on the long diagonal floor pattern. (*Pause . . . teacher then continues, calling three children each time. As when presenting floor patterns in previous lessons, the teacher utilizes considerable time and patience in presenting this concept of moving throughout space.*)

A second opportunity to move on the long diagonal is detailed in this diagram.

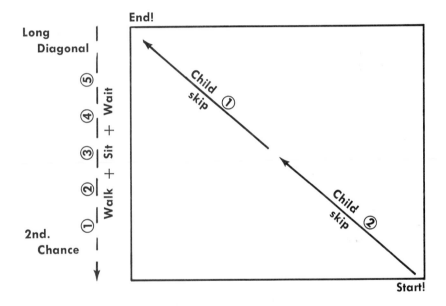

(*The teacher now beats several locomotor forms and step patterns on the drum, while the children become well acquainted with moving on the long diagonal floor pattern. Since this pattern was presented to the children through the activity of a skip, the teacher may find that the concepts of moving on the diagonal will be strengthened by developing the skip into several step patterns and continuing to do them on the long diagonal. For instance, the following combinations of locomotor forms and movement could easily follow the skip as presented above: four skips and four jumps; four skips and four jumps with bodily movement; four skips, stand still, and clap the rhythm of four jumps; four skips and four claps with bodily movement; four skips, four jumps with four claps and bodily movement. The teacher may continue to*

build on the step pattern of four skips and four jumps until it becomes as complicated and as exciting as the children can manage rhythmically and physically.)

Rhythm and Movement from Words:

Teacher: Listen to the rhythmic pattern of these words: house and a barn; red, white, and blue. (*She verbally repeats this phrase several times, and then urges the class to join her.*)

Teacher: Let's say and clap the rhythmic pattern of house and barn; and red, white, and blue. Make sure you clap on each sound or each word that you say. Let's accent the words barn and blue. (*Pause*) . . .

Teacher: Very well done. Instead of saying it and clapping your hands, let's say it and hit, or tap, different parts of our body. Watch me and do as I do. (*She leads the class in saying the phrase again, making sure to enunciate each syllable. She then proceeds to softly slap one part of her body as she says each syllable. For example, the first few times she says house and a barn; red, white, and blue, she may slap her shoulders on each beat. The next few times, she taps her head. She then proceeds to slap or tap various parts of her body, i.e. hips, knees, nose, chest, thighs, etc. The children follow and do the same.*)

Teacher: Let's continue to say, house and a barn; red, white, and blue, and step in place on each word. Make sure you accent the words barn and blue both verbally and in movement. (*By this time the rhythmic pattern is so well established that it has a somewhat hypnotic power which incites movement.*)

Teacher: Locomote to the rhythmic pattern of house and barn; red, white, and blue. Don't forget the accents. (*Pause*) . . . I see some children stamping on "barn" and "blue." I see other children accenting the words "barn" and "blue" by making a big movement with their whole body. Let's try both. Every time you say the words "barn" and "blue," stamp and make a big bodily movement. (*The teacher encourages the children to stamp hard and make a big bodily movement on the two words. Many of the children will now naturally execute a leap immediately after they say "barn" and "blue," without the teacher even mentioning the word leap, or instructing them to do a leap. The leap arises as the result of stamping down hard onto the floor and making a large bodily movement. The teacher should make sure that the children are stamping on the words "barn" and "blue" and not jumping. Those children who discover the leap first should be encouraged and positively reinforced so that the leaping movements become infectious, with the whole class doing them.*)

Teacher: You are all doing very well. Let's watch Jane move alone on the long diagonal floor pattern while doing house and a barn, etc. (*Pause*) . . . What can we call the locomotor form that Jane and all of you are doing on the words "barn" and "blue"?

Children: We are doing a leap.

Teacher: What have you done with your body in order to make the leap larger?

Children: We have made our body into a very big shape and stamped as hard as we can down onto the floor.

Teacher: That's right! Let's each take a turn on the long diagonal. Let's see how large you can make your leap on the words "barn" and "blue." Let's have all the children who are waiting and watching the movement be your rhythmic accompaniment. You will say "house and a barn; red, white, and blue," while each child moves to the rhythmic pattern. *The rhythmic pattern for house and a barn; red, white, and blue follows.*

	House	**And**	**A**	**Barn**		
6	1	2	3	4	⑤	⑥
	1	2	3	4	5	6

	Red	**White**	**And**	**Blue**		
6	1	2	3	4	⑤	⑥
	1	2	3	4	5	6

Teacher: Let's try moving to some other words. Listen to the rhythmic pattern that these words make when I say them. My mother belongs to the P.T.A. Say it with me. (*Pause*) . . . Make sure that you say every sound of each word. How many sounds or syllables are there in the words mother and belongs?

Children: There are two syllables in each word.

Teacher: Make sure that you sound out the two syllables in each. Clap the rhythm of "my mother belongs to the P.T.A.," as I say them. Ready, begin. (*Pause*) . . . Touch the space surrounding you to the rhythm of the words which I say, "my mother belongs to the P.T.A." (*The teacher repeats the words many times, to allow the children to experience the rhythm and the feeling through movement.*)

Teacher: Locomote as I say, "my mother belongs to the P.T.A." (*Pause*) . . . This time do not locomote, but move all parts of your body as I say it again. Remember, move your body twice for the words "mother" and "belong." (*Pause*) . . . Let's alternate locomotion with bodily movement as I say, "my mother belongs to the P.T.A." When I say it once you will locomote. When I say it the second time you will use bodily movement. Let's try it, ready, begin. (*Pause*) . . .

The Feeling Evoked from Words and Movement:

Teacher: How did you feel when you moved to the words house and a barn; red, white, and blue? (*Pause*) . . . Sit down and think a little bit now about the feeling that you got from your movement. Close your eyes. (*Pause*) . . . How did you feel when you moved to the words, my mother belongs to the P.T.A.? Think about it. (*Pause*) . . .

Teacher: Were the feelings from these phrases quite different from each other? Listen to me say each of them as you continue to keep your eyes closed and think about it. (*Pause*) . . .

Children: Yes, the feeling of each is very different.

Teacher: Open your eyes. What kind of feeling words can you use to describe how you felt when you moved to house and a barn; red, white and blue?

Children: Free, flying, exciting, different, happy.

Teacher: What kind of feeling words can you use to describe how you felt when you moved to the words, my mother belongs to the P.T.A.?

Children: Swingy, pleasant, easy.

Teacher: Let's combine both phrases. Let's do house and a barn; red, white, and blue, four times. Then, let's do my mother belongs to the P.T.A., four times, using bodily movement. Move anywhere you want in the space in this room. Be sure you have enough space for your own movement and be sure you leave enough space for the movement of the children near you. Ready, begin. (*The teacher may find that there is a need to review house and a barn, before combining both phrases. She now directs the children through the stages of progressive relaxation from the whole body stretch down to the sitting position. This indicates to the children that it is the end of the previous segment of the lesson, and that the following segment will deal with a new concept. As indicated in the section on teaching suggestions, chap. 3, pp. 100–119, several concepts are usually introduced and/or worked on in each lesson plan. This helps to prevent boredom, and keeps the chil-*

dren alert. It is however, of the utmost importance that the teacher return to original concepts one or more times in the course of ensuing lessons. The second presentation of an original concept should, however, be in the same form as the first presentation. This gives each child several chances to be cognitive of the concept and perform with medium to excellent proficiency. After this, the original concept may be presented in various ways as suggested many times throughout this book.)

Spatial Finger Painting:

Teacher: Pretend that you have icky, gooey paint all over your hands and fingers. Pretend too that the space around you, that is, the near space in front of you, above you, next to you, and behind you is your paper to paint on. Pretend that you are going to finger paint in the near space surrounding you. Show me that you're ready to paint by putting your hands somewhere in the space surrounding you. Are you looking at your hands, and ready to go? Begin. (*She allows the children to experiment with the idea of finger painting in the space surrounding them. Every now and again, she stops the children, emphasizing the need to watch what they are doing, and also emphasizing the need to use all parts of their hands, not just their fingers.*)

Teacher: You are doing very well painting in the space surrounding you. I would like you to continue to paint in the surrounding space. I will now call out different levels. You will go to that level and continue to paint in the space that surrounds you. Do not move there quickly. Continue to paint in the space surrounding you as you move to the other level, and when you get there. Ready to change your level and paint? Slowly, begin. (*She proceeds to call out the highest, high, medium, and low levels, while the children move to these levels and continue to paint in the space surrounding them.*)

Teacher: I love to watch you move. Your movement is very interesting and creative. It is creative because each one of you is doing his very own movement, and discovering movements that you have probably never done before. We are going to make an effort to make even more creative movements by adding another part. You will again move throughout the levels. Every time you come to the medium level, you are to continue to paint with your hands, but also locomote. Are you ready? Do you know what you are going to do? Ready, begin. (*Pause*) . . . Now we are going to add still another new part. When I play the cymbal, continue to move just as you were moving; that is, painting, moving through levels, and locomoting in the medium level. Try to get the feeling of the movement. Try to get the feeling of the sound of the cymbal in your movement. Let your feelings show. I will then play the piano as you continue to paint, move through levels, and locomote. I will play the piano percussively. Again, try to get the feeling of what you hear from the piano in your movement. It will probably be very different than the feeling you received when moving to the cymbal. Let the difference between your feelings of the sound of the cymbal and the sound of piano show in your movement. Ready, begin. (*Pause*) . . . Stay there! Very well done. You are dismissed.

LESSON PLAN 9

The Lesson

Locomotion:

Teacher: Sit on the floor and lean back on your hands. Now your feet will be free to move. Be ready to skip with your feet while leaning back on your hands. Let's do eight skips. Then, stop leaning on your hands, and skip your hands in the space surrounding you. Ready to skip with your feet? Ready to skip with your hands? Begin. (*Pause*) . . . Get up and do the same thing in the space in this room. Ready, begin. (*Pause*) . . .

Teacher: Very well done. How did you feel when you were moving? Don't tell me with words, show me with movement. Ready to do eight handskips, with feeling? Ready, begin. (*Since the children are expressing their feelings of their movement, it is best not to use music the first few times they do it. When music is selected, it is chosen by determining what feeling state is expressed by most of the children in the class. When music is ultimately used with a movement, a union of the two should occur, and the movement and the music should enhance each other, thereby expressing and emphasizing the best of each.*)

Sensory Perception and Movement:

Teacher: Sit here in front of the blackboard. Today I have brought something for you to touch. In order to help you be more aware of how it feels when you touch it, I have brought a blindfold for each one of you to wear. This way your sense of sight will not influence your sense of touch. You will think only of how you feel when your body contacts it, and not how it looks. You will put the blindfold on like this, making sure that you cannot see anything. (*Pause*) . . .

Teacher: I'm going to go to each one of you and let you touch a sweater with both of your hands. As you handle the sweater, be aware of how you feel when touching the sweater. Think and be aware of the feeling you personally get from touching the sweater with your hands. Touch the sweater as much as you want. Take your time and think of the feeling you are experiencing from handling it. (*Pause*) . . . Show me, by moving your hands in the space surrounding you, the feeling you experienced when you touched the sweater. (*Pause*) . . .

Teacher: Let the feeling of the sweater show in your movement. I see lots of interesting and creative movements. I see many movements with feeling. Take off the blindfold and stand up. Show me the same feeling that you got from touching the sweater by moving your whole body in the space in this room. Use any amount of space to move about in and through. Express that same feeling about touching the sweater that you did when you were blindfolded. Ready, begin. (*Pause*) . . . Stop, and stay there. (*The teacher stops the children's movement at various intervals, and then directs them to move again.*) Stop showing me your feeling in movement. Tell me, in words, the feeling you experienced when you touched the sweater.

Children: (*Respond verbally in one or more of the following ways:*). The sweater felt

—like a soft sweater.
—like soft wool.
—like touching cotton candy.
—like a soft warm breeze.
—like walking through soft, warm grass.
—like a soft kitten or bunny.
—(*using descriptive adjectives*) soft; fluffy; airy; gentle; smooth; slippery; furry.

Teacher: You can get a feeling from touching something, and that feeling can be described and expressed in words and in movement. How else can you express your feeling about something?

Children: We can cry. We can scream. We can be angry. We can laugh. We can love. We can hate. We can be jealous.

Teacher: Can one express his feeling about something by painting a picture?

Children: Yes.

Teacher: Can one express his feeling about something by composing a song about that something?

Children: Yes.

Teacher: Can one express his feeling about something by composing a dance about that something?

Children: Yes.

Teacher: When one composes a dance, a musical composition, a painting, or any other art form, one expresses a feeling or an idea. The dancer is telling us how he feels, not in words, but in rhythmic bodily movement.

Teacher: I have brought an iron for you to touch today. (*The iron should be plugged into an outlet, and be where the children can see it. The iron should be warm, not hot.*)

Teacher: No, it's not really a hot iron. But if it was hot, and you were about to test to see how hot the iron really was by touching it, how would you approach the iron and touch it? Who would like to show us? (*If time permits, this situation provides an excellent opportunity to give individual attention to each child that takes a turn touching the iron. The teacher asks the class to watch as each child touches the iron and points out the following*): (1) the approach to the iron is made cautiously and somewhat reluctantly; (2) the touch is short and fast; (3) the flight or escape from the iron is also fast; (4) the teacher emphasizes the words look—touch—go!

Teacher: Pretend that each one of you have a hot iron sitting on the floor in front of you. Look at the iron. Carefully, reach for the iron with your hand. Touch the iron. Take your hand away fast. If the iron was really hot, you would want to touch and go very fast. Show me again how you would approach the iron, and touch and go. Ready, look at the iron, begin. (*Teacher says touch and go several times, allowing the students to experience a cautious approach, and a quick touch and go.*)

Teacher: I'm sure if the iron was really hot, you would approach the iron very carefully, always looking at it. I'm sure if the iron was really hot, you would touch and go very quickly. I'm sure if the iron was really hot, you would watch every movement that you were doing. Let's try it again! Ready to touch and go with your hands? Ready, begin. (*Pause*) . . . This time, touch and go with your elbow. Watch it! Ready to look at the hot iron on the floor, begin. Touch and go. (*Pause*) . . . This time, stand up, and touch and go with your toes. Look, touch, and go. (*Pause*) . . .

Teacher: This time pretend that your hot iron is a spot on the wall in front of you. Touch and go with your toes and your elbow. Ready, look at the hot iron, touch and go. (*Repeat this movement often and let the children enjoy it.*)

Teacher: Touch and go with both hands. Are you ready? Ready, touch, and go. (*Pause*) . . . Add your hips. Touch and go with both hands and your hips. Look at the spot on the wall. Don't forget, it's a hot spot, watch it, touch, and go. Now find a hot spot in the space above you. Ready to touch and go with one hand? Look, touch, and go. (*Pause*) . . . Quickly, find another hot spot in the space surrounding you. Look, touch, and go. Quickly, find another hot spot in the space surrounding. Look, touch, and go. Ready, find another spot. Look, touch, and go. Look, touch, and go. Look, touch, and go. Look, touch, and go. . . .

Teacher: Recall the soft, airy sweater movement that you showed me earlier in the lesson today. I'm going to play the autoharp for the soft sweater movement. The sound of the autoharp has the same feeling quality that you showed me in your soft movement. Close your eyes, and listen to it. Can you recapture that movement in your thoughts while I play the autoharp? (*Pause*) . . . I'm now going to play the wood block for the touch and go movement. The wood block has the same feeling quality that you showed me in your touch and go movements. Close your eyes, and listen to it. Can you recapture the touch and go movement as I play the wood block? What sense were you making use of when you closed your eyes and listened to the autoharp and the wood block?

Children: The listening, hearing, or auditory sense.

Teacher: What sense did you make use of when you touched the sweater and iron?

Children: Our touching or tactile sense.

Teacher: Ready to do soft, creative rhythmic movement to the autoharp? Ready to do touch and go creative rhythmic movements to the wood block? Ready, begin. (*Pause*) . . . Freeze your last movement! Very well done, class. (*She now directs the children through the stages of progressive relaxation from the whole body stretch down to the sitting position where they are asked to just listen.*)

Teacher: I've enjoyed very much watching you discover your own movements today. You are truly a creative class whose movements showed originality and feeling. Sometimes it is necessary to exaggerate bodily movement. The dancer, pantominist, and actor very often find that they can express their feelings and ideas better if they exaggerate their movements. The audience seems to understand what they are saying if they exaggerate their movements. How do they exaggerate their movements? Have you ever watched a pantomimist? How does he communicate his feelings and ideas so that everyone watching him receives his message? (*The teacher looks for the following answer.*)

Children: The dancer, pantomimist, and actor make their movements either larger or more forceful in order to more readily express themselves.

Teacher: How can you make your movements larger?

Children: We can stretch them out. We could make bigger movements if we were taller.

Teacher: How can you make your arm movements bigger?

Children: I don't know. We could stretch and extend more. We could hold something in our hand; like a stick. This would make our arm longer.

Teacher: I have brought some ribbons to the class today. The ribbons are easy to move, and will not hurt anyone if they accidentally touch someone. I'm going to give each one of you a ribbon to hold in your hand. When you get the ribbon, find a space in this room which you can move about in without touching anything or anyone else. Experiment by moving the ribbon. Make the ribbon move, and if you watch the ribbon, you will find that the ribbon will move you. (*Pause*) . . . Are your movements becoming larger and exaggerated? Watch the movement of the ribbon wherever it goes. When the ribbon moves high, your eyes, head, and whole body should be stretched high and looking at the ribbon. (*The children continue to move with the ribbon.*)

Teacher: Stay there. Are you watching the ribbon? Ready, begin. (*Children again move with ribbons.*) Stop, and stay there. Are you watching the ribbon? When you watch the ribbon, as it moves, the ribbon will urge you to move. Let the ribbon help you to make larger movements. Ready, begin. (*Pause*) . . .

Teacher: (*The teacher intermittently stops and starts her pupils. She reinforces the children positively, all the while making sure that they are watching the ribbon when it moves and when it stops. Watching the ribbon, is an excellent and effective way to get a child to move his entire body, including that part of the body often neglected in movement education—the head. It is best not to use music the first few times the ribbon movement is introduced, but to attend to the concentration and awareness of bodily movement.*)

Make the ribbon move and . . . the ribbon will move you!

LESSON PLAN 10

The Lesson

Movement and Feeling:

Teacher: Most doors have a doorknob. If you want to open the door, what are some of the movements you must make with the doorknob and your body? What part of your body will you be moving the most in order to open the door? (*She looks for one of several answers, and especially for the word* twist.)

Children: The hand grabs the doorknob. (*or*) The hand, wrist, elbow, and whole arm twist the doorknob.

Teacher: Close your eyes. Pretend that there is a doorknob in the space directly in front of you. Take a hold of that doorknob. (*Pause*) . . . Twist the doorknob, as if you were opening the door. (*Pause*) . . . Twist the doorknob many times. Keep your eyes closed. Think of the movement you are making. It is a twisting movement. Think of the various parts of your arm twisting. Can you feel your wrist twisting? Can you feel your whole arm twisting and turning? Keep your eyes closed. Does the twisting movement go completely around? Or, does the movement go only so far in one direction and then back again so far in the opposite direction? (*Pause*) . . .

Teacher: Try the doorknob twist with your other hand and arm. Keep your eyes closed, and think about your movement. Be aware of each part of your arm twisting. (*Pause*) . . . Can you find one part of your body, which attaches to your arm, that remains motionless and stable and seems to support the twist?

Children: The shoulder.

Teacher: Very good. Open your eyes. The shoulder and arm bones are joined together at the shoulder arm joint. The shoulder bone and the muscles around it stay strong and motionless while your arm is twisting. The shoulder-arm joint is the axis for this movement. The arm rotates in the shoulder-arm axis. Try the doorknob twist, and watch your shoulder. Does it move? Put your hand on your shoulder, on the axis, and twist your arm again. Does it move? If the shoulder remains motionless and steady, how then is the arm able to twist?

Children: We don't know. (*Or, maybe they do know!*)

Teacher: The shoulder-arm joint is a ball and socket joint. It looks like this. (*The teacher holds up one hand and cups it. Within the cupped hand she inserts her other fist, and proceeds to rotate the fist.*) Try it! (*Pause*) . . .

Grasping the doorknob.

Teacher: The upper end of the arm bone is shaped like a ball, while the end of the shoulder, inside, is shaped like the middle part or pocket of a baseball glove. (*Teacher shows a baseball and baseball glove to the children and rotates the ball in the glove.*) This is called the ball and socket joint and it is found in many of the joints in our body. (*If time permits, the children may discover these joints by moving the various parts of their body and observing and identifying those bodily parts which twist.*) Some of you may be able to feel the ball rotating in its socket, by putting your hand on your shoulder, at the axis, and again twisting your arm. (*Pause*) . . .

Teacher: Close your eyes again and think carefully of your twisting movements. Try the doorknob twist again. What kind of feeling do you get from this twisting movement? Open your eyes, and stand up. Pretend the door is in the space in front of you. This time, pretend that the doorknob is huge. If you take ahold of this doorknob with both hands, you will need to twist your whole body in order to open it. Ready to take hold of the giant doorknob? Ready, and twist. (*The teacher should encourage the children to twist with their entire body.*)

Teacher: I see some children twisting with their whole body. I also see some children turning around. What is the difference between a twist and a turn?

Children: A twist goes one way, and then back the other way. A turn goes around one way, and continues to go in that same direction until it has gone all the way around.

Teacher: Good. Experiment with the twist and the turn until you are well acquainted with the difference between the two. (*Pause*) . . .

Teacher: We will be coming back to the full body twists later in the lesson, so don't forget them. As we said previously, a twist rotates this way and that on its axis. Let's think of the small doorknob again. Let's pretend that we have many doorknobs in the space around us. Sometimes you will twist a doorknob with one hand. Sometimes you will twist another doorknob with another hand. At times you may want to twist a doorknob with another part of your body. Let's try twisting open many doorknobs in the space surrounding us. Look at the first doorknob. Do you know which part of your body is going to grab that doorknob, and twist it open? Good for you. I can see that you're looking right at your doorknob and are ready to twist it open. Let's twist each doorknob eight times before going to the next. Begin. Twist, two, three, four, five, six, seven, and eight; and twist, two, three, four, five, six, seven, and eight. Each series of eight counts initiates a twist from another part of the body which is done in another area of space. (*The teacher repeats the above counts a number of times, allowing the children to open as many imaginary doorknobs as they wish.*)

Teacher: I like the way you look at each imaginary doorknob before you open it, and the way you twist each doorknob with a different part of your body. I also like the way you place your imaginary doorknobs in all the space surrounding you. I saw Jimmy opening an imaginary doorknob right behind his left ear. I saw Elizabeth opening an imaginary doorknob with her elbow in the space right behind her knees. You are being as creative as you know how to be. You are inventing all kinds of new movement, and I enjoy very much watching you do it.

Movement Composition:

Teacher: You are now ready to do a doorknob movement composition. Do you recall how a movement composition is formed? (Refer to lesson plan 3).

Children: A movement composition is formed by combining one or more step patterns with one or more movement patterns.

Teacher: Does a movement composition express both your feelings and ideas about something? If not both, does it express either one? Remember the dive and swim movements you did before in class?

Children: Yes, it expresses both.

Teacher: Your doorknob twist composition will have the following parts. I have written them on the blackboard for you to look at. (*Teacher reads each item to the class.*)

1. Knock on the door with any part of your body you wish to use.
2. Doorknob twist or twists with one or more parts of your body.
3. Open the door.
4. Move through the door, using any step pattern you wish.
5. Close the door any way you wish.

Teacher: I have also written a list of suggestions on the blackboard which will help you do your movement composition. (Teacher writes only the underlined portion of the following, and reads it to the class.)

SPACE. Confine your movement composition to a particular area of space. Then try to use that whole area at different times during your composition. (*Each child may outline his own space with chalk.*)

RHYTHM. You may do any part of the movement composition for as long a time or as little time as you wish. You will find that changing the tempo of your movement now and then <u>adds</u> <u>interest</u> <u>and</u> <u>excitement</u> to your composition.

MOVEMENT. Start and end with a good definite movement. The beginning and end movements are like book ends holding together everything in between. <u>Move any or all parts of your body</u>, and <u>compose a step pattern to locomote you</u> through the door.

REMEMBER <u>each part of your composition before progressing to the next</u>. You can <u>do this by</u> repeating each part often and <u>thinking of what your body is doing as you move</u>.

Teacher: Remember, the first list consists of all the ideas you are to express in your doorknob composition. The second list contains suggestions to help you compose. Right now, find a spot on the floor where you can move without touching anyone, and compose your doorknob twist composition. (*The teacher stations herself in one area of the room, where she can watch all of the students composing at one time. If there is a sturdy, high platform or stage in the room, it is an excellent vantage point from which the teacher can watch each child as he composes. The teacher encourages the children to respect the right of each child to compose by being silent, and to attend to their own composition. The teacher positively reinforces at every opportunity, without interfering with their progress. If the children are progressing well in composing their own movements, the teacher may go to each child and give individual help. However, it is much more helpful to the children for the teacher to stand high above them and collectively watch them, and make general remarks. It is most important to finish this first composition in one period, as it is difficult for children to remember the following day what they have composed. About fifteen minutes should be allowed for this composition. If the teacher now sees one or two compositions that meet the requirements stated above, she may stop the class and have those children share their composition with the rest of the class. On the other hand, sometimes the children will think that the composition shown to them is what pleases the teacher most, and they will copy the movements of that child. The teacher may find that it is better for half of the class to show their composition, while the other half watches. After this type of sharing of movement ideas, and after discussing these ideas, the teacher may want to encourage the children to go back to their space, and work on their compositions a little more. It is best to break up the period of composition into two or three periods of four to five minutes each. Each period is separated by comments from the teacher, questions and comments from the class, and a sharing of movement ideas. Positively reinforce the uniqueness* and creativity of each child. Find something good to say about each child's composition. Encourage the children to remember one move-ment by repeating it over and over again, before continuing on to the next. Encourage them also to allow one movement to grow or flow from the previous movement.) (*The teacher now completely changes the pace.*)

Locomotion and the Twist:

Teacher: I'm going to beat an elementary form of locomotion on the drum. Can you guess which one it is?

Children: (*Some will say*) skip, (*some will say*) gallop, (*and others may say*) slide.

Teacher: The skip, gallop, and slide all have the same rhythmic pattern and sound very much alike. How many sounds are there to a skip, a gallop, or a slide?

Children: There are two sounds to each.

Teacher: Is each sound equal to the other?

Children: No, one sound is longer than the other. One sound is long and the other is short.

Teacher: Who would like to demonstrate the skip? Who would like to demonstrate the gallop? Who would like to demonstrate the slide? (*The teacher selects three children to demonstrate the three movements: skip, gallop, and slide.*) Let's have all three of you moving at the same time, so we can see the difference. Ready, begin. (*Pause*) . . .

Teacher: What makes the slide different from any other locomotor form?

Children: The side of the body goes first.

Teacher: Let's do a slide slowly and smoothly. (*As the children execute a slow slide, the teacher says* side, close, side, close.

	side		close		side		close
	walk		walk		walk		walk
6	1	②	3	4	⑤	6
	1	2	3	4	5	6

Make sure your side leads. You can check yourself by facing your whole body toward this wall. As you move, make sure your body does not twist. Look at the wall while you are sliding. Now that we are all facing this wall, let's do slow slides toward the clock wall first. We'll do eight slow slides toward the clock wall, and then eight slow slides toward the piano wall. Ready, begin. (*Teacher says* side, close *eight times in each direction.*)

Teacher: Now let's do the same thing only faster. One, two, ready go! (*Teacher says:* slide and slide and:)

slide (and)	s (a)
walk leap	walk leap
2 1 ⊕ ah	2 ⊕ ah
1	2

Can you discover the leap in a slide?

When we speed up the slide, and put more energy into it, we have a little leap in our slide. See if you can discover where. Ready to do eight slides in each direction, begin. (*Pause*) . . .

Teacher: Let's add a part. Do eight slides toward the clock, stop, and do eight full body twists. Then, do eight slides toward the piano, and again do eight full body twists. Ready, begin. (*This movement goes well with a peppy Polka, and is a good climax and end to lesson ten or to any of the ensuing lessons.*)

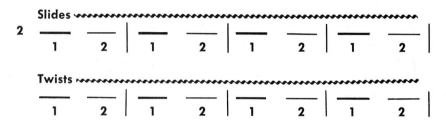

Repeat in Opposite Direction

five

Additional Ideas for the Teacher

Creative rhythmic movement suggested by, and to be developed from a rhythmic pattern

The teacher starts by beating any rhythmic pattern she chooses. To achieve the most success with this plan, the rhythmic pattern should be simple and of a medium tempo. In order to develop the rhythmic pattern, the following plan is suggested.

The first eight steps in the following procedure are simple enough for presentation during the first ten to fifteen lessons of a beginning CRM unit.

1. Beat the rhythmic pattern on the floor or on a percussion instrument.

	beat	b	b	b	b	beat	
4	1	2	+	3	+	4	⟵ beat!
	1		2		3	4	

2. Clap it.

clap	c c	c c	clap	
4	1	2 +	3 +	4	←— clap!
	1	2	3	4

3. Say it in longs and shorts, or in counts (numbers). Make sure that there is an utterance for every beat in the pattern, no matter how short it is.

long	s s	s s	long	
4	1	2 +	3 +	4	> ←—say!
	1	2	3	4	s = short

4. Move individual parts of the body to the rhythmic pattern. Make sure that there is a movement for every part of the pattern.

move head	move head	move head	m. h.	m. h.	move head	←—move head
4	1	2	+	3	+	4
	1	2		3		4

5. Move two or more parts of the body to the pattern.

move head + elbows	move h. + e.	m h. + e.	m h. + e.	m h. + e.	move head + elbows	←— move head and elbows
4						

6. Step in place to it.

step	step step	s s	step	←— step in place
4	1	2	3	4

7. Step in place to the pattern and say it. (See step 3.)

step	s s	s s	step	← do and say!
long	short s	s s	long	
4 ═══	═ ═ ═	═ ═ ═	═══	
1	2	3	4	

8. Step in place and move one or more parts of the body to the rhythmic pattern. (See step no. 4.)

step	—	move	hands and	hips
4	1	2 +	3 +	4
1	2	3	4	

The following three steps in this plan are more difficult to do. It is therefore suggested that steps 9, 10, and 11 be withheld from the children until they can do the previous eight steps with ease.

9. Locomote to this pattern. Make sure that there is a locomotor movement for each beat, or part, in the pattern. Remember, the skip, gallop, and slide are locomotor forms consisting of two beats each.

walk	jump j	j j	jump	← locomote
4 ═══	═ ═	═ ═	═══	
1	2	3	4	

10. Locomote, and say it. (See steps 3 and 7.)

long	short s	s s	long	say and
walk	j j	j j	jump	← locomote
4 ═══	═ ═	═ ═	═══	
1	2	3	4	

11. Locomote, and move one or more bodily parts to the rhythmic pattern. (See steps 4 and 8.)

	clap walk	move i i	hips and i i	arms jump	move and locomote
4	—	—	—	—	
	1	2	3	4	

12. Change the tempo. Do two measures of the above pattern slowly and four measures fast.

When first presenting this plan, it is best to go slowly, developing the rhythmic pattern by only one or two steps each lesson. If the children are in need of more practice, introduce several other patterns, and develop them up to the point that had been achieved when the additional practice patterns were introduced, before going on to the next step. Keep the rhythmic pattern simple and at a medium tempo. Refer to rhythmic patterns in this book for more ideas. The teacher may choose to stop the development of the rhythmic pattern into a movement pattern at any point. Or she may choose to change the order of the procedure, or leave some parts out. However, the procedure should always begin by simply beating, or clapping the pattern long enough for the children to acquire a strong feeling for it. The development of the rhythmic pattern in this plan, then, is built upon that acquired feeling, and not the rhythmic analysis of the pattern. After the children have frequently experienced the development of a movement pattern from a rhythmic pattern, the mathematical analysis of a rhythmic pattern is much more easily pursued.

The following steps, not to be presented until all of the above can be easily and readily executed, provide an excellent lead-in to the formation of a movement composition.

13. Combine the preceding pattern with another rhythmic pattern and go through all of the above procedures.
14. Exaggerate some or all of the movements, and let the feeling spread throughout the entire rhythmic and movement pattern.
15. Invent a floor pattern for it.
16. Do the pattern with one or more children relating the movement, and/or feeling evoked from it, to each other.
17. Play it on one or more instruments, as an accompaniment.

Creative rhythmic movement suggested by, and to be developed from, locomotion

The teacher may start with whatever elementary form of locomotion she chooses, and she will find that any form can be developed in numerous ways. The following methods are only a few of those ways, and will suggest others. The teacher may, in many cases, direct the development of a locomotor form by allowing the children to discover the answer through movement to such questions and movement problems as: How fast can you jump? How high can you jump? How far can you jump? What do you need to do with your arms in order to jump higher? If you changed your center of gravity when walking, what would your walk look like? Try it! Can you cross your feet at any time during the execution of a slide? Can you change the rhythm of a skip so that the walk and the hop, which a skip is composed of, are even beats instead of uneven beats? How many ways can you move your hanging foot while you are hopping on the other? The possibilities are numerous. The following is presented as a guide from which the teacher may draw ideas for inciting children to move, creatively and rhythmically, by starting with a locomotor form and extending it in one or many of these possible ways.

Start with any locomotor form; then try any or all of the following ideas.

- Change the tempo of execution, as, for example, doing a skip in slow motion; doing eight runs slowly, and sixteen runs quickly; running as fast as one can. What happens to the size of the running steps as one increases the speed of execution? What happens to the muscles of one's legs and entire body when one runs as fast as possible?
- Change the range of execution of all, or one part, of the locomotor form and see what kind of movement will develop. Examples are:

  a. Runs done with extended legs lead to leaps.
  b. A gallop leads to a step leap, by extending or reaching forward with the foot that always leads.
  c. A series of leaps leads to a step leap by reaching out with, or extending one leg further than the other.

- Change the placement of the body's center of gravity. Examples are: the execution of a leap changes drastically when the body's center of gravity is behind the base of support rather than forward of the base of support. It looks like one is leaning back, kicking up, but locomoting forward.
- Change the direction of execution. Examples are: three jumps forward and one jump backward, or walks done with the side of the body moving forward.
- Change the accent of execution. Examples are: change the walk from a heel, ball, toe movement to a toe, ball, heel movement. Or

reverse the steps of a slide, so that the side step is done swiftly and the close step is done slowly.

- Compose a pattern of certain quantities of a particular locomotor form. Examples are: do a walk as follows: eight walks, eight walks; four walks, four walks; two walks, two walks; one walk, one walk, one walk, one walk. Or do these same walks as follows:

a. Stamp, or clap, on the first walk of each series of beats.

	stamp	walk	w	w	w	w	w	w	
8	1	2	3	4	5	6	7	8	Repeat

	stamp	walk	w	w	
4	1	2	3	4	Repeat

	stamp	w	stamp	w	s	w	s	w	
2	1	2	1	2	1	2	1	2	

b. Say, or shout, something on the first beat of each series.
c. Change direction on the first beat of each series.
d. Move a part of the body on the first beat of each series.

The eight, eight, four, four, two, two, one, one, one, one pattern, being rhythmically easy to execute and leading to many fascinating movement patterns, is an especially interesting one. For example, if this same rhythmical pattern is done with the slide or gallop, it will lead to the execution of a polka.

Another interesting combination, numerically, is the six, six, three, three, three, three, pattern. Again, one may produce new and interesting movement patterns by combining with any of the movements a, b, c, or d above.

- Combine two or more elementary forms of locomotion. Examples are:

a. Combine one measure of one locomotor form with another measure of another locomotor form, i.e., four jumps and eight hops.
b. Combine one or more locomotor forms in one measure. For instance, combining a skip and a walk leads to an interesting step pattern. Combining three walks and one hop leads to the step pattern commonly known as the schottische.

Try these combinations:

	skip	step	skip	step	
4	1(+)ah	2	3(+)ah	4	or skip-a-step
	1	2	3	4	

	walk	w	w	hop	
4	1	2	3	4	or the schottische
	1	2	3	4	

	r r	r r	i i	i
4	1 +	2 +	3 +	4
	1	2	3	4

	slide	slide	i	i
4	1(+)ah	2(+)ah	3	4
	1	2	3	4

	jump		r r
3	1	(2)	3 +
	1	2	3

	skip	w	w	skip	w	w
3	1	2	3	1	2	3

	skip	w	w	i	i	i
	1	2	3	1	2	3

Creative rhythmic movement suggested and to be developed by arousing the imagination

The teacher may, by one method or another, stimulate a child's imagination, thereby inciting the child to express his inner imagery, outwardly. Whether or not the child expresses himself in rhythmic movement, or in writing, speech, poetry, painting, sculpture, music, or in acts of screaming and kicking, very much depends on how the teacher incites the child, and how the teacher helps to direct or channel the child's form of expression. Before suggesting ways in which the teacher may incite the child imaginatively, and encourage the child to release and express these images through CRM, let us examine some ideas and theories which pertain to imagination and children.

Imagination and Children:

- Children only express what has impressed them. Therefore, the teacher should choose ideas and methods of inciting a child's imagination by referring and relating to that child's world of experiences. In order to be sure that each child has had the opportunity to experience an idea, and has had the chance to create related images, the teacher should present to the child as many ideas, in as many ways as possible. Or, she may refer to particular material which she knows the child is studying, or has been studying in school.
- When a child's imagination is incited, he will extract bits and pieces from it, relate and unite it to his present situation, and create something new. This is an essential activity employed in the creative process.
- The child's new creation will be an outward expression of his inner self. This, however, does not mean that he has lost his imagery, but that he now has expressed and/or created something from it. This process helps to make him aware of the difference between imagination and reality by placing his imagery and the object of his expression in perspective to each other.
- Just as each child is different inwardly, based on his past experiences, each child's outward expressions will also be different; some quite drastically. Regardless of the differences in outward expression between the various children, a feeling of acceptance and respect for each child's endeavors should prevail in a class of creative rhythmic movement.
- The senses are particularly involved with imagination. Therefore, a method of calling forth children's images through the stimulation of the senses is usually successful.

- Feelings and emotions, and their meanings, are also involved with imagination. Therefore, a method of calling forth children's images, and what they signify, through stimulation of the child's feelings and emotions, is usually successful.
- Children's imaginations are usually more vivid and active than those of adults. Inciting a child to use his imagination, expressively and creatively is usually a simple, rewarding, and sometimes surprising experience for the teacher.

Ideas and theories pertaining to imagination and CRM

Although stimulating a child to use his imagination expressively and creatively is usually an easy task, it is not always easy for a teacher to induce the child to channel his expression toward helping himself to problem solve and become aware of a movement concept. Very often a movement response which has been prompted by inciting a child's imagination will result in a great deal of emotional and dramatic gesture, and less rhythmic bodily movement. How can the teacher help the child to express his inner self by moving rhythmically and creatively? She may begin by asking the child to exaggerate his movement without losing the feeling quality. Also, the teacher may facilitate this process by frequently changing the tone quality of her voice, or showing the children some examples of how a small movement or gesture can be made much larger by exaggerating it, spatially and dynamically.

For example, the teacher may begin by asking the children to shake their head signifying "no." She may then give the following directions: Say "no" with other parts of your body. Say "no" with your knee. Say "no" with your shoulders. Say "no" with your hands. Say "no" with your hands and shoulders, etc. Show me the largest "no" movement you can make with your body. Can you locomote while making this large "no" movement? How? Show me the tiniest "no" movement you can possibly make. Do it fast. Do it slow. Do it fast and locomote. Create a pattern of "no" movements. Select five large "no" movements and ten small, fast "no" movements. Locomote at any time during the movement pattern.

The above plan works well with all gestures. For example, waving good-bye may be developed as above, but may also be developed by such directions and questions from the teacher as:

Show me how you would say good-bye to your favorite pet when you are going to leave him for a month. What kind of movements would you make? Try doing that same movement with other parts of your body. How do you think you would feel if you had to leave your pet for one month? Wave good-bye to your pet with your head showing how you feel about leaving him for so long a period. Wave good-bye to your pet, with your whole body, letting that same feeling show. Wave good-bye to him with both arms, with feeling. Add good-bye head movements. What movement expresses your feelings the best? Let your feeling show in all of your movements. Exaggerate your feeling and your movements. Make them larger and sadder. Repeat these movements often enough so that you will not forget them.

The development may continue by exploring the movements of the pet, and then composing a movement pattern of sad, slow, good-bye movements and fast pet movements. The teacher should encourage the children to repeat the pattern often enough so that they can really concentrate on the feeling they want to express. The movement and the feeling should flow together.

The initial movement which results from the teacher arousing the imagination of the child depends on the method used to stimulate, the category of images conjured up, and the amount of previous experience the child has had in expressing his feelings and ideas verbally, as well as through other mediums. The category of images induced, and the method of evoking these images also depend very much on the physical, mental, social, and psychological age of the child and how well the teacher knows the child. For example: the teacher would not ask a class of sixth grade girls to express their ideas and feelings through movement by referring to the topic of playing with dolls. Neither would she ask a class to express their innermost feelings, ideas, and images through movement until children and teacher were well acquainted and working with each other well.

Because the expression of the inner self through bodily movement is a very personal one, for all to see, the teacher should also employ some caution in determining where to incite the imaginative mind in the unit. She should approach this means of expression with a warm friendly attitude, and appeal to the experiences and expressions in which she and the children have a common interest. For example, the teacher may begin by talking about an experience she had during the summer, and how she felt about it. This experience should provide an opportunity for her to use movement as a means of self expression in addition to verbalizing. Hopefully, several children in the class may have had similar experiences which they will eagerly want to relate. As the child relates his experiences verbally, the teacher utilizes every opportunity to invite the child to also express himself in movement. The child is encouraged to show how he feels, or what he means, through movement. She may then ask other members of the class to show, also through movement, how they would feel if this same thing happened to them. This is a good introduction to the imaginative approach, and it allows children to be aware of their common feelings and of the differences in the way others in the class express these feelings. The process may take three to ten lessons before a child feels comfortable expressing himself through movement. The teacher should progress slowly. always gently encouraging more movement and less talk.

The teacher may find that because of the unpredictable nature of children no one particular method of inciting a child imaginatively works well all the time. If the children are not responsive the first time, she may drop it, and try again next time. Be enthusiastic and patient, and always watch for a chance to encourage more movement, more feeling, and less talk. Inducing children to express their innermost feeling through movement is an activity which can begin in the classroom.

Suggested here are a few of the ideas which have been found to be successful with children in conjuring images that resulted in creative rhythmic movements.

- Finger painting, in many colors, in their surrounding space. The child should be encouraged to concentrate on his fingers, hands, and the space he is painting. The teacher may also refer to many different colors.
- Moving like a particular mechanical toy.
- Knocking on the door, twisting the doorknob open, opening the door, and slamming the door shut.
- Gathering things in, and spreading them out again.
- Pushing an elephant or a piano.
- Pushing or guiding a power-driven lawn mower.
- Pulling a sack of dog food.
- Tug of war between two or more children.
- Walking on the moon. Walking on the sun.
- Punching and ducking.
- Slicing a big piece of chocolate cake.
- Peeling a banana.
- Getting a pair of new shoes.
- Chocolate chip cookies.

The children are instructed to indicate how they feel about the above subjects, and not to portray the essential idea. For example, a child may move like a chocolate chip cookie tastes, looks, smells, or tactilely feels to him. He may also recall making cookies, and this may remind him of a warm kitchen, a rainy day, or a burned finger. Evoking an image by appealing to the senses is very often successful, and the teacher may find that she can achieve the greatest response by bringing chocolate chip cookies to class for the children to eat.

In order to express one's feelings, ideas, and imagery in movement in a way that accentuates the feeling qualities and minimizes the expression of the actual idea itself, try the following plan.

1. Do the movement in rhythm, and let the rhythm dominate the movement.
2. Exaggerate the movement spatially or dynamically. This may produce a very different feeling.
3. Exaggerate the feeling by over-emoting through bodily movement. That is, let the feeling show more until it almost dominates the movement. This may lead to larger and increased movement, or movement of a different quality.
4. Change the rhythm of the movement by changing the tempo, by accenting various parts, by stopping and starting again, or by sustaining one or more movements.
5. Change the range of space used. Make some movements tiny or huge. Use a limited amount of space, as in a box or tunnel. Use locomotion and levels.
6. Change the joint action. For instance, try the same movement with very little joint action, such as a stiff movement. Change the movement to an angular one; or change it to a round movement.
7. Reverse the order of occurrence of the movement events. Do last what was originally done first.

If each child expresses chocolate chip cookies differently, how does the child communicate the idea of chocolate chip cookies so that the viewer will understand? He doesn't. The child may communicate, roundness, bumpiness, pleasantness, and other feeling tones which he feels, but not the idea of chocolate chip cookies per se.

If the child wants to communicate an exact idea, he, like the pantomimist, should look for the universal feelings and movements of an idea, and express them. Obviously, the universal feeling qualities of a chocolate chip cookie are meager. It is therefore, not a good subject to communicate literally through movement. However, the subject of baking cookies has more depth, and it's literal idea can be communicated through gestures and pantomime.

Creative rhythmic movement suggested and to be developed by vocalizing words

Words which conjure up images (refer to the foregoing section, p. 220)
The very mention of a given word may conjure an image and bring

about an expression of that image via CRM. The following words, used either individually or in groups, have been found to be especially evocative:

1. *Movement Words:*
   sneak, climb, look, attack, good-bye, reach, grab, spin, stretch, fall, lift, drop, hammer, drip, twist, saw, peek, prance, wave, stagger, see-saw, and hang. The right combination of movement words may result in an interesting movement pattern. For example: dive, splash, and swim; or, look, reach, grab, and spin.

2. *Feeling and Emotional Words:*
   hurt, happy, friendly, exciting, homesick, patriotic, love, hate, jealous, affectionate, curious, frightening, gentle, rough, scary, lazy, hot, and sloppy.

3. *Sensory Words:*
   a. Taste: sweet, sour, sharp, devour, gobble, peck, swallow, and bitter.
   b. Tactile: gentle, rough, bumpy, hot, cold, warm, sharp, smooth, scratchy, and furry.
   c. Visual: beautiful, ugly, colorful, big, small, shiny, fat, skinny, bright, and dull.
   d. Auditory: screeching, moaning, groaning, high, low, piercing, tingling, noisy, static, vibratory, ringing, melodius, humming, loud, and soft.
   e. Smell: stink, reek, odoriferous, perfumed, delicious, and spicy.

   Very often the above words will produce only a slight movement response. The teacher may find that combining the words to produce a pattern of movement may be more stimulating. The words should be related, such as: sweet and sour, big and small, beautiful and ugly, or peck and gobble. Or, the teacher may find that repeating a word many times in a certain rhythmic pattern may be evocative. Or, the children may respond more if the words are used as comparisons or descriptions. For example, sour like a lemon; gobble like a turkey; skinny like a snake; scratchy like a sweater, etc.

4. Movement may also be evoked by referring to the following: animals, places, seasons, sports, professions, and so on. The teacher is again reminded that when creative rhythmic movement evolves from inciting and expressing images, the dramatic responses are often stronger than the movement responses. Therefore, in order to evoke more movement the teacher must try additional stimulating methods. (See the previous section on imagination, particularly p. 218.)

Movement evoked by rhythm derived from word vocalization

Every word consists of one or more syllables, or sounds. As each word is vocalized, one may discover how many sounds, syllables, or beats there are in each word. The child, vocalizing, is encouraged to move with each syllable. The rhythmic pattern which evolves from vocalizing each syllable of the word depends on how the child says the word. Therefore, the number of syllables, sounds, or beats to each word never changes; however, the rhythmic pattern may vary. The word "astronaut" may be said several different ways depending on what syllables are accented. Here are two examples. Be sure to say each word audibly five or six times to feel the rhythm.

```
                      ∧
   a s  —  tro  —  n a u t

 4    1       2       3      ④
 ___     ___     ___    ___

       1       2       3       4
```

                              or

```
   ∧
   a s—tro  — n a u t

 4    1 +      2      ③       ④
 ___     ___    ___    ___

       1       2       3       4
```

For the purposes of communication through movement, the children should look for the natural rhythm inherent in a word and move to it. The correct placement of the accent can easily be determined by looking in the dictionary. The teacher may find that dwelling on the way a word sounds, either rhythmically or emotionally, may help the child who is having difficulty in reading and spelling.

More interesting rhythmic combinations may be obtained by uniting two or more words. Some combinations of words, such as those that follow, have been found to be quite successful in evoking movement responses, creatively and rhythmically:

- peanut butter and jelly
- house and a barn, red, white, and blue
- get out, get out, get out of this house
- lions and tigers and bears, oh my!

- my mother belongs to the P.T.A.
- extra, extra, read all about it
- gee whiz! Charlie Brown!
- moonlight and candlelight; moonlight and stars
- don't cry, don't cry, your face is getting red

The teacher will find that keeping the combination of words simple will lead to clarity of movement. Encourage the children to both vocalize and move to each syllable. Some combinations of words go easier, and lead to more interesting movement responses, than others. The teacher should point out the feeling one gets when moving to words. The children should also be allowed to discover the differences in feelings and meanings evoked from different combinations of words or different ways of saying and moving to the same words. The feelings evoked from the words moonlight and candlelight, are quite different than the feelings evoked from the words get out, get out, get out of this house! In like manner, the same group of words sound quite different, and evoke a very different movement response when the emphasis is put on another part of the phrase. For example: "My mother belongs to the P.T.A.," may be said in a sing song rhythmical voice. It also may be said with a feeling of arrogance such as, "*My* mother . . . *pause* (not your mother) . . . belongs to the P.T.A." The feeling and movement evoked from each is very different, and so is the meaning.

The child who becomes aware of the close relationship between meaning and expression will gain a great deal of insight into his own self and the relationship between himself and others.

Movement evoked by feeling derived from word vocalization

Feeling and movement may be evoked by merely saying a word or a group of words. In this case, the feeling is evoked by the actual sound of the word. Or, the feeling and resulting movement may be evoked by the mechanics of saying the word. For instance, the sound of the word "pizza" might evoke movement from a child, for several reasons. The child might be incited to move rhythmically and creatively because he remembers the delicious taste of pizza. However, he might also be incited to express the feeling he gets by vocalizing the word "pizza" once or many times.

Sounds and nonsense words may also be used to evoke a movement response. (The teacher may collect a very impressive variety of sounds by recording the sound from television commercials.) When using this plan, the children should be encouraged to react immediately to the sound of the word. They will then not have time to recall an image associated with that sound. Some of the following sound effects have been found to be especially evocative: groans, cries, knocks, laughter, whistles, screams, clicks, bells, barks, other animal sounds, mechanical sounds, crashes, etc.

Movement evoked by word meanings

The teacher may choose a word, any word, and ask the children to think about what that word means to each one of them. She may then ask the children to express their feeling about the meaning of the word, not vocally, but in movement. It is an excellent opportunity for children who have difficulty expressing themselves verbally, to use another medium of expression.

Words associated with certain holidays are usually meaningful to children and evoke interesting creative rhythmic movement responses. For instance, the Christmas holiday has many words associated with it which not only calls forth many images, but the very sounds and significance of the words evoke movement. For example: bells ringing, singing, jingling, happy, happy, happy, toys, candy, Christmas trees, red, green, blue, yellow, lights, lights, lights, sparkling, twinkling, glittering, lights.

The teacher may bring a tape recorder to class, and the children may record their voices saying the words which are usually associated with the Christmas holiday. The children should be encouraged to repeat some of the words. They should also be encouraged to say the words in many different ways. For example, the words may sometimes be said very loudly or very softly. Or, they may be said in a high-pitched or a low-pitched voice. The children will enjoy recording their voices and later hearing and moving to their voices. Spontaneous laughter and giggling which may occur should also be recorded.

Movement evoked from a poem or story

Children may be prompted to move as the result of the feeling or meaning they get from hearing a poem or story. When the teacher chooses a story or poem to move to, she should look for the following qualities: (1) The poem or story should be simple and short. That is, the events which occur in the poem or story should not be complicated, numerous, or abstract. (2) There should be many movement words in the story. That is, such words as stretch, reach, run, blow, tramp, ooze, pour, boil, and so on, are the kind of words one should look for in a story which will tend to evoke movement. A good place to find this kind of story is in children's books. Another obvious possibility is for the children and the teacher to compose their own story.

The following stories are examples of the kind of narration which children and their teacher may enjoy composing together. Both stories have been left unfinished intentionally, so that the children may collectively or individually have the pleasure of finishing them as they desire.

The Story of Squeak and Creak

Once upon a time there were two mice by the name of Squeak and Creak. Squeak was always busy doing something. Squeak liked to jump, hop, skip, gallop, slide, roll, scoot, and run. He never sat still. And do you know what? Every time he moved he made a tiny high sound, like a squeak.

Creak was a very different kind of mouse. He moved as little as possible. He liked to lie in the shade of a tree and relax and snooze. The strange thing about him, was that when he did move, his bones made a sound like an old rocking chair creaking. Now, one day Squeak and Creak met. Just as Squeak came whizzing around a corner, and darting hastily from one spot to another, he bumped smack into Creak lying on top of a. . . .

A Story About the Wind

Once upon a time, there was a great big wind storm in the town of Blowing Heights. The wind blew and blew, day and night. It pushed and shoved and whistled throughout the town. It huffed and puffed so hard that it shook the leaves off the trees, and bent the trees into peculiar and ugly shapes.

The leaves blew everywhere. Sometimes, the leaves blew into little circles and the circle of leaves spiraled high into the sky. Sometimes, many leaves joined into a crowd of leaves and swished around corners and chased each other noisily around trash cans. Some leaves curled up into themselves and rolled merrily along the ground enjoying the excitement of a whole town set to movement. Soon the wind lost all its breath, and the movement slowly and quietly died down. . . .

Children may find it fun to compose their own story from a list of movement words. The children are instructed to use all the words in the list to compose a movement story, and then compose movement for the story. The words in the list should be somewhat related to each other. For instance, the following words may incite a provocative movement story: boom, explode, glow, burst, spiral, vibrate, ooze, squirt, and collapse. Another movement story may be composed from the following words: fast, bright, colors, flags, fresh, wind, sun, moving, birds, sky, planes, flying, circling, and climbing. The children may add any number of additional words that they wish, and may use the above words in any order they choose. Using the movement story plan for evoking creative rhythmic movement has several limitations, and the plan should not be used without forehand knowledge of these limitations.

Since the entire thrust of creative rhythmic movement is on self-awareness, and self-expression, through bodily movement, children should not be channeled into a structure as formed as a story or poem until they have had the freedom of expressing their own feelings and ideas through CRM—that is, until they have had plenty of opportunities to explore and discover movement for themselves.

If the children are asked to move within a structure such as a story, record, or poem, and if they have had little previous opportunity to discover themselves through movement, their composition very often results in dramatic and emotional gestures with a minimum amount of movement. Movement which does occur under these circumstances is very often stereotyped, and not a true expression of the child's feelings and ideas about the story. The child moves as he sees others move, or he moves the way he thinks he is expected to move.

Since all stories have a definite pattern, a good lead-up activity is to allow the children ample opportunity to move to a pattern of words. Or, the children should have ample practice in composing a pattern of movement from related words or phrases before forming an entire story of movement.

Movement evoked from a nursery rhyme

Nursery rhymes may also be used to evoke movement by placing the emphasis on their meaning, feeling, or rhythm. Again, if the teacher is interested in getting the most movement she can from the children as the result of using nursery rhymes, or poetry, for that matter, it is recommended that the children move more specifically to just the rhythmic pattern, and not to the feeling or meaning.

Let's look at the nursery rhyme, "Hickory Dickory Dock." This rhyme has many movement words in it. However, much more movement will result if the teacher follows this plan:

1. Say the rhyme with the children several times.
2. Then, while having the children repeat the rhyme several times on their own, encourage them to vocalize each syllable—to open their mouths and enunciate each syllable of each word. Do not proceed until each child enunciates each and all of the syllables. Each syllable equals one beat or one sound.
3. While the teacher says the nursery rhyme, the children clap to each syllable of the nursery rhyme.
4. While the teacher says the rhyme the accompanist plays the beat of each syllable, and the children punch, pat, or touch the space surrounding them to the beat of each syllable.
5. The children step in place to each beat of the nursery rhyme as the teacher says it and the accompanist plays it.
6. The children locomote and punch the space surrounding them to the beat of each syllable of the rhyme. The teacher's voice, the drum, or the piano accompany them.
7. The children select an even locomotor form which they do to each syllable of each word in the rhyme. They then select a particular part of their body to move. They combine the locomotor form and the bodily movement and move to each syllable of each word.

Movement suggested by sensory stimulation

Creative rhythmic movement offers a unique opportunity for children to experience, explore, and express their feelings. Through the external expression of their feelings they become more aware of themselves and others; through bodily movement rather than through discussion. This plan works especially well with children who have difficulty communicating verbally, and with those children who are capable of limited movement only due to physical or mental incapacities. The mechanics of using this approach can be found in lesson plan 9. Add to them the following few ideas:

• Touch something soft, like cotton. Touch something sharp, like a tack.
• Smell a pot of chicken soup. Smell a lemon. Smell some flowers. Smell an onion. Smell bacon cooking.
• Listen to various sounds, as mentioned in the section on words and feelings. Listen to the sounds of any moving object. Listen to the sounds of the street, or the sounds of the school. Listen to the silence.

- Taste a piece of candy, or a lemon.
- Look at a color, a photograph, or a painting.

Movement suggested and assisted by an object

Movement is sometimes facilitated or deterred by the use of an object. Use of an object to facilitate movement works especially well with children. It seems to create within them a new interest, or an awareness of what they are doing, and very often facilitates a movement by making it larger, smaller, rhythmic, emotional, interesting, purposeful, and/or creative. The teacher should however, be aware that children who only learn about movement with the help of objects and gadgets do not really learn about the actual inherent movement possibilities and limitations of their own body. In addition, they tend to think more about the gadget they are using than about being aware of their own bodily movement. For these reasons, the use of other objects in the study of movement education should be kept to a bare minimum, to be introduced only after the child has experienced and explored the movement of his body in space, in time, and with regard to force and feeling factors. The mechanics of this plan has been presented in lesson plan 9. The following are additional ideas for evoking and facilitating movement through the use of another object. Some of the following objects may be used to facilitate movement in various ways:

Beachballs: Each child is given a beachball, and encouraged to move with it. Since a beachball is very light in weight, the child will tend to move the ball in various ways in addition to bouncing it. The teacher may then help the child to achieve an awareness of his own movement in relation to the moving ball. The child may also become aware of the shape, or roundness, of the ball, and how it influences his movement. A beachball may be shared by two children to help each become aware of the interaction, or the give-and-take movement which exists when two people are moving with a common object. Interaction like this also tends to emphasize focal points.

Use of a large beachball works well to introduce small-group movement. The ball should be two to three feet in diameter for a group of four to six children. All the teacher needs to do is give a large beachball to a group of children, and stand back and watch the movement evolve. The teacher may stop the movement intermittently, and talk about the awareness and special relationships of each of the others in the group, about focus, and change of leadership within the group, about acting and reacting dynamically to the ball and to each other, and about the necessity for including every-one within the group movement. The teacher may also take one child out of the group at a time, and let that child become aware of some of the above points through observation.

After an ample amount of time has been allowed to explore movement with either the small ball or the large ball, it is taken away from the children. The children then try (without a ball) to recapture that same movement with all its same spatial, dynamic, and emotional qualities.

Cardboard disks or squares: The teacher may cut out colored circles (approximately eighteen inches in diameter) or squares from heavy cardboard and use them to stimulate the children to move. The circles should be approximately eighteen inches. Each child receives one, and is then asked to do all he can think of doing with the card-board object (but strongly advised not to throw it.) They may dis-cover new and interesting movements by using the cardboard in the following ways: (1) hold it in one or both hands and locomote; (2) hold it in one or both hands and move any or all parts of the body; (3) do either of the preceding while moving the object; (4) sit on it and locomote; (5) put one foot on it and locomote; (6) put both feet on it and locomote; (7) hold it between the knees and locomote.

Again, after a great deal of exploration the cardboard objects are taken from the children, and they are asked to recapture that same movement with all its same spatial, dynamic, and emotional qual-ities. (Refer to film *You Can Compose a Dance*—bibliography.)

Fly Swatters: The teacher may purchase one or two fly swatters per child, which may be used to stimulate the children to move. Use of the fly swatters to explore, discover, and facilitate movement is not recommended for children with behavioral problems. It is, however, an excellent activity to be used in a class that is cooperative and follows directions readily. The teacher starts by giving each child one fly swatter. The children sit on the floor at least four to five feet away from each other. The teacher demonstrates a beginning and a stopping signal, which is then practiced to absolute perfection. She then tells the children to beat the fly swatter on the floor as much as they want and in the immediate space surrounding them. This will create quite a bit of noise, but not as much as if each child had a drum or a stick. The teacher stops and starts their activity often. After the children have experimented with hitting the fly swatter by holding it in either hand, the teacher may continue as follows:

- She beats several measures of any time signature she chooses. The children beat exactly the same measures with the fly swatter on the floor along with her.
- She beats a rhythmic pattern. The children do the same with the fly swatter.
- She beats the underlying beat while the children beat the rhythmic pattern. Or vice versa.
- The children compose their own rhythmic pattern.
- They compose a locomotor pattern to go with the rhythmic pattern.
- They compose a movement pattern (which may or may not include movement of the fly swatter) to go with the rhythmic pattern. The movement of the fly swatter may consist of swinging it, touching or hitting at the surrounding space, or hitting the floor or oneself with it.
- Suggest spatial movement with the fly swatter. As the children beat it on the floor, they are encouraged to attend to the floor pattern which they are creating. The teacher may help them to become aware of this pattern by rubbing powdered chalk on the fly swatter before hitting it on the floor, so they will be able to see the design on the floor as they create it. This activity is an excellent lead-in to an awareness of floor patterns (but not an activity recommended for a large class or one which has many behavioral problems.) It is also an excellent activity to aid children in coming to an awareness of shapes, sizes, forms, designs, distance, perspective, depth, and other spatial perceptions. After the children have had plenty of time experimenting with making a floor pattern using chalked fly swatters, they are asked to stand up and do this same floor pattern with their feet. That is, they follow the exact design they created on the floor with fly swatters, by walking on it. The spatial pattern may be accentuated at one point by hitting the fly swatter on the floor, or at the surrounding space. More interest in the spatial pattern may also be gained through locomotion. For instance, a child may choose to walk on one part of the floor pattern, jump on a corner, and run the remainder of the way.

Rope movement. Refer to lesson plan 2, p. 130 for use of the rope in relation to tension and relaxation. The rope may also be used in many other ways; however, the teacher should be aware of all possible mishaps which may occur, and take every precaution to avoid them. A wonderful whipping movement may be discovered by mov-

How many ways can you swat a fly?

ing the rope. This whipping movement may also be executed with the whole body without use of the rope. The rope also makes an interesting snake-like and coiling movement. The children may also hop, jump, and skip with the rope, or it may be an excellent springboard for a group composition in movement, as it incites the children to move in all of the above ways.

Movement through awareness of basic movement education principles

Good movement, efficiently and effectively accomplished, comes from an awareness of one's own body and its parts, and how it works and rests. Children should be allowed the time and the opportunity to discover the many movement possibilities and limitations of their physical bodies. Children can and should be aware also of the comparison of movement between their body and that of a mechanical object. They should likewise be aware that the human body moves not only mechanically, but rhythmically and emotionally as well. The classroom teacher who has had some training mechanically and scientifically will readily think of interesting problem-solving lessons in movement education for the children. Also, several boys in the class who are interested in mechanics and physics, may think of methods and ways of effecting an awareness of some of the basic principles of motor learning to the rest of the class.

Balance

Achieving stability through the use of the turned-out position of the feet: The children may work with partners for this plan, or the teacher may use one or several children to demonstrate. Since the plan invites the children to push one another, the teacher will have to arrange the grouping carefully in order to avoid behavioral problems. She may also illustrate the whole theory on the blackboard.

Teacher: If you stood with your feet close together, and someone or something bumped against you, would you tend to lose your balance and fall over easily? Try it. One of you stand with your feet parallel and close together. Your partner will then walk up to you and gently give you a nudge. (*Pause*) . . . Exchange places, and do the same thing. (*Pause*) . . . •

Teacher: Now stand on one foot. Is it easier or harder for your partner to push you over? (*Pause*) . . . Exchange places, and do the same thing. (*Pause*) . . .

Teacher: If you do not want to lose your balance, and fall over, how could you change your standing position? Show me. (*She now looks for those children who have separated their feet and have widened their base of support.*)

Teacher: I can see that many of you have discovered that your body is more stable when you separate your feet out to the sides of your body, and put more space between your feet. Do you think it would be more difficult for you to push a person over with this kind of wide base of support? Try it. (*Pause*) . . . Exchange places, and try again. (*Pause*) . . .

Teacher: What is a wide base? What is a narrow base? What kind of object can you draw on the board which will have a wide base? What common geometrical figure has a wide base? Who can draw a triangle with a wide base? Would it be difficult to push this triangle over? How does the triangle relate to your body when you stand with your legs wide apart? Draw a triangle with a more narrow base. Is it easier to push over this triangle? Can a triangle remain in balance on one corner? For how long? Can your body remain in balance if you stand on a very narrow, or small, base? What is the smallest base of support you can stand on without losing your balance? Try it. Do you think you could stay in balance longer if you wore shoes with very hard toes and balanced yourself on your toes? (*The children may now draw on the blackboard or demonstrate with blocks how the stability of an object is increased by widening the base of support.*)

Teacher: Although it may be easy to stand with a wide base of support, it is not easy to locomote that way—with so wide a base of support. Get your feet about one yard apart. (*She holds up her hands to demonstrate a space of about one yard.*) How fast can you locomote with your feet this far apart? Try running that way. (*Pause*) . . . Now get your feet about one foot apart. (*The teacher holds up her hands to demonstrate a one-foot space.*) How fast can you move, or locomote your feet, when one is a foot away from the other? Try running. (*Pause*) . . . Now get your feet close together and side by side. How fast can you locomote them now? Try running. (*Pause*) . . .

Teacher: If you wanted to locomote your feet fast, and at the same time maintain a stable position, what kind of position, or shape, would you make with your feet? (*She looks for one of two answers.*) We could run with our feet slightly apart. We could run with out feet shaped like a duck, that is, the toes pointing diagonally outward while the heels remain closer together.)

Teacher: The duck-shaped position of your feet, is called a turn-out position. Using a turn-out position when you locomote increases your stability, yet does not slow down your speed very much. Each one of you will need to discover for yourself how much of a turn-out you will need to use in order to balance your bodily movement in relation to the rate of speed you wish to go.

Opposition:

It is recommended that the theory of opposition not be presented prior to the fourth grade. Most children will move naturally with opposition, and reference to the easy swing of the arms as the body moves should be all that is needed to stress opposition. The following plan is suggested for teaching the theory of opposition (to the children in the fifth and sixth grades) which not only exemplifies the theory through movement, but also provides a thorough stretch of almost all parts of the body.

To begin, the children form a circle and stand about five feet from their closest neighbor. The teacher stimulates their imagination in the following manner:

Teacher: Pretend that in the center of this circle there is a very large cake. The cake is so big that it uses all the space within the circle. Pretend that your whole arm is quite sharp, like a knife. Now, slice a large piece of cake right out in front of you. (*Most children will extend their arm above and in front of them, and make a large vertical movement* down to the floor. *Some children will take a big step forward and extend and flex their legs in order to make the movement of getting a large slice.)*

Teacher: Could you get a larger slice of cake if you stepped forward? Try it. *(Pause)* . . . *(Most children will take a large step forward with the opposite foot. That is, if they slice with the right arm, they will naturally step forward with the left foot. This is opposition. As soon as the teacher sees one or two children using opposition, she uses these children to demonstrate.)*

Teacher: Now, let's watch these three children slice a big piece of cake. *(She now chooses children who are using nonopposition to show their*

Opposition!

slicing movement.) How do they use their bodies differently than the first group? (*She looks and waits for one child to make the observation that one group is using opposition while the other is not. However, they will probably not use the word opposition.*)

Teacher: When one side of your body moves at the same time as the opposite side of your body moves, it is called oppositional movement. When two parts of your body on the same side of your body move at the same time, it is called nonoppositional movement. Let's all try slicing a big piece of cake using opposition. How big a slice can you take? Ready, begin. (*If some children do not use opposition at this point continue without calling their attention to it.*)

Teacher: Using opposition in movement is the most natural thing to do. Let's all try walking, and swinging our arms in opposition. (*Pause*) . . . Now, let's all try walking, and swinging our arms in nonopposition. (*Pause*) . . . We'd all look very different if we walked in nonopposition all the time. Let's try walking with opposition again. (*Pause*) . . .

Teacher: That looks much more comfortable. Let's go back to the slicing movement. Take a big slice, using one arm to slice and the opposite leg to step forward. (*Pause*) . . . What can you do with your feet in order to assist you in balancing your body while doing a very large slicing movement? (*The teacher looks and waits for the children to suggest that they use a turn-out position with their feet.*)

Teacher: We can now see that there are two basic ideas which concern our body during rest and movement which help to keep it in balance.

The slicing movement is a very useful one for children to learn. Besides using it to effect an awareness of counterbalance through the use of opposition, and balance through the use of the turn-out position, it is an excellent physical activity, as it stretches the whole body. The slice may also lead to many interesting variations. One of these is formed by combining two slow slices with four slices of medium tempo. Another interesting combination may result from changing the spatial pattern. For instance, the children may do the first pattern of slow slices two times in a forward direction. The teacher may then invite the children to do slicing movements anywhere in the space surrounding them. The pattern may again be varied by doing slices with either arm, or with both arms. The slices may also vary from oppositional movement to nonoppositional movement. The presentation and variation of slices is an activity which has so many interesting possibilities that it can be presented and worked on as a continuum study throughout the length of the unit.

Slicing!

After the children have been introduced to and experienced balance and opposition through bodily movement, they will tend never to forget these theories and their relationship to the movement and balance of all masses.

Following Through

The theory of following through in bodily movement may also be worked on very effectively by use of the above slicing movements. However, the teacher may discover many other ways of introducing the theory of following through, a theory which should be taught beginning in the early elementary grades, and constantly worked on. Use of the theory of following through begins in lesson plan 1, at which point the children are asked to look and touch space. Throughout all the lesson plans they are encouraged to follow their movement with not only their eyes, but with their entire body.

Moment of Execution

(See lesson plan 8, p. 180, for the moment of execution of a skip.)

Eye-Hand-Foot Coordination

Coordination between the eye and hand; or the eye and foot; or the eye, hand, and foot, also begins in lesson plan 1 and is stressed in all ten lesson plans.

Tension and Relaxation

Even children of kindergarten years may become aware of a tense and relaxed muscle through observing a working and a nonworking muscle. As children get to the second grade and beyond, they may seek and find the answers to questions like the following in regard to tension and relaxation: What muscles, or what part or parts of the body, does one tense in order to create a movement? When, during the course of doing a movement, does one alternately apply tension and relaxation, and how much does one need of each? How does one practice tension and relaxation in order to use this knowledge to create a movement in the most efficient and satisfying manner? At what given instant is tension applied to a movement in order to do the movement in the most efficient and satisfying manner? How does a tense or relaxed muscle affect one's feelings and one's ideas? See lesson plans 1, 3, 4, and 6 (pp. 123, 142, 150, 173) for ideas on teaching the basic principles of muscular tension and relaxation.

Space

Spatial awareness may begin as early as the kindergarten years and is done by moving within and throughout various amounts of space. Spatial awareness also involves discovering for oneself the physical and psychological feeling one experiences as he moves in space and how it effects bodily movement. Some of the questions which children will need to answer in order to be more aware of their body moving in and throughout space are as follows:

QUANTITY: How many ways can your body move in a very small space? How many ways can your body move in a very large space?

LIMITATIONS OF SPACE: How many ways can your body move in a very large box? How many ways can your body move if the ceiling was

Shaping the space!

lowered to one foot above the floor? How many ways can your body move if it were in a small box? (*The teacher may bring various size boxes to class and the children can move within them.*) How would your body move if it was suddenly let out of a box? How many ways can your body move if there is only one yard of space between your body and the body of another person, or persons? How would your body move in a hall after the walls were brought very close together?

SHAPES: How many shapes can your body make while lying on the floor? How many shapes can your body make while sitting, or standing? Can your body make the shape of certain letters in the alphabet? Can your body make the shape of certain geometrical figures?

> Here is a good lead-in activity to effect self-awareness of the contour of one's own body and how the body can take on various shapes:
>
> 1. Get a piece of paper large enough for a child to lie on. The child makes his body into any shape he desires.
> 2. Another child draws around the contour of the body of the first child, outlining it.
> 3. The shape is then cut out and put up on the bulletin board.
> 4. Each shape bears the name of the child so that it can be referred to.
>
> The teacher may ask the whole class to look at Cindy's or Charles's paper body contour on the bulletin board and then shape their bodies the same way. Or, she may ask one child to shape his body like one of the paper contours on the bulletin board, while the rest of the class guesses the identity.
>
> Drawing body contours on paper may also be used effectively with identifying and improving the execution of locomotor forms. If a child can get his legs as far apart while actually doing a leap as he can while lying down and stretching his legs apart, he has done a pretty good leap. If he has drawn the contour of his legs stretched out to their fullest and placed it on the bulletin board, it will be a constant reminder to him as the goal for a leap he may be able to achieve and can constantly strive for.
>
> Shadows may also be used to effect an awareness of bodily shapes. The best shadow is made by using one or more large bed sheets sewn together and hung on a horizontal line about six or seven feet high. There should be five to eight feet of space behind the sheet to allow the child ample space to move. The

Shadows and shapes.

teacher places a strong light about eight to fifteen feet behind the sheet. (A flood light such as that used for taking home movies works well, and a group of flood lights works even better.) One child is asked to go behind the sheet and make his body into any shape he desires, thus producing his movement shadow. Each of the other children may then go behind the sheet in order to try to duplicate the first child's movement shadow.

The use of shadows is an excellent way for children to become aware of the shape or contour their body can make in its surrounding space. It also may be the only strategy for effecting spatial awareness that works with some children.

SIZES: How much space can I cover with my body? How small can I make my body in order to cover very little space? How big, or small is my body compared to that of an ant, to a yardstick, a house, or a car?

How small can you be? How big can you be?

Direction

Understanding the concept of directional movement can be difficult for children (as it is for some adults.) The teacher should introduce it early in the unit and proceed with it slowly. The children should be completely aware of where the front of the room is and should have plenty of experience relating to it by means of bodily movement, before stressing other directions. The teacher should remain in the front of the room, and make that her home base location, until the children are very comfortable and secure in their awareness of direction. After achieving this primary goal, she may then change her home base position many times during a lesson while the children continue to relate their directional movement to the front of the room. After the children are well acquainted with both of the above procedures, she may change the location of the "front of the room" to any of the other three walls. The children who experience all the above procedures, through movement, will have a better awareness of the concepts and elements of space; especially those that pertain to three-dimensional space and directional movement throughout space. The teacher who has already used this procedure in the classroom will find that the children will move with an awareness of direction more easily than those children who have not had this previous experience. Questions like the following may be used to incite the children to discover, for themselves, the relationship between their bodies and other objects in space, and, the many ways they may proceed toward or away from another object, in an effort to become aware of direction: How many ways can your body move forward while locomoting on your feet? On your knees? On your stomach? On your back? Point to your forward direction. Why do you call this forward? Who, or what, determines where your forward direction is? Where is the front of your body? Show me the front of your body by putting your hand on it. Where is the back of your body? Can you move your body in a forward direction with the side of your body leading? How? Can you move your body forward while making a zig-zag floor pattern? Can you move in a forward direction while making a diagonal floor pattern? (The teacher encourages the children to explore movement in a backward and sideward direction by repeating the above questions in relation to these directions.)

Often, when children think about directional movement, they are not thinking about their body and how it moves rhythmically and creatively. It is just too much to think about all at once. For such reasons the teacher may avoid introducing directional movement until the children are ready for it. The teacher may choose to have the children move in the total space in the room by locomoting in a large circular floor pattern around the room. Or she may have the children move in a particular area which they will claim as their own, and have the freedom to move within that area of space any way they choose. Whatever plan the teacher elects to use, the child should be aware from the very first minute of the beginning of the unit that the front of the room is the whole wall behind which the teacher is standing. For more ideas on class movement please refer to the section on suggestions for teaching creative rhythmic movement.

Suggested Teaching Procedure for Directional Movement:

1. The teacher establishes the location of the front wall of the room on the first day. This is usually one of the long walls. She stands midway between the corners of this wall with her back to it. She announces the fact that this whole wall is the front of the room, and when the front of the child's body moves closer to the front wall, he is moving in a forward direction. She does not change this location until the children feel very secure moving in various directions in relation to this front wall.

2. She permits the child to discover and get well acquainted with each part of his body through movement activities.

3. The child indicates awareness of the front of his body and puts his hands on it. He also learns where the front of the room is, points to it, and moves forward toward it with the front of his body leading.

4. The child indicates awareness of the back of his body and puts his hands on as much of it as he can. He also learns where the back of the room is, points to it, and moves toward it with the back of his body leading.

5. The child indicates awareness of one side of his body and puts his hands on that side. He also discovers both sides of the room which may be further delineated as the window side or the piano side, etc. He is asked to point to the piano side of the room and move toward it with his side leading. These directions are reinforced by doing them with various locomotor movements.

Examples: Can you
—hop forward? —slide sideward toward the piano? —walk backward? —crawl forward? —roll sideward toward the windows?—run in place?

(Do not proceed until every child in the class can do the above with 95 percent accuracy.)

6. Walk forward and focus your eyes on an imaginary spot on the wall straight ahead. Walk forward and focus your eyes sideways, below, and above. Walk sideward and backward and change the focal point each time. (Repeat with other locomotor forms. Review directional terminology.)

7. Change the location of the "front of the room" to the opposite wall and repeat all of the above steps. Change the location of the "front of the room" to one of the side walls and repeat all of the above steps. Do not continue until 95 percent of the children can do the foregoing with 95 percent accuracy.

8. Return to the location of the first front of the room. The teacher may ask the child to perform the following in order to further his understanding of directionality.

    Can you move
    —in a forward direction with your side leading? —with your back leading? —to the left side with your front leading? —to the right side with your back leading and your focus front? —in a diagonal direction with your side leading?

9. Review the process of developing awareness of the front, side, and back of the body. Proceed with the following instructions:

    —Face the front of your body forward.
    —Raise your right hand—now lower it.
    —Your right hand is now next to your right side.
    —Face forward and slide to your right. Now slide to your left.
    —Face forward and focus right—now focus left.
    —Face the front of your body right—or right face!
    —Face the front of your body front—or forward face!
    —Face the front of your body left—or left face!
    —Forward face.
    —Face the front of your body to the rear. This is called about face!
    —Forward face.

10. The teacher now introduces several movement problems involving directionality, such as: Do four slides toward the right, about face, and do another four slides continuing to the same right wall, and do an about face.

11. The teacher now points out that some directions, which are done exactly the same, may be described two different ways.

    For example:

—Face left and walk forward.

or

—Walk to the side with the front of your body leading.

Usually when one changes his body facing he also changes his frontal location, and his directional movement is oriented to this new front. This is exemplified in the following commands:

—Right face, forward march!
—Left face, forward march!
—Right about face, forward march!
—Left about face, forward march!

Understanding the change in frontal positions is not difficult for the child to understand if he has slowly gone through all of the above steps in movement. It is much more difficult to explain directionality than it is to perceive it through movement. The teacher should proceed with the above slowly and cautiously.

FLOOR PATTERNS: What kind of shape, or pattern on the floor, will my feet make if they travel forward in a straight line? What kind of pattern will my feet make on the floor if they go from the piano to the window? What kind of pattern will my feet make on the floor while doing four skips forward, four slides sideways, and four jumps backwards? Can you draw this floor pattern on a large piece of paper?

TRACKING ABILITY: Watch John as he moves and makes a floor pattern. Where does he start his floor pattern? What part of his body moves first? In which direction does he move? Where does he end his floor pattern? Can you make the same floor pattern that John has made? Watch two children making a floor pattern. Watch them move from here to there. Can you and your partner make the same floor patterns? How far will your body be from your partner's body while moving? Can you draw your floor pattern, or the path of your movement, on a piece of paper so that someone else who has not seen it can follow it exactly? Do your eyes have to follow a path of words, phrases, and sentences while reading? Do your eyes look from here to there on a page while reading? What kind of path do your eyes follow when looking at a map? What kind of path do your eyes follow when looking at a circle—a dot—a line?

Force

All the forces which are produced by or result from movement may be taught to children from the second grade level and beyond.

The children are made aware of the action of these forces by means of bodily movement, and through the probing, seeking, and finding activity in which the children engage themselves in order to solve the problems or answer the questions which the teacher proposes. (Refer to page 45 for a more complete discussion of force.)

GRAVITY: Awareness of the force of gravity may begin in the lower elementary level by posing questions pertaining to stretches, falls, rises, lifts, drops, and the balance and stability of the body during rest and movement. Suggestions for introducing these movement problems may be found in the ideas on balance and stability. Other questions which can be proposed are as follows: How long can your body stay up in the space above you when you do a jump or a leap? Try it. Why doesn't your body stay up high in the space above you? Why does your body always come down again? What kind of movement can you make with the rest of your body in order to help you stay up there longer? Try it. Think about how your body falls over if someone or something hits you hard. Does your body fall down in one piece like a piece of wood? Or, does your body drop like a waterfall? That is, it comes down as perpendicularly as possible but in pieces, little by little. Choose partners and watch each other fall from the standing position to the lying down position (or the high level to the low level.) What level must each body go through when moving from the standing to the lying position? What position in the middle level does the body need to get into before lying down?

The study of gravity is an excellent lead-up activity to the study of falls, balances, and sequential movement. The teacher should call upon her knowledge of the force of gravity and propose additional questions all of which can be tried and tested by bodily movement.

ACCELERATION: How slow can you run? How fast can you run? What happens to the size of your steps when you run fast? Does it take more muscle force to run fast or slow?

MOMENTUM: How can you stop yourself from running very fast? When you stop your fast run, in which direction do you want to continue to go? Does momentum have something to do with following through? How much muscle force does it take to stop your movement?

ACTION AND REACTION: How hard can you push down on the floor with both hands? What happens to the rest of your body when you push down hard onto the floor with your hands? If you pushed harder onto the floor, will your body rise higher? If you bounce, or push a ball harder onto the floor, will it rise higher?

BIBLIOGRAPHY

Additional Reading Material For Teachers

Key to Subject Matter	Subject Matter
A.	Creative Rhythmic Movement and/or Dance for Children
B.	Creative Teaching—Problem Solving—The Creative Process
C.	Dance and Art
D.	Dance and Drama
E.	Dance and Education
F.	Movement Education and Motor Learning
G.	Physical Education as Related to Creative Rhythmic Movement
H.	Rhythm and/or Music
I.	Creative Rhythmic Movement in Special and/or Pre-School Education

Books

A,B,F,H, I.   ANDREWS, GLADYS. *Creative Rhythmic Movement for Children.* New York: Prentice Hall, 1954.

A,D.   BARLIN, ANNE, AND BARLIN, PAUL. *The Art of Learning Through Movement.* Claremont, Calif.: 1971.

B,F.   BARRETT, KATE ROSS. *Exploration—A Method for Teaching Movement.* Madison, Wis.: College Printing and Typing, 1965.

B,E.   BEECHHOLD, HENRY F. *The Creative Classroom: Teaching Without Text Books.* New York: Charles Scribner's Sons, 1971.

F,G.   BILBROUGH, A., AND JONES, P. *Physical Education in the Primary School.* London: University of London Press, 1963.

A,I.   BOORMAN, JOYCE. *Creative Dance in the First Three Grades.* New York: David McKay Co., 1969.

D.   BRUCE, V. *Dance and Dance Drama in Education.* New York: Pergamon Press, 1965.

I. pamphlet   CHERRY, CLARE. *Creative Movement for the Developing Child.* Palo Alto, Calif.: Fearon, 1971.

F.   CRATTY, BRYANT J. *Some Educational Implications of Movement.* Seattle: Special Child Publications, 1970.

C,E,H.   DALCROZE, ÉMILE J. *Eurhythmics, Art and Education.* New York: A. S. Barnes, 1930.

H.   DALCROZE, ÉMILE J. *Rhythm, Music and Education.* New York: G. P. Putnam's Sons, 1921.

F,G.   DAUER, VICTOR P. *Essential Movement Experiences for Pre-*

School and Primary Children. Minneapolis: Burgess Publishing Co., 1968.

A,H. DIMONSTEIN, GERALDINE. *Children Dance in the Classroom.* New York: Macmillan Co., 1971.

A,D,E. DIXON, MADELINE C. *The Power of Dance.* New York: John Day Co., 1939.

H. DRIVER, ANN. *Music and Movement.* London: Oxford University Press, 1958.

B.F. GERHARDT, LYDIA A. *Moving and Knowing.* Englewood Cliffs, N.J.: Prentice-Hall, 1973.

F. GILLION, BONNIE CHERP. *Basic Movement Education for Children.* Reading, Mass.: Addison-Wesley, 1970.

A,G. GLASS, HENRY "BUZZ". *Exploring Movement.* Freeport, N.Y.: Educational Activities, 1966.

B,F,G. HACKETT, LAYNE C., AND JENSON, ROBERT G. *A Guide to Movement Exploration.* Palo Alto, Calif.: Peek Publications, 1967.

B,F,G. HALSEY, ELIZABETH, AND PORTER, LORENA. *Physical Education for Children.* New York: Dryden Press, 1958.

H. HAWKINSON, JOHN, AND FAULHABER, MARTHA. Book One: *Music and Instruments for Children to Make;* Book Two: *Rhythms, Music, and Instruments to Make.* Chicago: Albert Whitman, 1970.

A,B,C, H'DOUBLER, MARGARET. *Dance a Creative Art Experience.* New
E,F,H. York: F. S. Crofts, 1940.

B,E,F,G. HUMPHREY, JAMES H. *Child Learning.* Dubuque, Ia.: Wm. C. Brown Company Publishers, 1965.

A,I. JORDAN, DIANA. *Childhood and Movement.* Oxford: Basil Blackwell, 1966.

F,G. KIRCHNER, GLENN; CUNNINGHAM, JEAN; AND WARRELL, EILEEN. *Introduction to Movement Education.* Dubuque, Ia.: Wm. C. Brown Company Publishers, 1970.

A,F. LATCHOW, MARJORIE, AND EGSTROM, GLEN. *Human Movement.* Englewood Cliffs, N.J.: Prentice-Hall, 1969.

B,C. LINDERMAN, EARL W., AND HERBERHOLZ, DONALD W. *Developing Artistic and Perceptual Awareness.* Dubuque, Ia.: Wm. C. Brown Company Publishers, 1964.

A,G. LOGSDON, BETTE J., AND BARRETT, KATE R. *Ready? Set? Go!* Bloomington, Ind.: National Instructional Television Center, 1969.

D. LOWNDES, BETTY. *Movement and Creative Drama for Children.* Boston: Plays Inc., 1971.

H. MAYNARD, OLGA. *Children and Dance and Music.* New York: Charles Scribner's Sons, 1968.

A. METTLER, BARBARA. *Children's Creative Dance Book.* Tucson, Ariz.: Mettler Studios, 1970.

A,E,H.   MURRAY, RUTH LOVELL. *Dance in Elementary Education.* New York: Harper & Row, 1953.

C,E,G.   MURRAY, RUTH L., AND GRAY, MIRIAM. *Designs for Dance.* Washington, D.C.: N.E.A., Division of the American Association for Health, Physical Education and Recreation, 1968.

E.   NADEL, MYRON H., AND NADEL, CONSTANCE G. *The Dance Experience.* New York: Praeger, 1970.

I.   ROBINS, FERRIS, AND ROBINS, JENNET. *Educational Rhythmics for Mentally and Physically Handicapped Children.* New York: Association Press, 1968.

A.   RUSSELL, JOAN. *Creative Dance in the Primary School.* London: Macdonald & Evans, 1965.

A.   SCHURR, EVELYN L. *Movement Experiences for Children.* New York: Appleton-Century-Crofts, 1967.

H.   SEHON, ELIZABETH, AND O'BRIEN, EMMA LOU. *Rhythms in Elementary Education.* New York: A. S. Barnes, 1951.

A,H.   SHEEHY, EMMA. *Children Discover Music and Dance.* New York: Teachers College Press, 1968.

B,E.   SMITH, JAMES A. *Creative Teaching of the Creative Arts in the Elementary School.* Boston: Allyn and Bacon, 1967.

B,F.   SWEENEY, ROBERT T. *Selected Readings in Movement Education.* Reading, Mass.: Addison-Wesley, 1970.

A,B.,   TILLOTSON, JOAN. "A Program of Movement Education for
E,F,G.   Plattsburg Elementary Schools," *Cord, Research in Dance: Problems and Possibilities.* New York: New York University Press, 1968.

B.   TORRANCE, E. PAUL. *Rewarding Creative Behavior.* Englewood Cliffs, N.J.: Prentice-Hall, 1965.

A,B,C,   WAMPLER, MARTHA MAYBURRY, ed. *Orff-Schulwerk: Design for*
E,H,K.   *Creativity.* Bellflower, Calif.: Creative Practices Council, 1966–68.

H.   WATERMAN, ELIZABETH. *The Rhythm Book.* New York: A. S. Barnes, 1936.

A,B,E.   WEINER, JACK, AND LIDSTONE, JOHN. *Creative Movement for Children.* New York: Van Nostrand Reinhold, 1969.

B,E,I.   WOODS, MARGARET. *Thinking, Feeling, Experiencing: Toward Realization of Full Potential.* Washington, D.C.: N.E.A., 1962.

Additional Reading Material For Children

The children's books listed here will give the teacher an idea of the various kinds of children's reading material which is available and appropriate to reinforce or motivate learning related to the concepts found in this book. Each book has a reference letter indicating its subject matter followed by numbers indicating its approximate reading grade level.

Key to Subject Matter	Subject Matter
A.	Anatomy and Body Awareness
B.	Movement Exploration and Discovery
C.	Emotions, Feelings, Sensory Awareness
D.	Dance a Story—Dramatic Play
E.	Mathematics, Reading and Social Studies
F.	Movement Education as Related to General Science
G.	Rhythm and Music
H.	Spatial Awareness

Subject Matter and Grade Level	Books
C. 1–3	ADLER, IRVING. *Taste, Touch, and Smell.* New York: John Day Co., 1966.
F. 3–5	ADLER, IRVING, AND ADLER, RUTH. *Things That Spin.* New York: John Day Co., 1971.
D.	ALEXANDER, MARTHA. *Bobo's Dream.* New York: Dial Press, 1970.
E,F,H. 3–6	BENDICK, JEANNE. *Shapes.* New York: Franklin Watts, 1968.
E,F,H. 3–6	BENDICK, JEANNE, AND LEVIN, MARCIA O. *Take Shapes, Lines and Symmetry.* New York: Whittlesey House, McGraw-Hill, 1962.
F. 1–3	BERGER, MELVIN. *Gravity.* New York: Coward-McCann, 1969.
A,B,C. 3–6	BORTEN, HELEN. *Do You Move as I Do?* New York: Abelard-Schuman, 1963.
C,H. 3–6	BORTEN, HELEN. *Do You See What I See?* New York: Abelard-Schuman, 1959.
A,F,H. 1–4	BRANLEY, FRANKLYN M. *New Sounds, Low Sounds.* New York: Thomas Y. Crowell, 1967.
	————. *Gravity Is a Mystery.* New York: Thomas Y. Crowell, 1970.

————. *Weight and Weightlessness*. New York: Thomas Y. Crowell, 1971.

E,H. BRENNER, BARBARA. *Mr. Tall and Mr. Small*. New York: Young
K–3 Scott Books, 1966.

A. ————. *Bodies*. New York: E. P. Dutton, 1973.
1–3

E,H. BUDNEY, BLOSSOM, AND BOBRI, VLADIMIR. *A Kiss Is Round*. New
Pre–2 York: Lathrop, Lee, Shepard, 1966.

D. FIONA, FRENCH. *The Blue Bird*. New York: Henry Z. Walck, 1972.

E,F. FROMAN, ROBERT. *Bigger and Smaller*. New York: Thomas Y.
1–3 Crowell, 1971.

G. HUGHES, LAMPTON. *Rhythms*. New York: Franklin Watts, 1954.
3–6

G. KETTELKAMP, LARRY. *Drums, Rattles, and Bells*. William Mor-
3–6 row, 1960.

E,F. LINN, CHARLES F. *Estimation*. New York: Thomas Y. Crowell,
3–6 1970.

B,C,D. MERZ, DIANE. *The Mockingbird Book*. New York: Harper & Row,
2–4 1962.

C. MUJOSKI, SEKIYA. *Singing David*. New York: Franklin Watts,
1–3 1970.

C. REDLAUER, RUTH, Ed. *Colors*. Glendale, Calif.: Bowmar, 1968.
Pre–K

G. REEVES, JAMES. *Rhyming Will*. McGraw-Hill, 1968.
Pre–2

E,H. RINKOFF, BARBARA. *A Map Is a Picture*. New York: Thomas Y.
1–3 Crowell, 1965.

C. SCHEFFER, VICTORIA B. *The Seeing Eye*. New York: Charles
Pre–6 Scribner's, 1971.

E,H. SHAPP, MARTHA, AND SHARP, CHARLES. *Let's Find Out What's
Pre–2 Big and What's Small*. New York: Franklin Watts, 1959.

C. SHOWERS, PAUL. *Follow Your Nose*, New York: Thomas Y. Cro-
1–3 well, 1963.

A. SILVERSTEIN, ALVIN, AND SILVERSTEIN, VIRGINIA B. *The Nervous
3–6 System*. Englewood Cliffs, N.J.: Prentice-Hall, 1972.

————. *The Muscular System*. Englewood Cliffs, N.J.: Prentice-Hall, 1972.

————. *The Sense Organs*. Englewood Cliffs, N.J.: Prentice-Hall, 1972.

————. *The Skeletal System*. Englewood Cliffs, N.J.: Prentice-Hall, 1972.

F.   SIMON, SEYMOUR. *Motion.* New York: Coward-McCann, 1968.
1–6

E,F,H. SITOMER, MINDEL, AND SITOMER, HARRY. *What Is Symmetry?*
3–6   New York: Thomas Y. Crowell, 1970.

C.E.   SPIER, PETER. *Crash! Bang! Boom!* Garden City, N.Y.: Double-
all ages day, 1972.

F.   SRIVASTINA, JANE JONAS. *Weighing and Balancing.* New York:
1–3   Thomas Y. Crowell, 1970.

B,D.   UCHIDA, YOSHIKO. *The Dancing Kettle and Other Japanese Folk*
Pre–3   *Tales.* New York: Harcourt, Brace & World, 1949.

B,C,D. UDRY, JANICE MAY. *The Moon Jumpers.* New York: Harper &
Pre–3   Row, 1959.

FILMS

CHILDREN DANCE. University of California Extension Media Center, 2223 Shattuck Avenue; Berkeley, Calif. 94720. Produced and co-directed by Geraldine Dimondstein and Naima Prevots. 16 mm, color, sound, 14″, rental $5.50, sale $80. Teacher-training film for K–third grade teachers. Explores space, time, and force through improvisations and dance studies. 1970.

DANCE YOUR OWN WAY. Bailey Films, 6509 De Longpres; Hollywood, Calif. Directed by Gertrude Copley Knight. 16 mm, color, sound, 10″; rental $6.00, sale $120. Children of elementary school age dance to ethnic music and rhythms. 1952.

LEARNING THROUGH MOVEMENT. SL Film, 5126 Hartwick Street; Los Angeles, Calif. 90041. Produced and directed by Ann and Paul Barlin. 16 mm, b/w, sound, 32″; rental $20, sale $165.00. The exploration of movement and some large group movement by children in grades 1–6. 1967.

LOOKING FOR ME. University of California Extension Media Center (FN), 2223 Shattuck Avenue; Berkeley, Calif. 94720. Writer and narrator, Janet Adler. Produced and directed by Virginia Bartlett. b–w, sound, 30″. Excellent film for movement therapists or students training for work with disturbed children. Useful in personality development classes. Stresses body language. 1970.

WHAT IS RHYTHM? Bailey-Film Associates, 11559 Santa Monica Blvd.; Los Angeles, Calif. 90025. 16 mm., color, sound, 11″. Simple examples of rhythm found in the surrounding environment. Preschool through third grade.

YOU CAN COMPOSE A DANCE. SL Film, 5126 Hartwick Street; Los Angeles, Calif. 90041. Produced and directed by Shirley J. Winters. 16 mm., b/w, sound, two parts, 10″ each. Rental for total $20.00, sale $165.00. This film constantly invites and encourages the child to get up and explore and discover movement and to compose a dance. The method for composition is the classic ABA and ABCA. 1971.

An excellent bibliography of MOVEMENT EDUCATION FILMS may be found in the following: SWEENEY, ROBERT T., *Selected Readings in Movement Education.* Reading, Mass.: Addison-Wesley, 1970. Also listed in Bibliography—Additional Reading Material for Teachers, p. 251.

index